HAUNTED HEART

Lisa Rogak

HAUNTED HEART
THE LIFE AND TIMES OF
STEPHEN KING

First published in Great Britain in 2009 by
JR Books, 10 Greenland Street, London NW1 0ND
www.jrbooks.com

First published in paperback, 2010

A catalogue record for this book is available from the British Library.

ISBN 978-1-906779-71-9

1 3 5 7 9 10 8 6 4 2

Printed by CPI Bookmarque, Croyden, CR0 4TD

FOR SCOTT MENDEL,
FOR DEALING WITH ME AND
MY FOIBLES FOR FIVE YEARS NOW

CONTENTS

HAUNTED HEART

I'M AFRAID OF EVERYTHING.
—STEPHEN KING

It's probably no surprise that his fears rule every second of Stephen King's existence. He's surrounded by them, and anyone who's read even one of his novels knows that the most innocent item can be a harbinger of terror.

At various times through the years, King has rattled off a veritable laundry list of his fears: the dark, snakes, rats, spiders, squishy things, psychotherapy, deformity, closed-in spaces, death, being unable to write, flying—fill in the blank, the list is long. He's described himself as having a permanent address in "the People's Republic of Paranoia."

His treatises on his fear of the number thirteen—triskaidekaphobia—are particularly revealing. "The number 13 never fails to trace that old icy finger up and down my spine," he wrote. "When I'm writing, I'll never stop work if the page number is 13 or a multiple of 13; I'll just keep on typing till I get to a safe number.

"I always take the last two steps on my back stairs as one, making thirteen into twelve. There were after all, thirteen steps on the English gallows up until 1900 or so. When I'm reading, I won't stop on page 94, 193, 382, since the sums of these numbers add up to thirteen."

You get the picture. King—he prefers to be called Steve—draws upon his fears quite liberally in his writing, yet at the same time, part of the reason that he writes is to attempt to drown them out, to suffocate them and put them out of their misery once and for all so he'll never be tormented by them again.

Yeah, right. He doesn't believe it either.

The only way he can block them out is when he's writing. Once he gets rolling and is carried along by a story about a particular fear, it's gone, at least temporarily. He writes as fast and furiously as he can because if there's one thing Stephen King knows after spending decades writing, it's this: the moment the pen stops moving or the computer switches off, the fears will rush right back, ready for another round.

Despite his fear of therapists, he once went to see one. When he began cataloging his fears, the therapist interrupted him, telling him to visualize his fear as a ball he could close up in his fist. It was all he could do not to run for the door. "Lady, you don't know how much fear I've got," he replied. "I can maybe get it down to the size of a soccer ball, but fear is my living and I can only get it so small."

In an exchange with Dennis Miller on his former TV talk show, Steve was thrilled to discover that he had found a kindred spirit in the Land of Fear. The men were discussing their shared dread of flying when King offered his theory about how the collective fear of people on a plane helps prevent a crash.

"Right," said Miller with a knowing nod. "The degree of rigidity in our body keeps the wings up."

Not quite, as Steve went on to explain. "It's a psychic thing, and anybody with half a brain knows that it shouldn't work. You have three or four people who are terrified right out of their minds. We hold it up. The flight you have to be afraid of is the flight where there's nobody on who's afraid of flying. Those are the flights that crash. Trust me on this."

A few nervous laughs came from the audience. Both men blinked past the glare of the lights and then looked at each other. They think we're *kidding*?

Without fear where would Stephen King be? It's almost as if he's hooked on his anxiety, just one more thing for him to mainline, like the booze and drugs he was hooked on for decades. In fact, he's made no secret of his lifelong struggle with substances.

"All those addictive substances are part of the bad side of what we do," he said. "I think it's part of that obsessive deal that makes you a writer in the first place, that makes you want to write it all down. Writing is an addiction for me. Even when the writing is not going well, if I don't do it, the fact that I'm not doing it nags at me."

One of the amazing aspects of Stephen King's life is that his copious drug and alcohol abuse didn't interfere with either the quantity or the quality of his prodigious output. However, while he would later acknowledge his surprise that his work didn't suffer—especially when the haze was thickest—he's also spoken with regret that he couldn't remember writing certain books, such as *Cujo*. This clearly bothered him, for he always fondly looked back on each of his novels and stories, revisiting them as if they were old friends, rerunning the memories of the nuances and the ideas of a world and people that he just happened to have pulled out of his head.

Writing horror and telling stories had become so ingrained in him over the years that cranking out thousands of words every day of the year was second nature to him, despite a daily input of booze and drugs that would easily have killed a college kid on a weekend binge. Indeed, some of the tall tales and denial extended to what he told interviewers. For years, he told them that he wrote every day, taking a break from writing only on the Fourth of July, his birthday, and Christmas. That was patently untrue. He later said that he couldn't *not* write every day of the year, but he thought telling fans that he allowed himself a whole three days away from writing made him seem more personable. He hadn't yet realized that admitting his addictions to his fans would make him appear even more human.

While he's long been an unapologetic admirer of everything mainstream—he's referred to himself as the Big Mac of authors—he isn't always comfortable on the pedestal. Steve's iconic position in popular fiction was cemented early on, only a few years after his first novel, *Carrie,* was published. And yet, he isn't above—or below—using his fame when it suits him.

King claims to hate being famous—his wife Tabby detests it even more, calling life with a celebrity spouse like being in "a goddamn fishbowl"—but even after three decades in the public spotlight, he still talks to journalists from media large and small, gives public talks, attends Red Sox games, and conducts book signings. After all, with more than thirty years in the business, his ability to sell books has little to do with whether he gives a bunch of interviews. Though he claims to be shy, he's still as open and self-deprecating as he was when he first started out.

Then, of course, there's the flip side: "When you get into this business, they don't tell you you'll get cat bones in the mail, or letters from crazy people, or that the people on the tour bus will be gathered at your fence snapping pictures."

Because he lives a life that is so out and about, pick a random New Englander and chances are he'll have a story about a Stephen King sighting.

A New Hampshire man who regularly visited Fenway Park knew that Steve had season tickets to the Red Sox games. For several years, he kept an eye out for Steve, but he never spotted him. One day at the stadium, he saw King walking toward him and he froze. He couldn't think of anything to say. Finally, all he could come out with was "Boo!" as they came eye to eye. Steve said "Boo!" back and headed for his seat.

"He's just a competitive guy who wants to be the best at what he does," says Warren Silver, a friend from Bangor.

This, after sixty-three books published in thirty-five years, including collaborations, short-story collections—and having *The Green Mile* count as six separate books. Since the publication of *Carrie* in 1974, none of his books has been out of print, an accomplishment that can be matched by few bestselling authors. Proof still that his fears loom large.

Does he write for a particular person? While he admits that he writes to vanquish his fear, and writing for an audience of one—himself—he has occasionally provided a glimpse of the real man behind the curtain, a man whom Steve has no real recollection of: his father, who walked out of the family home one evening for a pack of cigarettes and kept on going, leaving his wife and two sons—David, age four, and Steve, two—to fend for themselves throughout a childhood of wrenching poverty and great uncertainty.

"I really think I write for myself, but there does seem to be a target that this stuff pours out toward," he said. "I am always interested in this idea that a lot of fiction writers write for their fathers because their fathers are gone."

Steve coped with a difficult childhood by turning first to books and then to writing his own stories. And as he put it, it's a world that he has never really left.

"You have to be a little nuts to be a writer because you have to imagine worlds that aren't there," he said. "You're hearing voices, you're making believe, you're doing all of the things that we're told as children not to do. Or else we're told to distinguish between reality and those things. Adults will say, 'You have an invisible friend, that's nice, you'll outgrow that.' Writers don't outgrow it."

So who is Stephen King, really? The standard assumption of casual fans and detractors is that he must be a creepy man who loves to blow things up in his backyard. Loyal fans usually go a bit deeper, knowing him to be a loyal family man and a benefactor to countless charities, many around his Bangor, Maine, home.

His friends, however, present a different, more complex picture.

"He's a brilliant, funny, generous, compassionate man whose character is made up of layer upon layer," says longtime friend and coauthor Peter Straub. "What you see is not only not what you get, it isn't even what you see. Steve is a mansion containing many rooms, and all of this makes him wonderful company."

According to Bev Vincent, a friend whom Steve helped out with Vincent's book *The Road to the Dark Tower,* a reference guide to King's seven-volume magnum opus, his self-image is somewhat surprising: "Steve still sees himself as a small-town guy who has done a few interesting things but doesn't think that his personal life would interest anyone."

And he doesn't understand why anyone would want to read an entire book about him—let alone write one. On the other hand, he has no problem if people want to discuss his work, either face-to-face or in a book.

But we all know he's wrong. Stephen King has led an endlessly fascinating life, and because we love, admire, and are scared out of our minds by his books, stories, and movies, of course we want to know more about the man who's spawned it all. Who wouldn't?

This is a biography, a story of his life. Of course his works play into it, they are unavoidable, but they are not the featured attraction here. Stephen King is.

Through the years, Steve's fans have been legendary for taking him to task whenever he's gotten the facts wrong in his stories. For instance, in *The Stand,* Harold Lauder's favorite candy bar was a PayDay bar. At one point in the story, Harold left behind a chocolate fingerprint in a diary at a time when the candy contained no chocolate. In the first few months after the book was published, Steve received mailbags full of letters from readers to inform him of his mistake, which was remedied in later editions of the book. And then of course, the candy company began to make PayDays with chocolate. Though some might claim Steve was prescient, you can't blame the man; after all, this is a guy who isn't exactly fond of doing research when he's deep into the writing of a novel. "I do the research [after I write]," he said. "Because when I'm writing a book, my attitude is, don't confuse me with facts. You know, let me go ahead and get on with the work."

On the other hand, his lack of concern with the facts of both his fictional and real lives has proved to be more than a bit frustrating to me and other writers. In researching this biography, I've attempted to check and double-check the facts of his life, but whether it's the natural deterioration of memory that comes with age or two solid decades of abusing alcohol, cocaine, and other drugs in various combinations, the guy can't be faulted for fudging a few dates here and there.

For example, in *On Writing,* he wrote that his mother died in February 1974, two months before *Carrie* was first published. However, I have not only a copy of his mother's obituary but her death certificate, both of which show that she most definitely died on December 18, 1973, in Mexico, Maine, at the home of Steve's brother, Dave.

Once I knew I was going to be writing about King's life, I got busy. I dug up old interviews in obscure publications that only published one issue back in 1975, read numerous books, and watched almost all of the movies based on his stories and novels—good and bad, and, boy, the bad ones can be a hoot. I also plunged into the many books that have been written about him and his work since the early eighties. As with the films, there are some good ones and some that are not so good.

The thing that struck me was not the blood and guts and special effects; the gory scenes in his books and movies weren't as bad as I'd imagined they would be. And it wasn't his ability to draw and develop characters; I already knew that was one of his particular talents.

What really got me was how funny the man is. I mean, really funny. Yes, his use of pop-culture references and brand names can be amusing when placed side by side with a guy who has a cleaver sticking out of his neck, or as with a corpse in an office setting with an Eberhard pencil stuck in each eye, but his sense of humor just knocked me over. I fell off the couch when the ice cream truck in *Maximum Overdrive* started playing "King of the Road," and again in *Graveyard Shift* when rats are trying to stay on top of broken planks coursing down a fast-moving stream in the middle of a mill's floor and the music playing is "Surfin' Safari" by the Beach Boys. King did not write the screenplay for the latter, but you just know his long arm of influence made it into the film.

Steve has gone on the record countless times to say that the one question he hates most is "Where do you get your ideas?" To me as a biographer, all you have to do is ask, "Is it authorized?" to make my face screw up like King's after an awestruck fan has asked him the idea question.

No, this biography is *not* authorized. The running joke among biographers is that if it is authorized, the book makes a good cure for insomnia. King does know about this book and told his friends that they could talk with me if they desired. I visited Bangor over several gray, bleak November days in the fall of 2007 to check out all of the key Stephen King haunts. In other words, all the highlights on the local Stephen King tours. It was sheer serendipity that one morning I found myself sitting in his office in the former National Guard barracks out near the airport, with his longtime assistant Marsha DeFillipo grilling me about my aim for this book.

For most of that half-hour interrogation, the man himself hovered just outside the doorway, listening in on our conversation but never once stepping inside.

In the end, perhaps the most surprising thing about Stephen King is that he is a die-hard romantic, which is evident in all of his stories. And to the surprise of his millions of fans, he would be the first to admit it, though to hear him explain it, maybe it's not really much of a revelation.

"Yes, I am a romantic," he said back in 1988. "I believe all those sappy, romantic things, that children are good, good wins out over evil, it is better to have loved and lost than never to have loved at all. I really believe all that shit. I can't help it. I see a lot of it at work."

However, the most romantic hearts are often the most haunted. I chose *Haunted Heart* as the title of this biography because it's clear that Stephen King's childhood indelibly shaped him for both good and not so good.

In an interview with the BBC, when Steve talked about his father and growing up without him, he began with a bit of an edge, a defiance as if to say, "Why are we talking about this? I'm *so* over it and have been for decades." Once he got going, however, things got painfully intimate, revealing the hurt, petulant boy that still exists close to the surface beneath Stephen King's skin. During his childhood, the other kids had fathers and he didn't, he explained. Male relatives were around, to be sure, but it wasn't the real thing. It would *never* be the real thing.

"At least the father in *The Shining* was there, even though he was bad," he said. "For me, there was a vacuum that was neither good or bad, just an empty place." At that point, his face crumpled a little, he distractedly ran a hand through his hair, and he looked away from the camera, which remained focused on him for a second or two before abruptly cutting away.

In short, Stephen King has never gotten over feeling like an abandoned child and he never stopped being a child permanently haunted by his father's absence. That's something that will never change. It has affected his entire life, from his childhood and his marriage to his books. *Especially* his books.

Keep this in mind as you read both this book and Steve's novels, and you'll find that it will go a long way toward a deeper understanding of the man and the worlds he's created.

APT PUPIL

By all accounts, Stephen King should never have been born.

His mother, Nellie Ruth Pillsbury, who went by her middle name, married a captain in the merchant marines named Donald Edwin King on July 23, 1939, in Scarborough, Maine. But given Donald's frequent and lengthy absences due to the encroaching war, their marriage was on shaky ground from the start.

Doctors had informed Ruth that she would never bear children, and so the Kings did what many presumably infertile couples did back then and applied to adopt a child.

David Victor was adopted shortly after his birth in Portland, Maine, on September 14, 1945, a month after the end of the war.

Despite her doctor's diagnosis of infertility, in the midwinter of 1947, Ruth discovered she was pregnant. Stephen Edwin King was born on September 21, 1947, two years to the day after David's adoption was finalized. He shares the birthday with H. G. Wells, author of such sci-fi classics as *The War of the Worlds,* who was born eighty-one years earlier.

Nellie Ruth Pillsbury was born on February 3, 1913, in Scarborough, Maine, to Guy Herbert and Nellie Weston Fogg Pillsbury. She was the fourth of eight children.

Ruth's ancestral roots ran deep in her seaside hometown of Scarborough, Maine. Her great-great-grandfather Jonathan Pillsbury moved to town before 1790 just after the American Revolution ended, married a local woman, and raised a family. Ruth's ancestors owned property, farmed, and built ships and houses in Scarborough for many generations. The family lived on Prouts Neck, a peninsula a fifteen-minute drive from Portland, whose population was a mix of summer people and locals whose roots went back at least several generations. As a young girl, Ruth was surrounded by her siblings, cousins, aunts, uncles, and grandparents. Artist Winslow Homer, who died in 1910, had his studio and retirement home near Guy Pillsbury's home.

In the nineteenth century, Scarborough was an active seaport. In addition to farming, townspeople participated in fishing and shipbuilding. A dike was built in 1877 to control overflowing tidal marshes, but it changed the seascape around Scarborough from a port to a salt marsh.

The town recovered and gained popularity as a summer destination in the early 1900s when regular trolley service brought tourists from Boston and New York. Vacation establishments known as shore dinner houses sprang up along with tourist homes and hotels and motels. A majority of the population worked at jobs in the tourist industry for the summer, including a hotel known as the Pillsbury House, run by some of Ruth's relatives from 1915 to 1932. In the early 1900s, Ruthie's father, Guy, supplemented his main income as a carpenter by shuttling tourists from the station to their hotels in a horse-drawn carriage.

Nellie, Ruth's mother, had worked as a schoolteacher before her marriage, and the entire Pillsbury family placed a high importance on education and music for their children. Ruth's siblings would go on to attend Bowdoin, Northeastern, and Emerson.

In 1931, the Depression was deeply entrenched in coastal Maine. Natives were already used to making do with what they had, but the Depression brought even less hard cash to down-east households as fewer tourists could afford to travel to the state for vacation. Guy Pillsbury had a houseful: his oldest daughter, Mary, at twenty-three, was still living at home, as were his other children, Mollie, Lois, Mary, Guy Jr., Carolyn, Ethelyn, and Ruth. It was time for some of them to move on. Ruth was only too happy to set off to see the world.

After her idyllic childhood, Ruth studied piano at the New England Conservatory in Boston for a time. Little is known about her life during the Depression, but clearly she didn't have an easy time of it when it came to her personal life.

A couple of years after she left Scarborough in 1931, Ruth got married, but the marriage quickly soured and she filed for divorce. In the 1930s, divorce was rare in the United States, and many men would automatically have viewed a divorced woman as damaged goods. A few years later, she met Donald Edwin King, who was born on March 11, 1914, to William R. and Helen A. Bowden King, in Peru, Indiana, and Ruth's history as a divorced woman didn't seem to bother him.

Ruth and Donald were married on July 23, 1939, in Scarborough, Maine, with her family present. Shortly after the wedding, the couple moved to Chicago to live with Donald's family at 4815 Belle Plaine Avenue. The honeymoon quickly wore off as Ruth found herself homesick for her native Maine. She was frequently alone while Donald continued to travel around the world as a merchant marine.

Over the next six years, the couple moved frequently. After spending a couple of years in Chicago, they moved to 17 Terrace Place in Croton-on-Hudson, just north of New York City. But again, Don took off, leaving Ruth to fend for herself for a few years while her husband visited sporadically.

She put a brave face on things and decided to pursue a musical career. Every Sunday morning, she ferried herself to Manhattan's Rockefeller Center to play the organ on a radio show called *The Church Today* on the NBC network, a weekly broadcast of a traditional church service. If Donald objected to his wife's career, it didn't stop her. After all, Ruth was a headstrong woman. Besides, he wasn't around enough to be bothered by it.

When it was clear that World War Two would soon end, the Kings returned to Maine and Donald retired from his footloose life. The couple fell into an uneasy truce in their modest home in Scarborough, Maine, an hour's drive from Ruth's relatives in Durham. Ruth had never learned to drive a car and depended on her husband to get around. He didn't care for her family, so visits were infrequent. The couple's unhappiness grew.

Donald took a job as a door-to-door salesman around Portland, pushing Electrolux vacuum cleaners to housewives who were establishing families and contented households as they settled into the beginnings of the postwar baby boom. Knowing that he'd spend each night in the same house, with the same woman, did nothing to soothe the restlessness Donald had indulged during the years he roamed all over the world, during stints at sea that lasted for months at a time. "As my mother once told me, he was the only man on the sales force who regularly demonstrated vacuum cleaners to pretty young widows at two o'clock in the morning," said Steve years later. "He was quite a ladies' man, according to my mother. In any case, he was a man with an itchy foot, a travelin' man, as the song says. I think trouble came easy to him."

Neither an adopted nor a biological child could keep Donald with his family. He was stuck in a place he didn't like with a family he didn't particularly want. And the housewives who invited him into their homes for more than his vacuum cleaners couldn't hold him either. He missed the adventure of the open road and sea, and waking up in the morning—or in the middle of the night—and never knowing which enemies he'd face.

So one night, when Steve had just turned two, Donald casually told his wife that he was going to the store for a pack of cigarettes. He walked out the door and kept on going. They never saw him again. The drama of his departure would be comically cliché, if not for the permanent damage it did to every member of the King family.

Ruth was a resourceful Mainer, frugal and practical by nature.

After her husband walked out, Ruth packed up her two kids, swallowed her pride, and depended on her relatives, as well as Don's family in Chicago, to put them up for a short time each while she looked for a job to keep them afloat. Steady jobs for a once-divorced, once-abandoned female pianist with two small children were not in great abundance, even in the great economic boom of the postwar years, so she took what she could get, which most often was menial labor as a housekeeper or bakery clerk.

The small King family would stay in a room in an aunt's or cousin's house or apartment until Ruth felt they were about to wear out their welcome, then they'd move on to the next sympathetic relative with a room to spare. Their perambulations took them far beyond Maine. During the first four years after Donald left and while Stephen was two to six years of age, they lived in Chicago; Fort Wayne, Indiana; Malden, Massachusetts; and West De Pere, Wisconsin.

Sometimes, to Ruth's great consternation, she had to split up the family. At one point Steve stayed with Ruth's younger sister Ethelyn and her husband, Oren Flaws, in West Durham, Maine, while Dave stayed with Mollie, another sister, in Malden, Massachusetts.

Ruth King rarely let her boys see her dejection at their poverty and constant moves. Instead, she dealt with their circumstances with a sense of humor and by telling her young sons stories. Both her optimism and storytelling would have a lasting influence on Steve.

The boys often shared a bedroom, more often a bed, and had to deal with threadbare hand-me-down clothes and broken toys from cousins who were often resentful at the attention Steve and David received. In the midst of such tumult, and with a few relatives who were clearly not thrilled about having a couple of youngsters underfoot, the two young boys quickly learned to look after each other, finding a comfortable refuge in books. They often read to each other. When Ruth got home from work, she'd grill them to make sure that they'd been reading the whole time she was gone.

In later years, Steve told a story from when he was four years old and playing outside with a friend who lived near a railroad line. He was supposed to wait to be picked up or to call Ruth when he wanted to come home, but he showed up back home an hour later, clearly in shock, his face white as a sheet.

While they were playing, Steve's friend had wandered over to the tracks and been hit by a freight train. "My mother told me they picked up the pieces in a wicker basket," he said years later. "My mom never knew if I had been near him, and I have no memory of the incident at all, only of having been told about it some years after the fact."

The family's constant changes of address continued. When Steve was in kindergarten, Ruth packed up the family to live with Donald's family in Chicago for a time. This was something new, a real connection to Steve's father. Through all their moves, Steve and Dave had learned to keep quiet whenever they were around grown-ups, but it became especially important when they were staying with Granny Spansky, Donald's mother. Steve was even better behaved around her for two reasons.

First, if he kept his mouth shut and just listened, maybe he'd hear her talk about why his father had left. After all, she was Donald's mother, she *had* to know what happened to him. But if she did know the whereabouts of her son, she wasn't talking.

Second, she was nothing like his mother's relatives back in Maine, who were reserved, quiet, and steered away from uncomfortable and difficult subjects. Granny Spansky reminded Steve of the evil witches in the stories he and Dave read to each other. "She was a big, heavyset woman who alternately fascinated and repelled me," he said. "I can still see her cackling like an old witch through toothless gums. She'd fry an entire loaf of bread in bacon drippings on an antique range and then gobble it down, chortling, 'My, that's *crisp!*'"

After they left Granny Spansky's house, they moved to West De Pere, Wisconsin, to live with Ruth's sister Cal for a while, then they moved on to Fort Wayne, Indiana, where they lived with Don's sister Betty for a few months before finding an apartment of their own nearby. But Steve already knew it wouldn't last. Either they'd be evicted—once they were kicked out of an apartment after the babysitter fell asleep and a neighbor saw Steve crawling on the roof of the building—or they'd wear out their welcome and the sisters would be calling each other long-distance to see who would take Ruth and the boys *this* time. Before long, it was time to move again.

When Stephen was six years old, Ruth and her sons moved to her sister Lois's house in Stratford, Connecticut. Finally, it looked as if Ruth's fortunes were starting to turn. After working for a few months, she had saved enough money to rent an apartment of their own nearby.

Once Steve got to school, he was always the new kid in the class, often more than once in one school year. But he quickly learned how to cope. If one of his classmates began to pick on him, it didn't last that long; Steve combined his intelligence and wit to gently disarm his fellow students—always in a nice way, he'd been on the receiving end of nasty and knew it only made the target hate the tormentor more—along with his teachers, and so he rarely had any trouble.

But from the beginning, Steve was a sickly kid. Whether from the stress of the family's constant moves or living in poverty, he spent most of the first-grade year home from school, confined to his bed. First he came down with measles, followed by strep throat, which then spread to his ears. He ended up with a nasty ear infection that wouldn't go away no matter how many antibiotics he took.

To combat boredom while at home, he devoured every book he could get his hands on, including a wide assortment of comic books of the day, but he also began to create his own stories. One day he copied the words out of the cartoon balloons into a notepad, adding some description about setting or a character's appearance whenever he felt it was necessary. He gave it to his mother, who read it and showered praise on him, until he admitted that he didn't really write it after all, it was mostly copied.

A flash of disappointment crossed her face. She told him those comics were mostly one-note: "He's always knocking someone's teeth out. I bet you could do better. Write one of your own."

Steve immediately got to work, scribbling out a story entitled "Mr. Rabbit Trick," about a white bunny who drove around town with his three animal pals looking for little kids in trouble to help. When he handed it to Ruth, the first question she asked was if he had written it himself. He answered yes. She told him it was good enough to be in a book, and he was so jazzed by her approval that he sat down and wrote four more stories about the rabbit and his buddies. She read them, smiled and laughed in all the right places, then gave Steve a quarter for each story.

It was the first money he made as a writer.

When he was engrossed in writing, he forgot he was sick. Though his stories made him feel better, they did nothing to clear up the infection. Ruth brought him to an ear doctor who recommended that his ears be lanced by sticking a sterilized needle into the eardrum to drain the moisture so the infection could heal. The doctor told the young boy to lie still on the exam table and be quiet. But he also assured Steve it wouldn't hurt. "The pain was beyond anything I have ever felt," he wrote years later. He howled and screamed as the tears ran down his face. But more important, he tried to absorb that the doctor had lied to him.

He returned to the doctor's office a week later, and again the doctor said it wouldn't hurt. "The second time I almost believed it," he said. But he was again betrayed. The third week when the lie was repeated, Steve kicked and thrashed on the table, anticipating the searing pain while realizing that he could do nothing to prevent what was about to happen. What made matters worse was that the doctor never got his name right, calling him Robert instead of Steve.

"In my panicky child's way, I'm thinking, 'Of course it will hurt! You're even lying about what my name is!'"

After his ears cleared up, his tonsils flared up next. After they were removed, he recovered, and he never again had to face a doctor with a needle pointed at his ear. But Steve had missed so much school that he had to repeat the first grade. To further embarrass him, that same year his brother, David, was doing so well that he was allowed to skip the fourth grade.

After Steve's father left, the only reference anyone in the family made to Donald was with a kind of shorthand: he became known as Daddy Done, short for Daddy Done Left.

"It was like he was an unperson," said Steve. Whenever Ruth had to leave Dave and Steve with various relatives, the boys would occasionally overhear a cousin or an aunt whispering among themselves that she'd had a nervous breakdown, and the only way she could get better was to go off and rest someplace for a while. The truth was that Ruth was actually working two and three jobs to pay off the debts Donald had accumulated during their marriage.

While she never wanted her kids to find out, Ruth did engage them in a bit of conspiracy before they entered elementary school. In the 1950s, for a husband to leave a wife, or to get a divorce, was the ultimate shame, especially in a small town, where neighbors would gossip about the real reasons and typically blame the woman. Only a widow could hold her head up high.

And so Ruth pulled her two young sons aside and told them what to say whenever anyone asked where their father was: "Tell them he's in the navy."

"We were ashamed not to have a father," said King. "I think my mother was deeply ashamed to have been left with these two young boys when her other sisters kept their husbands."

At one point Ruth had a job working the midnight shift at a bakery. Her sons would come home from school and have to tiptoe around so she could sleep. Desserts, a rarity before, now came in the form of broken cookies from the bakery.

Ruth lacked the time or the energy to chastise her children—she expected David to help her to raise his younger brother. But when Steve began to show interest in science fiction stories and horror comics, she told him she disapproved, though she never gave either of her children an outright no. Instead she preferred to let them make their own decisions and perhaps learn a lesson.

Steve's mother did forbid him to listen to radio broadcasts of Ray Bradbury's science fiction stories, but Steve eavesdropped anyway upstairs from his bedroom through a heating vent after he was supposed to be in bed as his mother listened to the radio downstairs. Afterward, he was so scared that he couldn't sleep in his own bed so he slept under his brother's.

As his appetite for books grew, a few started to make a huge impression on him. When he read *The 500 Hats of Bartholomew Cubbins* by Dr. Seuss, Steve realized that strange things could happen to perfectly normal people often for no reason at all.

He loved the comic-book series *Castle of Frankenstein* and bought the new installments every time one appeared on the newsstand.

Steve and his brother discovered E.C. Comics, which stood for Entertaining Comics, in the midfifties. The boys loved the ghosts, zombies, and ghouls that were featured in the bimonthly *Tales from the Crypt, The Vault of Horror,* and *The Crypt of Terror.* The publisher of E.C. was Bill Gaines, who would create a new kind of comic book in 1956 with *Mad* magazine. The narrators of E.C. comics would often start with an aside directed at "Dear Reader." This would later be echoed in Steve's work with the use of the salutation "Constant Reader" in his stories and novels.

"One of my favorites was when a baseball team was disemboweling the bad guys and lining the base paths with their intestines," Steve said. "They used his head for the ball, and this one eye was bulging out as the bat hits it."

Though Ruth was tolerant of her son's choice of reading material, she hated E.C. comics. She finally put her foot down when he began to wake up in the middle of the night screaming from his nightmares. She confiscated all of Steve's copies and refused to give them back, so he bought more and hid them under his bed. When she caught him, she'd ask why he was wasting his time with such junk. "Someday, I'm going to write this junk," he replied.

In addition to reading comic books and writing stories, Steve also loved the movies. When he was living in Connecticut, he watched the *Million Dollar Movie* on WOR, broadcast out of New York, as much as he could. This nightly program featured a black-and-white movie, usually from the 1940s, that was often repeated every night for a week. Steve was glued to the screen and began to study the structure, language, and special effects in each movie, and he began to apply the lessons he learned to his own writing. "I began to see things as I wrote, in a frame like a movie screen," he said.

He also saw *The Snake Pit,* a 1948 movie starring Olivia de Havilland, about a woman who is in an insane asylum but doesn't know how she ended up there and as a result is driven insane. Steve's wife, Tabby, later said that the movie made a lasting impression on him: "I think it may have infected him with a belief that you can go insane quite easily."

Steve agreed: "As a kid, I worried about my sanity a lot."

He also went to the movie theater as much as he could. He particularly loved the B-grade horror flicks such as *I Was a Teenage Werewolf* and *I Was a Teenage Frankenstein* and cheesy sci-fi movies like *Earth vs. the Flying Saucers* and *The Creature from the Black Lagoon.*

Though some people enjoy watching horror movies for the schlock value, even back then Steve never denied that he was scared out of his wits by these movies, while continuing to go back for more. "I *liked* to be scared, I liked the total surrender of emotional control," he said. "I'd been raised in a family where emotional control was a really important thing. You weren't supposed to show you were afraid, you weren't supposed to show that you were in pain or frightened or sad.

"There was a high premium on keeping yourself to yourself—on maintaining a pleasant exterior—saying 'Please' and 'Thank you,' and using your handkerchief even if you're on the *Titanic* and it's going down, because that's the way you were supposed to behave."

While being scared out of his wits, he was also studying the technical effects in the films. "I got a little more discriminating in my ability to detect special effects, if not necessarily my sense of taste," he observed. "Even when the flying saucer appeared to be a Kool cigarette filter tip with a sparkler stuck in it, it looked real to me because I was at a young and very credulous age."

But he wasn't too discriminating in his movie tastes: he also loved World War Two movies such as *Halls of Montezuma, Sands of Iwo Jima,* and *Gung Ho!*

In fact, the first movie that terrified him wasn't even a horror film, but one from Walt Disney. After he saw *Bambi* in 1955, the forest-fire scene gave him nightmares for weeks.

It wasn't just the movies that scared him; the normal things in everyday life did as well.

Perhaps Steve's greatest fear was what would happen to him and his brother if Ruth fell ill and couldn't take care of them. Or worse. It was clear that the relatives didn't want children. Steve thought he and Dave would end up in foster care or a place like the insane asylum in *The Snake Pit.*

Steve was learning that the world was a scary place—both the real one and the make-believe one—and as a result, his fears were beginning to multiply exponentially. He was afraid of spiders, falling into the toilet, older kids, what-if-his-mother-suddenly-walked-away-too, everything. He was afraid that he'd die before he was twenty years old. He was also scared of clowns. "When I was a kid, I saw other kids cry about clowns too," he said. "To me there's something scary, something sinister about such a figure of happiness and fun being evil."

Ruth did her part to contribute to her son's fears as well. "One of the reasons I've been so successful is that I was brought up by a woman who worried all the time," he said. "She'd tell me to put on my rubbers or I'd get pneumonia and die."

But back in the 1950s, some bona fide fears appeared as well, including a nationwide polio epidemic for which no vaccine existed. Most people refrained from swimming in public pools because of the fear of contracting the disease. And then there were the Russians. The general anxiety about the Communists was pervasive throughout the culture. And the fears of having an atomic bomb fall on your town were amplified with every school air-raid drill, which sent kids scurrying under their desks for protection.

One Saturday afternoon in October 1957, Steve was at a Saturday matinee when suddenly the movie screen went dark. The audience started to make noise, believing that the film strip had broken or the projectionist had switched to the wrong reel, but suddenly the lights came on overhead and the manager walked down the aisle and stood in front of the screen. "He mounted the stage and in a trembling voice, he told us that the Russians had just launched a space satellite into orbit around Earth called *Sputnik,*" said King. The United States was supposed to be number one when it came to everything—military strength and technology among them—and so when it was clear the Russians had taken the lead, the nation felt as if it had been punched in the gut.

In addition to warning Steve and Dave about the dangers of catching cold, Ruth King was fond of giving her children advice by offering up pithy sayings such as "You'll never be hung for your beauty" and "You need that like a hen needs a flag." After a particularly grueling day at work, she'd caution her children to "hope for the best and expect the worst."

Though Steve brushed some of the sayings off, two in particular he took to heart, while providing them with a little bit of a spin: "If you think the worst, it can't come true" and "If you can't say something nice, keep your mouth shut."

Fortunately, Ruth never said he couldn't *write* things that weren't nice.

Throughout his childhood, Steve continued to write and Ruth continued to pay him a quarter for each story. He wrote his first horror story at the age of seven. Spending almost every weekend and every weeknight sitting slack-jawed in front of a movie screen had begun to affect his subject matter.

"I had internalized the idea from the movies that just when everything looked blackest, the scientists would come up with some off-the-wall solution that would take care of things," he said. So he wrote a story about a dinosaur that was creating a lot of damage and havoc when one of the scientists came to the rescue. "He said, 'Wait, I have a theory—the old dinosaur used to be allergic to leather.' So they went out and threw leather boots and shoes and leather vests at it, and it went away."

However, all of the movies and comics and horror stories Steve devoured also had a downside: they often caused nightmares. "My imagination was too big for my head at that point, and so I spent a lot of miserable hours," he said. "With the kind of imagination I had, you couldn't switch off the images once you'd triggered them, so I'd see my mother laid out in a white-silk-lined mahogany coffin with brass handles, her dead face blank and waxen. I'd hear the organ dirges in the background, and then I'd see myself being dragged off to some Dickensian workhouse by a terrible old lady in black."

At the age of eight, he had a dream where he saw the body of a hanged man on a scaffold atop a hill. "When the wind caused the corpse to turn in the air, I saw that it was my own face, rotted and picked by the birds, but still obviously mine. And then the corpse opened its eyes and looked at me."

He woke up and started screaming and couldn't stop. "Not only was I unable to go back to sleep for hours after that, but I was really afraid to turn out the light for weeks. I can still see it as clearly now as when it happened."

In 1958, Ruth moved the family from Connecticut to West Durham, Maine, a small town about thirty miles north of Scarborough, so she could care for her ailing, elderly parents, who were both in their eighties.

It was her sisters' idea. The arrangement was that her siblings would offer Ruth food and a place, an old, rickety farmhouse with an outhouse out back. Steve, Dave, and Ruth would share the house and receive spare food and canned goods in exchange for caring for Mama and Daddy Guy, as they were known, who were beginning to have trouble taking care of themselves. Ruth's sister and brother-in-law Ethelyn and Oren Flaws also lived nearby.

Ruth accepted the offer, and the three settled in West Durham in a neighborhood near Runaround Pond that Steve later described as consisting of "four families and a graveyard."

Once the family had settled in, Steve discovered he was surrounded by relatives and the family history, exaggerations and gossip characteristic of small towns—including a few good ghost stories. By listening to the tall tales and rumors, he learned that people liked to invent truths where there were none. It was a valuable lesson for a budding writer.

Ruth came from a long line of Methodists, so her children dutifully attended services and Bible school several times a week at the tiny, two-hundred-year-old Methodist church next door to their house.

Fewer than twenty families attended the church, so the parish had no funds to retain a full-time preacher. The church drew on members of the congregation to lead services and preach sermons, a rotating selection that occasionally included Steve, though several times a year when they were feeling flush, parishioners would invite a traveling preacher to conduct services.

Hanging on one of the walls of the parish hall was a poster with the words METHODISTS SAY NO, THANK YOU. At Sunday school, children would dutifully learn their Bible verses and recite them from memory. For their efforts, they were rewarded with unadorned miniature crucifixes that the children could paint as they desired, deciding for themselves whether to add the bloody thorns on the hands and feet.

"I listened to a lot of fire and brimstone as a child," Steve said. "Part of me will always be that Methodist kid who was told that you were not saved by work alone, and that hellfire was very long." One story he heard that described the afterlife was about a pigeon that flies to a mountain made of iron to rub its beak on the metal only once every ten thousand years, and the time it took the mountain to erode is the equivalent of the first second of hell. "When you're six or seven years old, that kind of stuff bends your mind a little," he said, readily admitting the images from church have long influenced his stories and novels.

Stephen attended fifth and sixth grades in the Center Grammar School, a one-room schoolhouse a few doors down from his own. Because he had repeated the first grade, he was not only the biggest kid in the class but also the oldest. Despite his childhood illnesses, he'd shot up to a height of six foot two by the age of twelve.

West Durham was so small that it lacked a library, but once a week the state sent the Bookmobile to the town, a mobile library in a big green van. To Steve, it was a vast improvement over the library in Stratford, Connecticut, where he had only been allowed to check out books from the children's section, most often Nancy Drew and Hardy Boys novels. With the Bookmobile, patrons could take out three books a week, and the kids could borrow books from the adult section. While browsing the adult shelves, Steve discovered several police-procedural novels by Ed McBain. A few pages into the first one he took home, a scene described the cops interrogating a woman standing in the doorway of her slum apartment dressed in nothing more than a slip. The police turn away and tell her to go get dressed, but instead she pushes her breast toward them, saying, "In your eye, cop!"

"Immediately something clicked in my head," said Steve. "I thought, that's real, that could really happen, and that was the end of the Hardy Boys and all juvenile fiction for me."

From McBain, he progressed to Edgar Allan Poe and John D. MacDonald, running through the classics of horror, crime, and speculative fiction. Soon he was always the first in line when the Bookmobile rolled back into town.

As he had done back in Connecticut, Steve spent many Saturday afternoons sitting in the dark at the movies, and the Ritz Theater in Lewiston was one of his regular haunts. Since he was so tall for his age, the ticket clerk tried to charge him the adult price. He got in the habit of tucking his birth certificate into his pocket so he could verify his age.

As time passed, Steve began to retreat more into his books and movies. Even though the family was together with little chance of splitting up again, life at home was harder than in Connecticut, especially for Ruth.

For nearly a decade, the Kings had lived on very little cash, subsisting on barter and whatever their relatives could spare—a bag of groceries here and some hand-me-down clothes there. In summers, the farm's well would inevitably dry up and they'd have to tote water from Ethelyn's house a half mile away. Their own house had no bath or shower, so in the winters the boys would take a bath at their aunt's house, then walk home through the snow, their bodies still steaming.

Steve would later compare their life to a sharecropping arrangement, where his mother worked long hours for little reward. "Those were very unhappy years for my mother," he said. "She had no money, and she was always on duty. My grandmother had total senile dementia and was incontinent." Ruth used an old wringer washing machine to do the laundry, and when she hung the diapers on the clothesline in winter, her hands started to bleed because the combination of the lye and the cold water dried out her skin. She had still not learned to drive a car and so was always dependent on others around her who did.

An unspectacular intimacy with death no longer so familiar to most Americans also characterized Stephen's formative years. This became especially true once the Kings moved back to Durham. In rural Maine of the 1950s and '60s, families still dealt with their dead at home, instead of relying on a funeral home. Besides, most residents didn't have the money to pay for an undertaker. Steve had seen a number of dead bodies—mostly elderly relatives laid out at his friends' homes—along with the body of a man who had drowned in a pond in Durham.

In the late 1950s, the saga of Charles Starkweather captured the attention of the American public. With his fourteen-year-old girlfriend, Caril Fugate, the nineteen-year-old Starkweather went on a rampage, killing eleven people in Nebraska and Wyoming—including Fugate's mother, stepfather, and sister—over two months in the winter of 1957–58. Starkweather was caught, tried, and executed in 1959, and Fugate was sentenced to life in prison and paroled in 1976.

Young Steve was fascinated and revolted by the serial killer and started to keep a scrapbook of newspaper clippings about Starkweather's exploits. He'd sit for hours, staring at the photos of the condemned killer, trying to figure out where he'd gone wrong. As usual, Ruth thought it wasn't something her eleven-year-old son should be following so closely.

"Good God, you're warped," she told him when she found his scrapbook. But as he explained to his mother, he studied Starkweather so that if he ran into someone with the same deadened eyes on the street, he'd be able to recognize the killer and stay far away. But he realized even at that early age something else was at play.

"There's always the urge to see somebody dead that isn't you," he said. "That urge doesn't change because civilization or society does, it's hardwired into the human psyche, a perfectly valid human need to say, 'I'm okay,' and the way I can judge that is that these people are not.

"To me, Charles Starkweather was totally empty. I was examining the human equivalent of a black hole, and that's what really attracted me to Starkweather. Not that I wanted to be like him, but I wanted to recognize him if I met him on the street and get out of his way. You could see it in his eyes, to a degree. There was something gone in there. But I also understood that it was in me, and it was in a lot of people."

But something else was behind his fascination with Starkweather. "There was a little voice inside my head that said, 'You're gonna be writing about people like this your whole life, so here's the starting line, GO!'"

On the surface, Steve's childhood looked similar to other boys' lives in the 1950s: he hung out with his friends, tinkered with cars, and listened to rock and roll. The first record he owned was an Elvis Presley 78 with "Hound Dog" on the A side and "Don't Be Cruel" on the flip side. He wore out both sides of the record playing it over and over. "It was like finding something that was very, very powerful, like a drug," he said. "It made you bigger than you were. It made you tough even if you weren't."

But once he became a teenager, he stood out for being just a little bit eccentric. For instance, he'd head out to spend the afternoon at a friend's house and show up in his bedroom slippers, probably because so much was going on in his head that he forgot to change into shoes.

He often felt like an outcast, though he had learned at an early age to keep his mouth shut about it. "I kept that part of myself to myself," he said. "I never wanted to let anybody get at it. I figured they'd steal it if they knew what I thought about certain things. It wasn't the same thing as being embarrassed about it, so much as wanting to keep it and sort of work it out for myself."

He found that the only way to do that was to write about it.

In 1959, David got hold of an old mimeograph machine, and the two boys decided to publish a local newsletter. Selling it for a nickel, they wrote and distributed *Dave's Rag* to their neighbors in West Durham. Dave wrote news stories about people in the neighborhood while Steve wrote reviews of his favorite TV shows and movies as well as a few short stories. The response was favorable, with most neighbors buying a few copies, but after a few months, Dave's interest waned.

Steve wasn't too disappointed, for that meant there would be more time for writing his own stories and reading. In West Durham, Steve began what would become a lifelong habit of taking long afternoon walks while his nose was stuck in a book. Both Ruth and Dave shared his love of reading—it wasn't unusual to see the family sitting around the dinner table, each reading a paperback—but Steve devoured more books than his brother and mother combined. He got lost in the stories, but he was also starting to note how each author told the story and how he built suspense and made Steve care—or not care—about the characters. He learned something with each book he read, and he simply couldn't get enough.

He also started to write as much as he read. Every free moment when he wasn't in school or helping his mother with some of the chores, he was writing or reading.

When Ruth bought him a behemoth, secondhand Underwood typewriter for $35, he knew he had everything he needed to start on his path as a writer, and he began to submit his stories to the pulp thriller and mystery magazines he'd been reading for years. He wrote after school and on weekends, and during summer vacations he rarely left his attic bedroom. "I'd be upstairs during the summer pounding away in my underpants, streaming with sweat," he said. He typed so much that the letter *M* broke off, and he had to write in the missing letters by hand on each manuscript page.

The more he wrote, the better he felt. He had a way to deal with the images and thoughts that he knew his family and society wouldn't understand. His stories were full of blood and gore and inhumane impulses—just like the stories he loved to read—but writing them, getting them out, was better than keeping them inside.

"As a child, Stephen King saw and felt too much for his age," said George Beahm, author of several books on King and his work. "Consider how sensitive children generally are: they don't have a way to edit, to filter, to take a critical stance on experience around them. I would say that the reason why these images come out so powerfully in his fiction is because as a child he had no way to filter. Everything just came in, and it affected him deeply."

His childhood friend Chris Chesley believes that Steve's sense of isolation had as large an effect on his writing as the movies he saw, the books he read, and the murderous impulses he often felt. "His mother worked and his brother was older and off with his friends, so Steve spent a lot of time by himself," said Chesley. "In that respect, he was different from many of us who knew him because he was more isolated than we were."

Even though he had just started to submit stories to the pulp magazines of the day, Steve was calmly convinced of his talent and future success even at the age of fourteen. Chesley would sit with Steve in his friend's bedroom, reading, writing, and smoking. They'd take turns at the typewriter, one reading a book while the other cranked out a couple of pages. One day, Chesley remembered, Steve finished his stint at the typewriter and glanced over at him with a cigarette dangling from his mouth.

"You know what I'm gonna do the first time I hit it big, Chris? I'm gonna get myself a great big Cadillac!" Steve would laugh, light another cigarette, and return to the typewriter, even though it was Chris's turn.

Steve encountered a relative in Durham who reminded him of the way Granny Spansky had kept him spellbound for hours, though while his grandmother had captivated him because she reminded him of a fairy-tale witch, Uncle Clayton's stories were what mesmerized young Steve. "Some of the best yarns in those days were spun by my uncle Clayton, a great old character who had never lost his childlike sense of wonder," he said. "Uncle Clayt would cock his hunting cap back on his mane of white hair, roll a Bugler cigarette with one liver-spotted hand, light up with a Diamond match he'd scratch on the side of his boot, and launch into great stories, not only about ghosts but about local legends and scandals, family goings-on, the exploits of Paul Bunyan, everything under the sun. I'd listen spellbound to that slow down-east drawl of his and I'd be in another world."

Uncle Clayton, who wasn't really a relative, but a family friend, had a few other talents that kept Steve fascinated. The old man was able to track a bee from a flower to the hive—a skill called lining—and he knew how to dowse for water by using a Y-shaped piece of wood to locate a good place to dig for a well.

Steve had already started to file away the stories of these eclectic, eccentric relatives. He knew he might use them one day.

Writing was not only helping Steve to survive a childhood riddled with instability and poverty, but he was also beginning to use his skill to define himself and who he was. By the time Steve was fourteen, a few key facts had already cemented themselves in his young mind: Writing allowed him to forget the physical and emotional discomforts in his life, and it was good enough for someone to pay him for it. Yeah, it was his mother, but at least it was a start. The connection between writing and financial self-sufficiency had been made. He also knew that judging from the crowds at the movie theater and the popularity of books of scary tales, other people enjoyed being scared just as much as he did.

Rural Maine was filled with stories, and death was everywhere. And so, the general shape of Stephen King's life and creative gifts were cast.

Even though Ruth thought her youngest son was a bit too intrigued by horror stories and movies, she herself enjoyed a really frightening story or movie. However, she despised what she called an Alfred Hitchcock ending, where, after getting a viewer sucked into the lives of the characters up on the silver screen, Hitch chose an ending that was deliberately murky and unclear. Young Steve filed that opinion away.

One day Steve asked his mother if she had ever seen a dead body. She nodded, then told him two stories.

The first time, she was standing outside the Graymore Hotel in Portland when a sailor jumped off the roof twelve stories above the street. "He hit the sidewalk and splattered," she said.

The other time was while growing up in Scarborough. One day she went to the beach and saw a crowd of people standing on the shore and several boats attempting to go out to sea. A woman had been swimming, and a riptide had drawn her out to where she couldn't swim back on her own. The boats were unable to reach her since the current was too strong. Ruth said, "People stood on the beach and listened to that woman scream for hours before she finally drowned." It sounded like a story Steve would read in one of his E.C. comics, and it stuck with him for years.

Spurred on by his mother, Steve continued to write whenever he had a free moment. Though he had already begun to submit some of his stories to magazines, his work would be greeted by form rejection slips. So he decided to take matters into his own hand, and when he was fourteen, he wrote a sixteen-page novelization of the movie *The Pit and the Pendulum,* which had come out in 1961, starring Vincent Price and Barbara Steele based on the Edgar Allan Poe story. Steve typed up the story—replete with misspelled words—and added his own touches, remembering his mother's advice to make up his own story, so much so that it didn't come close to resembling the movie. He ran it off on an ancient copy machine, brought the copies to school, and hawked it to his classmates for a quarter apiece, since his mom had established that as the going rate. By the end of the day, he had a pocket-ful of quarters. He was suspended from school not because of plagiarism, but because his teachers and the principal thought he shouldn't be reading about horror, let alone writing about it.

He apologized effusively to his teachers, the principal, his mother, and to the students who'd plunked down a quarter to read his writing. He wanted everyone to like him, and Ruth thought that his desire to please was hard-wired into his system. One of his mother's favorite lines was "Stevie, if you were a girl, you'd always be pregnant."

But in Steve's mind, he wanted to please his mother in particular because he knew how hard her life was. They ate a lot of lobster while Steve was grow-ing up—back then it was considered to be poor man's food. A family would often keep a pot of stew on the stove for several days, reheating it when neces-sary and adding more lobster meat, potatoes, onions, and carrots when the pot ran low. Though it provided necessary sustenance, many families were embar-rassed at having to rely on it.

"If the minister visited, she took it off the stove and put it behind the door, as if he wouldn't be able to smell it," said Steve, "but the smell was all through the house and got in your clothes, your hair."

Nineteen-sixty marked a huge leap into the modern world for Steve as he moved from the one-room schoolhouse to a new building where nothing was a hand-me-down, from the desks and chairs to the books. Durham Elemen-tary was for grades one through eight and opened to much fanfare in a town that had previously had two run-down one-room schoolhouses. Steve joined its first class of seventh graders.

On the first day of school, the kids were most excited about having flush toilets and running water indoors. For many students, it was the first time they rode a bus to school.

Lew Purinton first met Steve in the seventh grade when Durham Elemen-tary opened. Since they lived on opposite ends of town, they had attended different one-room schools.

Steve was hard to miss. "He was the biggest kid in the class," said Purinton. "I remember seeing him walking down the aisle between the desks, and I asked him how old he was, since he looked so much bigger than the rest of us. He looked down at me and said, 'I'm old enough to know better, but I'm too young to care.'"

With that acerbic remark, Purinton knew he had a new friend. They were in the same class of twenty-five students, and soon they began to hang out outside of school.

Purinton visited Steve at his house, which he remembers was an old farmhouse much different from his own home. "It was obvious that they didn't have money, that they were struggling," he said. "The house wasn't neat and clean."

However, the thing that stood out in his mind was Steve's tiny bedroom, where literally hundreds of paperback books were stacked around the edges of the room and even at the end of Steve's bed, with no bookshelf in sight. Most of the books were science fiction and horror.

When Lew asked his friend about them, Steve said he'd read every one of them. Scattered through the piles of books were numerous volumes by H. P. Lovecraft, a horror writer from the early twentieth century widely considered to be the genre's successor to Edgar Allan Poe.

Steve was thirteen when he first discovered Lovecraft, which he later maintained was an ideal age to start reading his work. "Lovecraft is the perfect fiction for people who are living in a state of sort of total sexual doubt, because the stories almost seem to me sort of Jungian in their imagery," he later said. "They're all about gigantic disembodied vaginas and things that have teeth."

With Lovecraft and his other favorite authors around, Steve viewed his room as a sanctuary away from the pressures of school and the need to fit in as an unathletic kid with bad eyes and little coordination and no success with girls. He wasn't popular, yet he wasn't totally stigmatized such as two girls who lived in his neighborhood.

One was a girl whose mother entered every single sweepstakes and contest that came down the pike. She won prizes regularly, but they tended toward the unusual: enough pencils or tuna fish to last for a year. The most expensive and prestigious prize she won was Jack Benny's old Maxwell car, though she never drove it and let it sit beside the house to slowly rust and rot into the ground.

Even though she had enough money to buy postage stamps to enter all the contests and sweepstakes, she apparently had little left over for her kids. The children were given one set of clothes that had to last from September through June. Obviously, they were an easy target of ridicule for the other kids.

Sophomore year, the girl broke ranks and wore a completely different outfit after returning from Christmas vacation. Her usual outfit—black skirt, white blouse—was swapped out for a woolen sweater and a skirt that was in style.

She'd even permed her hair. "But everybody made more fun of her because nobody wanted to see her change the mold," said Steve.

He had taken to doing odd jobs for neighbors. A couple of times, he was hired to dig a grave at the local cemetery. His friend Brian Hall's father oversaw the graveyard and hired the boys to do the job, which paid twenty-five bucks, a fortune to a teenage boy in the early sixties.

Another time, he was hired by the mother of the other outcast girl, who tried to make herself as small as possible whenever she had to walk down the halls of high school. The family lived in a trailer near Steve's house in West Durham. When Steve went into the trailer to do an odd job for the mother, he was dumbfounded by the enormous crucifix that towered over the living room. The Jesus figure was particularly realistic, with blood dripping from the hands and feet and an anguished look on his face.

The girl's mother told Steve that Jesus was her personal savior, then asked him if he'd been saved. He said he hadn't and left the house as quickly as possible.

When he started to write *Carrie,* the memory of these two outcasts inspired his portrayal of the main character. He later discovered that both girls had died by the time he began writing the story; the girl with one outfit for the entire year shot herself in the stomach shortly after giving birth to a child, while the other, an epileptic, had moved out of the trailer after graduating from Lisbon High, but had suffered a seizure in her apartment and died alone.

From the time he was ten years old, though Steve loved to play sports, he wasn't athletic. At his new school, the students spent recess and lunchtime out on the playground playing games.

Baseball was a popular choice for these informal recreation times, and Steve loved to play baseball, but when it came time to pick sides, he was inevitably one of the last kids picked.

However, he was actively recruited for football because of his size. "I *had* to play football, because if you were big and didn't play football, that meant you were a fucking faggot," he said. "All I was good for in football was left tackle." Though he had a few good friends he hung out with, that didn't stop him from feeling different from the other kids at school.

He was also unofficially banned from joining the Boy Scouts since he didn't have a father to help the boys out.

If Steve was bothered by being excluded—first the ball field, then Boy

Scouts—he didn't show it. One day in the fall of 1960, he'd made an important discovery in the attic above his Aunt Ethelyn and Uncle Oren's garage. The musty space had long been a catchall for old stuff that various family members no longer had any immediate use for but, being frugal Mainers, wouldn't throw away. After all, you never knew when somebody might be able to put something to good use.

The children in the family—including Steve and his brother, David—were discouraged from going into the attic. The wooden planks of the floor had never permanently been attached to the beams, and in a few places there were gaps.

Nevertheless, one day Steve decided to go exploring and got the biggest surprise of his life so far. His mother had stowed away most of the artifacts from her ill-fated marriage to Steve's father in the attic years earlier after it was clear that Don had gone AWOL for good. Steve discovered that his long-gone father had a penchant for the same kinds of pulp paperbacks—mysteries and horror—that he devoured.

What was even more shocking was that in another box, young Steve found a stack of rejection slips from magazines with hastily scribbled notes of encouragement asking Don to try again.

His father had been an aspiring writer too!

Steve continued to dig through the other boxes, but didn't find any of his father's manuscripts or published stories. He ran downstairs to confront his mother, accusing her of hiding the truth about his father from him. Ruth calmed him down and explained.

"My mother told me that he wrote lots of really good stories, that he sent them off to magazines, and he got letters back saying, 'Please send us more.' But he was kind of lazy about it and never really did very much," Steve said.

Then she delivered the one-two punch that would remain with Steve all his life. "Steve," she said, kind of laughing, "your father didn't have any persistence. That's why he left the marriage."

Steve saw what his father's laziness had done to his mother and his family, and he swore he would never be like that.

But he was also intrigued by what he shared with his father. Maybe writing—and getting published, Steve's dream—would be a way to connect with the father he'd never known.

Steve thanked his mother for telling him the truth and excused himself from the room. He made a beeline for the attic back at their old, ramshackle farmhouse with the peeling paint, sat down at the desk under the alcove in the attic, and slipped a fresh sheet of paper into the typewriter.

In the spring of 1962, Steve graduated from eighth grade at the top of his class. He would later wryly say it was because "there were only three of us in the class, and one of them was retarded."

In the fall, King entered the freshman class at Lisbon High School in Lisbon Falls, eight miles away from West Durham.

Lisbon High had approximately five hundred students in grades nine through twelve, many of them, like Steve, coming from surrounding towns that had no high school. Two of Steve's classmates from elementary school entered in the same freshman class: Lew Purinton and Pete Higgins, whose dad was the principal at Lisbon High. The school had three official academic tracks: the A group, for students who planned to go on to college; the B track, for business-oriented students; and the C track, called the commercial track, where all the other students ended up, similar to the vocational/technical high school programs offered today. Occasionally a student would move from one track to another, most often downward from A to B, or B to C, when he started to fall behind. Steve, Pete, and Lew were in the college track, and so they were in all of the same classes, including algebra, English, and French.

Other unofficial tracks at the school were hammered out according to social strata: the athletes, the hoods, the nerds, and everybody else.

Though he always had his nose stuck in a book and never tried to hide his intelligence, Steve didn't fall into the nerd group because he liked people and was a bit of a ham in school. He excelled in English and easily earned straight A's in his classes, but his grades were lower in his science classes: C's in chemistry and B-minuses in physics. "I was never a geek, but on the other hand, I saw a lot of movies in the fifties like *The Thing* and *Them!*" he said. "I know that radiation causes monsters, and most important of all I know that if we mess around too much with the unknown, something awful will happen."

He obviously wasn't the James Dean type for the same reason he didn't fall into the athlete category. "I wasn't too cool," he said. "I wasn't the kind of kid who would get elected to student council, but neither did I lurk around the lockers looking like I was just waiting for somebody to haul off on me."

According to Pete Higgins, Steve fell into the catchall group of everybody else, but he traveled freely between the three other groups primarily because of his quick wit and offbeat sense of humor.

"He was a little bit different because he was taller than most of the kids," said Higgins. "He also wore those dark black glasses, and judging from his appearance, it was obvious he didn't come from a lot of money. But he was always ready to add something to a class discussion that would make the kids or the teacher laugh."

Steve also learned how to disarm those students who would otherwise have felt inclined to pick on him. "He gained a certain amount of confidence in high school," said Lew Purinton. "Kids accepted him more once they realized that he was intelligent and he could do a lot of things. And he was a genuinely nice guy."

Despite his efforts to make classmates feel comfortable, some students and teachers still misunderstood him. Prudence Grant, who taught at Lisbon High School when Steve was a student there, remembered that he was often teased by a few of the older boys on his way home from school. "He was the butt of a lot of pranks," she said. "They'd hide in a hollow, and as Stephen came down over the hill, they would jump out at him or scare him." Later on, when she read *Carrie,* she immediately recognized that he had based several characters in the novel on teachers at the school.

"I know that *Carrie* was heavily based on Lisbon High down to several faculty members," Grant said. "We had a bumbling assistant principal, and he's portrayed in the book as the guy who closes the file-drawer door and slams his thumb in there. There were other teachers who were portrayed in the book, but I didn't make the story, which is fine by me."

Peter Higgins remembered one kid in particular who was a thorn in Steve's side who fell into the James Dean–wannabe category. "In study halls, he'd bug Steve and call him Mickey Mouse because he said that's what Steve looked like." Higgins added that the other kid would tease Steve under his breath so the teachers wouldn't hear, and that the other students were well aware of what was going on. "But no one stepped in to stop it because they were afraid that the guy would turn to them next," said Higgins.

"I hated school," said Steve. "I always felt I was wearing the wrong clothes, or like I had too many spots on my face. I don't trust people who look back on high school with fondness; too many of them were part of the overclass, those who were taunters instead of tauntees."

Steve got through his freshman year and spent the summer upstairs in the attic of the old, creaky farmhouse, banging away on the typewriter without an *M.* He dutifully continued to send out stories, receiving a steady stream of rejection slips. He collected so many that he drove a nail into the wall above his desk and stabbed the slips on it. Most notices came back with no personal comments, but occasionally he'd get one with a hand-scribbled note that said, *Terrible story, shows some talent.* "At least I knew it wasn't just robots reading my work," he said.

On September 12, 1963, Steve had just started his sophomore year in high school when he came home from school one day and checked on his grandmother as usual. Her room was eerily still. He called her name, but she didn't respond. He froze for a moment, then recalled a couple of movies where a character held a pocket mirror up to a person's mouth to see if it fogged up. He tiptoed over to her dresser and grabbed a compact and held it up to her mouth. It stayed clear. Nothing. He sat down in a chair across the room and stared at his grandmother's body. He'd seen corpses before, but only for fleeting moments or from across the room at the wakes at his friends' homes.

So this was what a dead body *really* looked like.

He lost track of how long he sat there before his mother came home to find him.

Despite being forced to discontinue selling his novelization of *The Pit and the Pendulum* in seventh grade, Steve resumed offering his stories to fellow students, though this time he was smart enough not to sell them. At the time, *The Man from U.N.C.L.E.* was a popular TV show, and during study hall Steve would make up a story of his own using the characters Napoleon Solo and Illya Kuryakin from the program. Lew Purinton witnessed the process several times.

"He'd start writing, and when he was done with a page, he'd hand it to me, and I'd start reading," Purinton remembered. "By the time I got down to the bottom of the page, he had the next page ready. He brought other kids in the class into the story and set it in Lisbon Falls and Durham. Every time I was finished with a page, he'd have another one for me. He loved to write, and he was always writing."

Finally in 1965, the long-awaited day arrived: a letter arrived from the magazine *Comics Review,* telling him they wanted to publish his story "I Was a Teenage Grave Robber." The story was about a mad scientist who cultivated human-size maggots and hired an orphaned teenager to dig up fresh corpses for them to feed upon. Steve drew on his experience digging graves to add a note of realism to the gravedigging part, and revenge ensued when the maggots attacked and ate the scientist and the teenager escaped.

The only compensation the magazine offered was a couple of copies of the magazine, and the editor changed the title to "In a Half World of Terror." Steve didn't care, he was thrilled that someone wanted to print his work.

Being a published author did nothing to advance him in the eyes of the female students at Lisbon High. Whether it was his gawky looks, his obvious poverty, the lack of a car, or some combination of these, he struck out with the girls more often than not. The logistics of living so far out in the country in the early sixties obviously didn't help. Hitchhiking was a possibility, though a clearly unpalatable option for everyone involved.

"We could thumb it, but things were more complicated than that," King explained. First, he went to one of his friends who owned a car to see if he wanted to go to the movies, and Steve offered to pay for half the gas if his buddy would play chauffeur or bring his own date. "He'd agree, so I'd go ask some pretty girl out and she'd say she was busy." Or else the friend would have a girl with him and Steve would be dateless. "After I got my license, I can remember going to the drive-in a couple of times, and I'm behind the wheel all by myself while they're making out like crazy in the backseat," he complained.

But he didn't have much time to spend feeling sorry for himself. Between his studies, his reading—Purinton remembered Steve reading a book as he walked down the hallways from class to class—and his writing, in the tenth grade he became the editor in chief of *The Drum,* the school newspaper at Lisbon High. Then, as now, Steve was more interested in fiction as opposed to stories that required facts and research—and therefore had to be 100 percent true—so his heart wasn't in it. He did write several stories for the paper including "The 43rd Dream" and "Code Name: Mousetrap," but he raised eyebrows when instead of publishing an issue every week or two as his predecessor had, he produced only one issue over the year.

During one slow night at the newspaper's office when his attention wandered to all of the comics, horror flicks, and detective novels he could be reading—or writing—instead of slogging through class reports and navel-gazing adolescent poetry, he got a brainstorm: why not publish a newspaper that kids will want to read? Of course, it went without saying that it would be something he actually enjoyed writing. And so *The Village Vomit,* a four-page satirical broadsheet where thinly disguised stories of his least favorite teachers and students appeared above the fold—in other words, an exact parody of *The Drum*—was born.

Steve printed it up and distributed copies around the school, and it was an instant hit. In one story, he poked fun at a business teacher, a prim and proper old maid, by having the Wolf Man—then a popular horror-movie character—carry her off.

He neglected to put his name anywhere in the paper, but word quickly spread who was responsible. He was suspended from school for three days and had to apologize to every teacher he'd made fun of. His notoriety earned him new respect among his classmates, even among those who had teased and bullied him before. Steve learned that his writing could serve as a shield, to deflect attention from people who didn't like him for whatever reason.

A few days after his suspension ended, the administration met to discuss how they could help Steve channel his talent, and he landed a job working part-time as a sports reporter for the *Lisbon Weekly Enterprise,* writing up high school football and basketball games. He enjoyed his work, but all the while he was watching the games, dutifully taking notes and interviewing fans, he wished he could be playing the games instead of reporting them.

"He loved sports, but he wasn't athletic," said Purinton. "I think that was a big frustration for him, because he really wanted to be a good athlete." He did play football one year, but perhaps a greater obstacle for Steve than his lack of athletic ability was that he lived so far from school and lacked both a car and a license.

With no bus service, Steve usually took Yanko's Taxi Service, a local livery company hired specifically to ferry students the eight miles back and forth to school. But getting home after school was a different story. If he missed the afternoon taxi service, he'd have to grab a ride with someone who was heading his way or hitchhike. And if no one stopped, he'd have to walk home, often after it had turned dark and cold.

To Steve, the best thing about the taxi service—run by a Slovakian man named Yanko—was that part of the fleet was made up of old Pontiac and Cadillac hearses from the 1940s and '50s. The girl who lived a few houses away from Steve's, whose living room contained the life-size crucifix, rode along. Steve and the other students were sure to be first in line when the taxi arrived. "There was a rush to get the best seat," said his neighbor and classmate Brian Hall, "because no one wanted to ride all the way to Lisbon with her on his lap."

In high school, Steve's musical tastes continued to develop. Elvis notwithstanding, in 1963 the majority of music played on the radio harkened back to the fifties with easy-listening instrumentals and doo-wop pop hits. Henry Mancini and Barbra Streisand won Grammys that year, but so did a little-known acoustic trio by the name of Peter, Paul, and Mary, who won Best Performance by a Vocal Group for their song "Blowin' in the Wind." Folk music was starting to spread across the country, even to rural outposts such as Durham, Maine.

Steve and his buddies took notice of the new trend. Along with his friend Chris Chesley, Steve began to explore folk music and was particularly drawn to singers such as Dave Van Ronk, Bob Dylan, and Tom Paxton. "We were crazy about Phil Ochs because he sounded the way we felt most of the time, pissed off and confused," said Steve. "The music had an urgent, homemade feel that spoke to our hearts. When I started smoking Pall Malls a year or two later, I did so because I was sure that my hero, Dave Van Ronk, smoked them. What other brand could the elucidator of 'Bed Bug Blues' possibly smoke?"

Chesley had a Gibson guitar and taught himself how to play, and between odd jobs and borrowing a few dollars, Steve managed to retrieve a guitar he had hocked earlier at a Lewiston pawnshop. He, Chris, and a few others formed a ragtag band and played together at a few school functions, but they never got good enough to play at the high school dances.

Steve was more a wallflower than a Fred Astaire, but the common practice at the school was to cruise the girls, not gravitate to the dance floor. The guys would stand on one side of the gym and the girls on the other—though some girls would always be out dancing—and they'd walk around the perimeter of the dance floor, flirting and laughing at whomever they wanted to impress.

According to Pete Higgins, Steve was far from being a ladies' man, and he was much more interested in going to some of the unofficial parties. A few classmates organized the after-hours parties at a cluster of abandoned houses a few miles from where Steve lived, and one of the houses was supposedly haunted; the last family to occupy the house went by the name of Marston.

After the students grew bored with the music and tired of being hounded by chaperones at the high school dance, they'd get three or four carloads of their classmates together and head over to the Marston house to scare the girls, drink, and make out. The drinking age in Maine at the time was eighteen, so it wasn't too difficult to buy beer and whiskey, especially with a hulking six-foot-three-inch student in your midst. Someone would suggest a drive to a liquor store in Lewiston, thirteen miles away, and if the clerk refused to sell booze to Steve, they'd hover outside the door until they found someone to buy it for them, in the time-tested ways of teenagers everywhere. Or else, some kids would bring booze along from their parents' stock.

On February 5, 1965, Steve saw his second dead body in just over a year when his grandfather Guy Pillsbury died. The death of her father meant Ruth was free from the grueling manual labor and subsistence living the family had been dealing with for almost seven years. Or so she thought. The family continued to live in the house, and she sought work in the area.

But as before, all she could find was menial, mind-numbing manual labor. Though she was no longer tied down to the house and her parents and was now earning cash instead of canned goods and hand-me-down clothes, the family was no better off than before.

Though it had been more than a decade since her husband had walked out on the family, Ruth never gave up trying to track him down, at least in order to receive some child support or an official divorce. But she never found him.

With her hard schedule and being away from home now, Ruth had no patience for pretense, especially when it came from her own sons. One day, she passed by Steve's room and saw him preening in front of the mirror, playing with the lapel of his shirt and pushing up the cuffs of his sleeves, and something struck a nerve inside his mother. She rushed into his room, pushed him against the wall, and said, "Inside our clothes, we all stand naked. Don't ever forget it."

He was just trying to figure out how he could dress for the upcoming senior-class trip so that he wouldn't stand out as much in the big city, but her words stuck in his head. However, as it turned out, he didn't have to worry about standing out. The whole class did.

Two busloads of seniors from Lisbon High and a number of chaperones headed south for a weeklong trip to see the sights of New York City, Washington, D.C., and York, Pennsylvania, in April of 1966. The first stop was in New York for a couple of nights before heading to York. The class would spend a night each in Pennsylvania and Washington, then return to New York for two days before heading back to Maine. They stayed in hotel rooms, visited all the usual tourist attractions such as the Empire State Building in Manhattan, the Washington Monument and the Smithsonian in D.C., and Gettysburg in Pennsylvania.

What's the one thing that high school seniors are going to do when they're away from home in the big city—many for the first time—and easily able to dodge the chaperones? Find alcohol. Steve and his friends were no exception. The drinking age in New York was eighteen, the same as it was in Maine, and since Steve and some of the other students were already of age, they had no problem buying beer and liquor. But in York, Pennsylvania, where the drinking age was twenty-one, things got tougher.

"Steve was big and he looked older than the rest of us, so the choice was unanimous," said Lew Purinton. "We sent him into the liquor store to buy beer and liquor. I remember him coming out of the store and looking very proud."

Back in New York on the return trip, the high school seniors were feeling full of themselves with their success on the road, but their luck soon changed. They went into a bar in Times Square, but the bartender recognized trouble in the large group of cocky, out-of-town teenage boys and refused to serve them. So they headed to a pizzeria, where Pete Higgins noticed a beer named Tiger's Club, a Bavarian black beer. They ordered a pizza and a round of Tiger's Club for the table.

"It was absolutely the worst, bitterest stuff I've ever had in my life," said Higgins, who, with Steve, forced down a few swallows before giving up. Next, they headed for a steak house, and when the waiter asked for their drink orders, booze was the last thing on their minds.

"Chocolate milk," said Steve.

The waiter, an African-American man, snorted. "Man, down here we don't call it chocolate milk, we call it black or white milk."

So Steve said, "I want a black milk." The waiter asked the next boy what he wanted to drink and he replied, "A black soda." Purinton thought that made sense. "He thought if they called chocolate milk 'black milk,' a Coke would be a 'black soda,'" he said.

All of a sudden, the waiter got mad. "Are you trying to be funny? If you are, my gang's waiting outside for you."

The boys panicked and left the restaurant before their drinks arrived. Whether the waiter was serious or if he was pulling their legs, Purinton didn't know, but the table of self-described hicks from Maine got a quick lesson in life in the big city.

The students arrived back home a few days later and had another week before they had to return to school, after the weeklong April vacation.

Steve'd done well enough in high school to be offered a partial scholarship to Drew University, a Methodist college in Madison, New Jersey. But his mother couldn't afford to send him, so in 1966 he applied to the University of Maine at Orono.

Though he was awarded a full scholarship to the University of Maine, Steve couldn't afford to laze around for the week off. He still needed money for textbooks and other expenses, so he started his summer job two months early at the Worumbo Mills and Weaving in Lisbon Falls. He mostly worked in the bagging area, where other workers would blow fabric up into huge bins on that floor above, and it was Steve's job to stuff the fabric into bags. When school started up again, he would maintain a breakneck schedule until he graduated, attending classes during the day and working at the mill full-time.

Somehow, he still found time to write a one-act play for the annual Senior Night in May. Past classes had performed skits, played musical instruments, and presented awards such as Class Clown and the like to individual students.

Luckily for Steve, the faculty members who said it was okay for him to write a one-act play for Senior Night had short memories, because Steve's play turned out to be little more than a G-rated version of *The Village Vomit*, where he returned to poking fun at teachers and students with his thinly disguised parodies.

The play was called *Fat Man and Ribbon*, a takeoff on the popular *Batman* TV series, which first went on the air in January 1966. "Steve played Fat Man and the play was set at Lisbon High," said Peter Higgins. "Fat Man and Ribbon were at Lisbon High trying to catch a disruptive student named Lew Corruptington, who wore a black leather jacket and was clutching a beer bottle." Higgins played his own father, the principal. His name in the play was Principal Wiggins and he came out wearing a fright wig.

Although many students had read their copies of *The Village Vomit* and roared with laughter, a number of people at the school, mostly faculty, didn't appreciate Steve's play.

He earned a newfound respect from some of the students and a sigh of relief from many teachers who were glad to see this brilliant troublemaker on his way out the door. At his high school graduation, Steve was relieved as well, since it meant that he could solely focus on reading and writing in college, a step he hoped would bring him that much closer to living his dream of being a full-time writer.

While Steve was working at Worumbo Mills, he was fascinated by the hordes of rats that constantly wandered throughout the mill. "While I was waiting for my bin to fill up, I'd throw cans at the rats," he said. "They were big guys, and some of them would sit right up and beg for it like dogs." His supervisor asked him to join a cleanup crew to work in the basement over the July Fourth weekend, but he declined. However, the following week he heard loads of stories from those who had worked over the holiday about aggressive rats, the water running through the basement, and a particularly sadistic supervisor, and Steve filed them away.

In late August of 1966, he headed north to Orono to enroll as a freshman at the University of Maine. He signed up as an English major and took courses at the College of Education so he could become certified to teach in case his dream of writing full-time took a little longer to materialize.

His brother, David, had entered the university several years earlier. When both were students, Ruth would send them $5 each week so they'd have some spending money. "After she died several years later, I found she had frequently gone without meals to send us the money that we'd so casually accepted," he said. "It was very unsettling."

On the first day of freshman orientation, Steve met up with several of his buddies—Lew Purinton and Pete Higgins—from the college track at Lisbon High who had also signed up at the university.

According to Higgins, Steve almost got kicked out of school before classes even started. It was the custom on campus for fraternities to hold a "smoker," where groups gathered in a lounge or a living room to look over the freshmen. "They were evaluating the students to see if they wanted to accept any," said Higgins.

Pete, Steve, and a few other students from Lisbon went to one smoker together where they met a student who wanted to light some fireworks he had left over from the Fourth of July and asked if they wanted to watch.

The group from Lisbon High stood and watched while their new friend lit the first fuses. "We ran like crazy when they went off," said Higgins. "They weren't just bottle rockets and sparklers, but meaty kaboomers loud enough to shatter a number of dormitory windows. The administration was called and announced if they found whoever was responsible for the fireworks, they would be kicked out of the incoming class of 1966 before they could start. We would have been disciplined because we were standing right there when the fireworks went off, and if Steve was caught, it could have stunted his whole career."

THE GUNSLINGER

The first time Rick Hautala, another freshman English major, saw his new classmate, Steve was standing in the lunch line with his nose buried in a paperback book. "He was reading the kind of junk I liked to read," said Hautala. "At suppertime he'd be in the line again, but with his nose in a different book. It seemed like he read three books a day since he always seemed to be reading a different book at every meal."

Though both were English majors, their paths of study were widely divergent. "Steve stuck more with modern poetry and twentieth-century literature, while I focused more on Renaissance and medieval literature," said Hautala. "His writing stood out from what the majority of students were writing. He wasn't trying to be pretentious or artsy, he was writing real stories instead of precious little reminiscences."

"Steve had a very strong point of view," said classmate Michael Alpert. "He didn't believe in the official canon—the Harvard curriculum—at all. He thought many of the more popular writers had more to say. He didn't just talk about subject matter, he talked about language. His sensibility was already formed even back then."

Jim Bishop had King as a student in freshman English. "He was never without a paperback book, and he talked about authors of popular fiction the other students and professors had never heard of," said Bishop. "Even then, he saw himself as a famous writer and thought he could make money at it. Steve was religious about writing, and he wrote continuously, diligently. He created his own world."

In the turmoil of living away from home for the first time and getting accustomed to a whole new slew of classes and a variety of students who were nothing like those back home—i.e., they had money and would occasionally lord it over the others—Steve managed to write his first novel, "The Long Walk," during his first two semesters of college. He polished it in the summer between his freshman and sophomore year, and then in the fall of 1967, he heard about a first-novel competition run by the noted editor Bennett Cerf at

Random House. He sent off a copy of the manuscript, and it came back with a form rejection slip and no scrawled notes from the editor, which he had gotten used to from his submissions to the pulp magazines. He became discouraged and tucked the manuscript away in a drawer.

However, not all was bad news. Steve made his first professional sale to a pulp magazine, *Startling Mystery Stories,* for a story called "The Glass Floor." They paid him the princely sum of $35. By his own count, before making the sale, he had received about sixty rejection slips.

He was on his way. Someone besides his mother and his classmates thought his work was good enough to pay real money for it.

Steve had first showed up on campus with a Barry Goldwater bumper sticker on his car, evincing his family's stalwart Republican roots. Between his sophomore and junior years, Steve discovered that the political beliefs of his youth had been challenged, not only by the Vietnam War, but by the peace movement that was inundating much of the country. He'd gone from the rock-ribbed Republicanism of his youth to a radical form of liberalism that was sweeping across college campuses everywhere, even in a remote corner of Maine.

In August of 1968, Steve decided to head for Chicago to go to the Democratic National Convention to support his preferred candidate, Eugene McCarthy, a senator from Minnesota running against President Lyndon Johnson, who had promised to pull American troops out of Vietnam if elected. At the time, the country was in chaos. Martin Luther King had been killed in April and Robert Kennedy in June, so the stage was set for a contentious convention. With a hundred bucks for spending money, Steve headed for Chicago, staying at YMCAs along the way.

At the convention, word quickly spread that police were taunting the protesters, and vice versa, which resulted in violent clashes between the two groups. Steve was demonstrating outside the convention hall with thousands of other people when tempers suddenly flared and he was maced. He couldn't see, but he somehow found his way back to the YMCA where he was staying.

In the aftermath of the convention, he became swept up in the political fury and turmoil that was escalating. When he returned to Orono for the start of his junior year in the fall of 1968, it seemed that overnight all the rules had changed. The university was not immune to students demanding radical change in classes and throughout the entire campus. And when it came to the stodgy curriculum of the English Department, Steve was one of the lead instigators.

The University of Maine had the reputation of being an old reliable school where the focus was on mechanical engineering. Any English courses that were offered didn't stray far from the reliable canon of Dead White Men English literature and composition classes.

Encouraged by the unorthodox demands and requests from some of the undergraduates—Steve included—some of the professors thought it was time for a change as well. Two of Steve's professors, Burt Hatlen and Jim Bishop, designed a workshop in contemporary poetry that was geared more to graduate students than undergrads. Each workshop met after hours and was limited to twelve students, who had to be approved to attend. They wrote, read, and discussed poetry and literature, and here King was first exposed to the work of Steinbeck and Faulkner.

"Burt was more than a teacher to me, he was a mentor and a father figure," said Steve. "He made everyone feel welcome in the company of writers and scholars and let us know there was a place for us at the table."

George MacLeod was one of the students in the workshop. "It was a discussion class held in a living room, which was something completely different than had been offered at the time," he said. The second thing that stood out about the class was Steve, both his appearance and his contributions to the workshop.

"He was a larger-than-life kind of guy," said MacLeod, describing how Steve was tall but always seemed to be trying to hide his height by slightly stooping over. It was also hard to miss his long, black, oily hair reaching to his shoulders, his Coke-bottle glasses, and his sloppy manner of dressing. "He sat on the edge of the circle and he'd harrumph and make comments about a poem or what the other students were saying," MacLeod added. "He always had a different opinion and seldom concurred with the group. He liked to argue with people just to be different."

Steve was equally contentious with the faculty. One day the faculty invited a few students to offer their input on the future curriculum of the English Department, and it didn't take long for Steve to offer his two cents. He stood up and immediately criticized the department because of the total absence of popular culture in the courses. He complained that there was no class where he could read a Shirley Jackson novel for credit.

He became known for walking around the campus with a John MacDonald book or a collection of short stories by Robert Bloch. "Some asshole would always ask why was I reading that, and I'd tell them that this man is a great writer," he said. "But people would see the picture on the front with some lady with her cakes falling out of her blouse, and they would say, 'It's garbage.' So I'd ask, 'Have you read anything by this guy?' The inevitable reply would be 'No, all I gotta do is look at that book, and I know.' This was my first experience with critics, in this case, my teachers at college."

He always liked that kind of fiction, he'd grown up with it, and he knew that those were the kind of stories that he wanted to write. Even so, it was a bit of a hard sell to some of his professors.

Even when he was in college, Steve told everyone that his dream was to write popular fiction. "And there he was, spending so much time reading seventeenth-century English literature that he felt was a total waste of time," said MacLeod. "He definitely had this anti-snob thing going on, and I think that a lot of what motivated him politically was that he was from the wrong side of the tracks."

Steve shocked the faculty even more when he offered to teach a class about popular fiction, which sent the professors into a tizzy. Many objected not only to including commercial fiction in a college-level course, but also to the idea of an undergraduate teaching it. After the faculty discussed the proposal, they agreed to let Steve teach the course—Popular Literature and Culture—along with Graham Adams, an English professor.

Soon after, MacLeod struck up a friendship with Steve. They both needed to find a new place to live at about the same time, so they looked for an apartment together off-campus with a couple of other students.

They rented a duplex on North Main Street in Orono with each roommate paying forty bucks a month. Downstairs there was a living room and a kitchen, and upstairs were four bedrooms—turned into five when one of them was partitioned with a blanket.

"It was a terrible apartment," said MacLeod. "In winter, there was ice on the floors. And no one ever used the shower, it was so filthy. Everyone was dirt-poor, but Steve took it in stride since he obviously had grown up that way. He had very low expectations of his environment. We had one roommate who was better off than the rest of us since his parents were paying for his education. He had his own closet and kept his food in it, and the rest of us would filch it on a regular basis.

"But Steve had his own alternative universe in his reading and his books," MacLeod continued. "He read books like the rest of us breathed. He could tell you how many books John MacDonald had written because he had read all of them. He absorbed every part of a book, and his focus was legendary."

On virtually every college campus in America in the late sixties, drugs were a fact of life. Whether pot, pills, or acid there was always something around for whoever wanted it, and the apartment on North Main Street was no exception. One day, word spread across campus about a new kind of hallucinatory drug that someone had in a nearby dorm and was willing to share, with one caveat. According to MacLeod, the substance messed with your equilibrium, so he cautioned that anyone who took it should make plans to stay put for a while. "You had to sit on the couch and just wait for it to pass," he said. Steve took some along with other students, and soon everyone became lost in the experience, talking, listening to music, and laughing.

After a while, someone asked where Steve had gone. They looked around the house, but no one could find him. MacLeod suggested that he had wandered off somewhere on campus and that maybe he was so stoned he couldn't find his way home. Despite that the effects of the drug were not favorable for conducting a manhunt, his roommates organized a search and began to comb the campus.

They searched the bars, the alleys off Main Street, some of the dorms, and the English Department. After several hours, they gave up and returned to the apartment, where they found Steve in the living room reading a book. "He was sitting in a three-legged easy chair with his feet up on a cranking kerosene heater, which was in the process of melting his rubber boots, and he was oblivious to it all," said MacLeod. "I think he was reading *Psycho*. On this particular drug, no one else could even manage to turn the pages, but Steve was sitting there reading, totally safe in his own little cocoon of fiction."

Later on, Steve would detail his drug consumption during his college years. "I did a lot of LSD and peyote and mescaline, more than sixty trips in all," he said. "I'd never proselytize for acid or any other hallucinogen, because there are good-trip personalities and bad-trip personalities, and the latter category of people can be seriously damaged emotionally."

No matter what kind of drug the guys at the apartment took, if the munchies arose, they were a short stumble from Pat's Pizza and the Shamrock, two of the regular hangouts for students in Orono. Pat's offered pizza and food cheap enough to fill a poor college student's belly, while the Shamrock just sold beer, which Steve often referred to as poor man's Valium.

"The Shamrock was just tables and beer," said MacLeod. "It was in a basement with no windows, and no light, just three beer taps and the football players who worked them."

One day between drugs and visits to Pat's and the Shamrock, Steve called

MacLeod into his room, where he pulled open a dresser drawer and revealed hundreds of pulp magazines stashed away in his bureau. It was all the stuff he had read when he was a kid. He pulled out the copy of *Startling Mystery Stories* with his story in it and told MacLeod that he planned to go to the next level. MacLeod, who also wanted to be a writer, was particularly fascinated by the other magazines, which he recognized as being at least a couple of decades old. Steve's enthusiasm for writing and pop fiction would in turn fire George up, and they'd often head to the journalism office since neither one owned his own typewriter; Steve had left his at home.

"We'd head over late at night and sit there and bang on these big manuals, and soon it became a routine," said MacLeod. Sometimes, instead of working on his own stories, he'd watch Steve. "When he sat down at a typewriter, he would just go. He was so incredibly focused that if you hit him with a brick, he wouldn't notice."

That same focus and confidence extended to Steve's work in the classroom. Even back then, he believed in his work. Whenever a professor or student criticized his work for being too modern, he took it in stride.

"This is me and this is who I am," he'd respond. And if it bothered him, he'd write an essay or crank out an article for the school paper, the *Maine Campus*.

Between Steve's classwork, reading and writing, and social life, more than a few of his classmates wondered when the guy slept.

And he still watched as many movies as he did when he was a kid. He had just entered his junior year in college when *Night of the Living Dead* came out, and one afternoon he went to see it. Kids filled most of the seats, and Steve would later say it was the first time in his life when he sat in a theater full of kids where they were so quiet it was as if they weren't there. "They were simply stunned by the gore and violence," he said. "It was the best argument for the rating system that I have ever seen. I don't have anything against either of the *Dead* movies or *The Texas Chainsaw Massacre,* but it's not something you just hand to kids. You have to be old enough to take it, and these kids just weren't prepared for it."

He vowed when he had kids, he'd do it differently. Even though he had cut his teeth on horror movies, the movies of ten years ago were totally different from *Night of the Living Dead*. He felt that the film left little to the imagination, and that it was better if you had to imagine some things on your own. He followed the same philosophy in his own writing.

He was also starting to crystallize other ideas about what writing should and shouldn't do for the reader. "Literature is supposed to be a sweaty, close-up thing," he said. "I want it to reach out and grab you and pull you into a sweaty embrace so you can't let go. I've always strived to hurt the reader but exhilarate him at the same time. I think a book should be something that's really alive and really dangerous in a lot of ways."

He was becoming a keen study of human character. And he wasn't afraid to ask people why they did certain things because he hoped he'd eventually be able to use it in his fiction.

One day, he ran into a girl he'd known in high school, and she had a bruise under her eye. He asked her what happened, but she refused to talk about it. He pressed the matter, asking her to join him for some coffee.

"She told me she'd been out with a guy, and he wanted to do some stuff that she didn't want to do, and he punched her," Steve said. He was fascinated and revolted at the same time, so he grilled her gently.

"I can remember saying to her that it takes courage to go out with a guy," he remembered. "Maybe you're attracted to him, but basically you're saying, 'I'm going to get into your car, I'm going to go somewhere, and I'm going to trust you to bring me back in one piece.' It takes courage, doesn't it? And she said, 'You'll never know.'

"I never forgot that. It became the basis for a number of different stories I've written."

After writing a few articles and essays for the *Maine Campus,* Steve decided to approach the editor, David Bright, about writing a weekly column. Bright gave him the go-ahead, and his first column appeared on February 20, 1969. Steve christened his column "The Garbage Truck" because, as he put it, "You never know what you're going to find in a garbage truck."

From the beginning, Bright liked Steve's writing, but he wasn't overly fond of the nerve-racking style in which Steve cranked out his columns. An hour before the deadline with no column in sight, Steve would show up at the paper's office. Bright, wringing his hands, would tell Steve how many column inches he needed to fill for that issue. Steve would then sit down at one of the big, hulking green typewriters in the newspaper office and bang out his copy, letter-perfect with no cross-outs, no corrections, no crumpled-up pieces of paper, and meet his deadline with moments to spare.

His subject matter ran the gamut, and he clearly used the column to see how the population at large regarded his view of the world. In his column dated December 18, 1969, he wrote, "It just may be that there is a hole in our world, perhaps in the very fabric of our Universe, and Things cross back and forth. It may be that in some other world all of our ancient boogey men exist and walk and talk—and occasionally disappear into our own realm."

Indeed, in that same column he mentioned the story of a whole Vermont village called Jeremiah's Lot that had seemingly vanished into thin air in the beginning of the nineteenth century, and he described a theory by Shirley Jackson, one of his favorite authors, that houses and buildings can be inherently evil. A few columns later, he offered profuse kudos to the university's activity guild for scheduling a bumper crop of horror movies that semester. *Rosemary's Baby, Psycho, Dracula, Frankenstein, The Pit and the Pendulum,* and *The Hunchback of Notre Dame* were all featured films, among others. He didn't say whether the majority of students shared his glee at the slate of movies.

It's evident he didn't much care about what other students and faculty thought of his column; he viewed it as a pebble in the shoe of people on campus, and his aim was to get them thinking, no matter how much they disagreed with his ideas.

Another possibility is that he used it as a screening device so he could find out who his true friends were. That certainly seemed to be the case with his November 13 column, where he first admitted to liking the cops, then said that in contrast he didn't much care for leftists and liberals. In the tinderbox of the sixties college campus, no matter where you were in the country at the time, this was akin to throwing a jug of kerosene on an already blazing fire.

He then chastised fellow students who supported Huey Newton, a Black Panther who shot and killed a policeman in 1967.

"Cops are the people who stand between you and chaos of an insane society," he wrote. "In my book, the guy who goes around calling cops pigs is a pig himself, with a filthy mouth and a vapid mind."

He also took a surprising viewpoint toward sex and birth control. "Birth control demeans the act of sex," he wrote. "It's like jumping into your car, starting it up, and driving like hell in neutral. Birth control is a little gutless. It doesn't seem right to laugh them away with a little round plastic case. Abortion is the only really moral way it can be done. If nothing else, it would force the person involved to come to a serious decision about birth control."

But he didn't always write his column to stir up the bee's nest or test out his supernatural views of the world. Occasionally, Steve would present a laundry list of his favorite songs and albums and movies. In late 1969, he devoted an entire column to naming what he thought were the best albums of the year—Bob Dylan's *Nashville Skyline* and *Abbey Road* from the Beatles—and songs: "The Boxer" from Simon and Garfunkel, and surprisingly, "Sugar Sugar" by the Archies. He detested anything by Blood, Sweat, and Tears or Glen Campbell.

He also contributed short fiction to the college literary magazines, such as *Onan* and *Moth*. "The stories that he published in the student magazines had some power to them," Rick Hautala remembered. "You couldn't ignore them, but, at the same time there was a little voice that said, 'Wow, these are really violent. Is this guy sick in the head? Why do the stories have to be so bloody and gory?'" Hautala added that Steve's stories stood out so much from the others it was almost as if they were typed in a different typeface and color.

Because of his "Garbage Truck" column, Steve was pretty well-known on campus, and even the top brass at the university were keeping track of him. President Winthrop Libby even spoke with Professor Ted Holmes about Steve's prospects for making his living as a writer. "Ted was not especially complimentary on that point," said Libby. "He said that while Steve certainly had a knack for storytelling, he wished that Steve would write more than horror stories."

Some of the students were after Steve to expand his platform from the paper to live performances. He played guitar and sang just as well as he played sports in high school, but he relished the chance to get onstage.

An off-campus place called the Coffee House attracted the beatnik crowd. People would get onstage and read poetry—their own or someone else's—and metaphysical fiction. Steve was invited to read one night, and he chose a story he had written about a guy who had eyes all over his hands, and the audience offered up polite applause. The next time he was asked back was for the Halloween performance, where he read a few more of his horror stories. When the audience started to laugh at certain parts, Steve was dismayed and thought something was wrong with his stories, but most likely the audience laughed from discomfort and anxiety and because the stories were so different from what the others read aloud.

After that, Steve didn't go back to the Coffee House and opted instead to attend the open mike at the Ram's Horn, a coffeehouse on campus. But instead of reading stories, Steve brought his guitar and accompanied his singing. "Steve would always sing country-and-western songs about this terrible loser who never had any luck," said Diane McPherson, a classmate who participated in one of Burt Hatlen's poetry workshops with King. "I remember thinking at the time that Steve was singing about a version of himself that rang true."

Due to his weekly soapbox in the college paper, other students were starting to view Steve as not just a columnist but as a leader on campus.

"He was a loose cannon as far as politics go," said MacLeod. "He was a noisy radical opposed to Vietnam, but at the same time, he was an odd person: on one hand very private and yet public in a loud way."

"When the antiwar stuff came along, Steve just jumped in and was a leader," said Rick Hautala. "Whenever we had a student strike, he never seemed to have any qualms about grabbing the microphone and expressing himself."

There was a military draft at the time, to which many college students were vehemently opposed even though they were protected from conscription, albeit temporarily, since undergraduates and graduate students automatically earned deferments. However, academic achievement was part of the deal: the Selective Service spread the word that they would not hesitate to draft a college student who was carrying less than a B average.

When college deferments ended in 1969, the protests that had been happening on college campuses across the country since the midsixties immediately escalated. Poor physical condition or any untreatable disability such as myopia or flat feet would get a man classified as 4-F—prime condition was awarded a 1-A—and automatically exempt a candidate from service.

Later on, around 1971, a lottery was instituted to make the draft fairer across the board, according to birthday. Birth dates were randomly pulled and assigned a number in order from 1 to 365. The lower the number, the greater the chances of getting drafted.

While some students shied away from participating in campus protests in the hopes that if they kept their heads down and maintained a good grade point average, they wouldn't be noticed and perhaps earmarked for the draft, others such as Steve didn't care and didn't hesitate when it came to riling up the others. He may already have had an idea that he was 4-F and exempt from the draft due to his poor eyesight, which may have been why he felt freer to be outrageous and fling himself out there.

In addition to his column, he posed for a cover for the *Maine Campus* that appeared on the issue dated January 17, 1970, holding a double-barreled shotgun, with long, wild hair and a wild gleam in his eye that earned him a comparison by more than a few students to Charles Manson, with the caption *Study, Dammit!!*

In his junior year, Steve was elected to the Student Senate with the largest vote ever in the history of the student elections. One of the responsibilities of the position was to regularly attend meetings of the student affairs committees. President Libby respected Steve's drive and sense of fairness when it came to dealing with faculty and students and sympathized with some of the tensions that simmered between them, but he picked up on Steve's true colors early on. "He was essentially a very gentle person who acted the part of a very wild man," said Libby.

It wasn't a surprise that academics took a backseat to all of the other things that were happening on campus, and in the world, in the late sixties. Indeed, many students had trouble keeping their minds on their studies. And with all of his various activities, in school and outside of school, Steve didn't necessarily strike his friends as a particularly stellar student. "We never really talked about it that much," said MacLeod. "We all studied, but it was very much in the background. Everything was politics and poetry and recreational drugs, and rock and roll."

With students in larger cities and more well-known colleges all over the country closing down campuses and going on strike, Steve used his position as the head of the student/faculty coalition to make demands of the faculty and administration that would essentially reorganize the university. One night, he organized a march on the president's house to make a slew of demands that various groups on campus had requested, ranging from more independent studies, bail options, and even free degrees for everybody with a minimum of academic work. He even entertained suggestions from the Students for a Democratic Society, one of the more radical student groups across the country, who wanted several issues admitted to the package Steve would present to Libby.

On a cold, damp spring evening in 1969, Steve led the march across campus brandishing a torch and wearing a wet, ratty, full-length beaver coat followed by a ragtag group of protesters. Counterprotesters chanted slogans and threw eggs and rotten vegetables at students who were marching.

In the end, Libby listened to the demands and promised to meet with Steve and other students to hammer out a compromise, but the protest soon became less important to Steve as he turned his attention to two things that felt much more pressing: his senior year, and Tabitha Spruce.

Steve King and Tabitha Jane Spruce first met at Jim Bishop's writing seminar, though they both also worked part-time in the Fogler Library. "I thought she was the best writer in that seminar, including myself, because she knew exactly what she was up to," he said. "She understood syntax and the various building blocks of fiction and poetry in a way that the others didn't. They wanted to go off into metaphysical frenzies about how they were freeing the voice in their soul and a lot of bullshit like that."

She had been aware of him since she arrived on campus as a freshman in the fall of 1967. Before he started writing his column, he'd written a letter to the editor of the *Maine Campus* and the paper had printed it. She'd read it and thought, boy, this guy can write. "But at the same time, I was mad that he got a letter into the paper before I did," she said.

"He was that rare thing, a Big Man on Campus who was not an athlete," said Tabby. "He really was literally the poorest college student I ever met in my life. He wore cutoff gum rubbers because he couldn't afford shoes. It was just incredible that anybody was going to school under those circumstances, and even more incredible that he didn't care.

"Right from the beginning, I thought he was as good as any published writer I knew. I think it impressed him that I appreciated what he did. He also was hot for my boobs."

"Tabby looked like a waitress," he concurred. "She came across, and still does, as a tough broad."

George MacLeod provides a little background: "When Steve and Tabby met, she was already involved with another student in the workshop, but he dumped her and she was alone when she met Steve. Some of us got the impression that Steve felt sorry for her, but they really clicked; it was two loners and two writers who really understood each other who hooked up."

Before long, they began to spend all of their free time together. Within a few months, she moved into a small apartment in Orono with him.

Tabitha Jane Spruce was born on March 24, 1949, to Raymond George Spruce and Sarah Jane White in Old Town, Maine, just up the road from

Orono. Tabby, as she would be called, was the third of eight children in a Catholic family and attended Catholic grammar school and John Bapst Memorial High School. Her father worked at the family's general store, R. J. Spruce & Sons, on Main Road in Milford, a stone's throw across the Penobscot River from Old Town. Tabby's grandfather Joseph Spruce had purchased the store with his older brother sometime in the early 1900s.

The Spruces were French-Canadian and had changed their name from Pinette in the late 1800s because French Canadians were an easy target for discrimination at the time. The Ku Klux Klan was then active in northern New England and recent immigrants from Quebec—one derogatory term that was often flung at them was Frog—were regularly refused work in the local mills.

All the Spruce kids worked at the store. "I grew up listening to people talk over potbellied stoves," Tabby said. "I used to cut chunks of chewing tobacco for old guys. My dad cut beef in the back room of the store. At one point my grandmother ran the post office from part of the store."

Tabby grew up a self-described loner, introspective and independent, and she loved to write: she kept a diary and wrote letters to friends. Like Steve, she was an inveterate reader. "Once I discovered the public library, I was rarely at home," she said. "One time, the librarian called home to say that I'd been reading adult books, and my mother told her if I understood them, it was okay, and if I didn't, they couldn't harm me."

Also like Steve, Tabby wouldn't care if she never saw another lobster in her life. As a teenager, she worked at a tourist seafood restaurant near Bangor called Lobsterland and often ran the lobster press, where all of the lobster left over from customers' plates was gathered and dumped so it could appear on new plates the next day as lobster salad or lobster roll. She grew to detest the way the stale seafood smell permeated her skin, hair, and clothes, but it was the only work open to her at the time.

"When I grew up in Old Town, there wasn't any women's movement," said Tabby. "I learned real early that whatever I did, the basic problem was I was female, and being a female who wore glasses was a real downer. Then I grew boobs and that didn't get me anywhere either." She graduated from John Bapst Memorial High School in Bangor in June of 1967. After graduation, she proceeded to the University of Maine, the typical path for smart high school students from families with little money to send their kids to an out-of-state college. Like Steve, she attended UMO with the help of scholarships and part-time campus jobs. Once she got to college, she hoped to find freedom from the restraints that had held her back intellectually. Instead, she encountered new forms of sexism. She recalled how one professor would regularly scrawl across the top of the term papers of female students, *Drop out and get married*.

Persevering, she brushed such slights aside despite not being sure of her academic focus. For a while, she changed her major about once a semester. She eventually settled into English and history. After graduation she planned to pursue a master's in library science and become a full-time librarian.

At least that was the plan. Meeting Steve changed all that.

"I knew Tabby was my ideal reader from the first time that I gave her something to read, before we were married, which was a story called 'I Am the Doorway,' and she told me it was really good," he said. "That's usually the extent of her comments, if she likes something." Of course, he would in time find out that if she didn't like something, she wouldn't hesitate to tell him and follow it up with suggestions for how he could improve his work.

From the first time they met—Steve got loaded on their first date—they were joined at the hip. They understood each other and were interested in the same things.

By dating Tabitha, Steve instantly joined a big family, the kind he'd never had but always dreamed of.

As part of the requirements to earn his certificate to teach high school when he graduated, Steve started student teaching in January of 1970 at Hampden Academy, a public high school in nearby Hampden, Maine. Though it added significantly to his workload, he continued to take classes, study, read, and write while also teaching English.

By this time, he and Tabby were living together at the Springer Cabins by the Stillwater River in Orono. They were notoriously cheap accommodations, but since they were both in school and money was rare, it was all they could afford. This was especially important since Tabby was already three months pregnant. She continued to go to classes despite stares of disapproval, especially from her male professors. Though *Roe v. Wade* was still three years down the road, abortions were available if inquiries were made through the right circles. Since free love ran rampant in the late sixties and early seventies, many women opted for abortion rather than for birth, because motherhood was viewed as "square" in many circles at the time.

Which described Steve and Tabby to a T. Although Steve had taken more than his fair share of drugs and led marches to the president's house to make outrageous demands, his worldview hadn't strayed far from that of his conservative childhood. Abortion was *not* an option. Besides, Tabby was raised Catholic and they had already planned to marry after Steve graduated from college.

Most likely, to Steve, aborting a child was the same as abandoning one, and he swore he would refuse to do anything that smacked of his father's behavior toward his family. So Steve and Tabby soldiered on. Though Steve had never had any trouble finding the motivation to write, now he had even more incentive. Writing, he believed, would be their ticket out of a difficult life. He had recently started to send some of his short fiction to men's magazines such as *Gallery* and *Cavalier,* and he began to sell a story here and there. They paid only a couple of hundred bucks, but to Steve, it was a fortune.

One day in March, Steve was working at the library when the librarian set out several reams of bright green paper for students, free for the taking. It was easy to see why the staff had no use for the paper: the sheets were as thick as cardboard and wouldn't easily roll through typewriters. They measured seven by ten inches, an irregular size that professors would frown on.

Most of the students passed, but Steve took as much as he could. While he knew that most people viewed a blank sheet of paper with abject fear, to him it represented great promise. He regarded the paper, with its unusual size and color, as a gift. He wanted to save it for something special and ran his fingers over the reams as he giddily compared himself to "an alcoholic contemplating a case of Chivas Regal, or a sex maniac receiving a visit from a couple of hundred willing young virgins." He took the paper back to the cabins, rolled the first sheet into the same Underwood typewriter he had banged away on since childhood—he'd finally brought it down from Durham—and typed the first line of a novel whose idea he had based on a Robert Browning poem, "Childe Roland," about a young man's quest through an unfamiliar and dark landscape to a faraway tower.

"The man in black fled across the desert and the gunslinger followed."

In addition to the detective, horror, science fiction, and comic books King was reading, he was exploring another genre popular at the time: fantasy, most notably Tolkien's *Lord of the Rings* series.

"I was just knocked out by the magic of the stories, by the idea of the quest, the broadness of it, and how long it took to tell the tales," he said. Naturally, he thought about writing his own book along the same lines, and as he worked on the first of a projected seven-book series, he knew he had to consciously avoid Tolkien's style and stories. At the same time, he knew he wanted the books to have one foot in the fantasy world and one foot in the real one.

While he began to explore the world of the character Roland Deschain, he worked feverishly on other stories and novels while also finishing up the course work he needed to graduate. He continued to tell anyone within earshot that his goal was to become a full-time writer. Unlike many of his fellow students, who were succumbing to the pessimism of the Vietnam War period, Steve was still incredibly optimistic about his future. As a result, he saw opportunity and ideas in absolutely everything that crossed his path, even in a bunch of paper that nobody else wanted.

It would take twelve more years, but that oddly shaped green paper would serve as the genesis of his *Dark Tower* series.

DESPERATION

One month before his college graduation, Steve was arrested by the Orono, Maine, police in a bizarre incident involving three dozen rubber traffic cones. He'd been drinking heavily at a local bar, and on the way home he'd hit a traffic cone so hard that it had snagged the muffler from the dilapidated Ford station wagon he was driving at the time. Earlier in the day, he had seen that the town highway department was painting new crosswalk marks all over town and had set the cones so motorists and pedestrians would know to watch for the wet paint.

Not Steve. He was so indignant that he had to buy a new muffler for his car that he decided to teach the town a lesson. "With a drunk's logic, I decided to cruise around town and pick up all the cones," he remembered. "The following day, I would present them, along with my dead muffler, at the Town Office in a display of righteous anger."

He'd collected about a hundred cones in the back of his wagon before running out of room. He knew he was far from finished, however, so he went back to his apartment to clear out his car and deposit the cones before returning to the streets to round up the rest of the offenders. He had gathered up a good number on his second run when a cop spotted him and turned on the blue lights. The policeman spotted enough cones in the back of Steve's car—even on the second cone run—to arrest King for larceny. "Had I been caught with the hundred or so already stashed in my apartment building, perhaps we would have been talking grand larceny," he said.

A trial date was set for August.

Stephen King graduated from the University of Maine at Orono in the spring of 1970 with a BS in English and a certificate that qualified him to teach at the high school level. A draft board examination conducted immediately after he graduated declared him to be 4-F and unsuitable to be drafted due to his high blood pressure, limited vision, flat feet, and punctured eardrums.

Undoubtedly, for the first time in his life, instead of looking back at the sadistic doctor of his childhood with revulsion, he may have been just a wee bit thankful.

Even though he was no longer a student, Steve continued to write for the *Maine Campus*. One of the stories was "Slade," the story he'd started writing on that odd-size green paper a few months earlier.

Tabby's first child, Naomi Rachel, was born on June 1, 1970, just after Steve's graduation but a year before her own. Though he and Tabby were thrilled, they were understandably nervous about how they would be able to support a child when they were having trouble supporting themselves. As he had planned to do all along, Steve applied for a teaching position at Hampden Academy, and when he found no openings, he applied at a few other high schools in the area, only to be told the same news.

He had to make some money and didn't want to return to work at Worumbo Mills, so he got a job pumping gas at a service station in Brewer. The working conditions were intended to keep the attendants on their toes. If a customer filled up his or her tank, Steve had to morph into salesman mode.

"With a fill-up you got your choice of The Glass—an ugly but durable diner-style water tumbler—or The Bread, an extralong loaf of spongy white," he said. "If we forgot to ask if we could check your oil, you got your fill-up free. If we forgot to say thank you, same deal. And guess who would have to pay for the free fill-up? That's right, the forgetful pump jockey."

After footing the bill for several customers' free fill-ups, Steve learned his lesson, even though the job was incredibly boring. In August, his trial came up for cone theft, and he took the day off from work to go to court. But he didn't want his boss to think she had hired a miscreant, so he said he needed the day off to attend the funeral of one of Tabby's relatives.

He headed to Bangor District Court, defended himself without a lawyer, and was promptly found guilty. The judge fined him a hundred bucks, but he'd recently sold a horror story to *Adam* called "The Float" about four college students who swim out to a raft in the middle of a lake one fall day only to encounter a creature beneath the murky water, so he used the check to pay the fine. If the judge only knew where the money had come from . . .

The next day when he showed up for work at the gas station, he was fired for lying about the reason for his absence the day before. One of the boss's relatives had followed Steve in the court docket and told his aunt that her employee had been in court the same day.

He needed to find another job immediately, so he applied at several different places and was offered a job that paid $1.60 an hour at the New Franklin Laundry, which handled laundry from commercial establishments and businesses.

He thought long and hard before accepting it. After all, at one point his mother had worked in a laundry, and the last thing he wanted was to replicate his mother's life, something she would wholeheartedly agree with.

Despite his college degree, he was well on his way down Ruth's depressing path: supporting a wife and a newborn created a lot of stress for Steve. Although he knew in his heart the easy way out would have been to replicate his father's life, to excuse himself after dinner one night to go buy a pack of cigarettes and then put his head down, keep walking, and never look back, he knew he could never go down that path.

Besides, he had made contact with an editor in New York who liked his work and who thought he had a future as a novelist.

Since graduating from college, Steve had been working on a novel he called *Getting It On,* the story of a high school student who kills two of his teachers and holds his entire algebra class hostage. He finished it over the summer and thought it was as good—or better—than a lot of the paperback novels he was reading at the time and decided to send it to a publisher. He'd recently read a novel called *Parallax View* by Loren Singer that he admired. He saw similarities between his own novel and Singer's, which was published by Doubleday, so he packaged his up and addressed it to the "Editor of *Parallax View*" at Doubleday in New York. Unbeknownst to Steve, that editor had since departed the house, so his manuscript landed on the desk of a fiction editor named Bill Thompson.

Thompson wrote back to say that he liked Steve's novel but that it needed some work, spelling out the changes he wanted the young author to make. Excited beyond belief, Steve made the changes and sent the revised manuscript back to Thompson. After a few months, the manuscript came back with a note that the other editors on staff wanted to see a few more changes. Steve fixed the story for the second time and sent the manuscript back.

Thompson sent it back a third time, apologetically asking for yet more changes that were this time requested by the editorial board. Steve hesitated, but he figured this was what publishing was like, so he dutifully followed the board's suggestions and returned the manuscript.

When the thick package came back a fourth time with the Doubleday return address, Steve's spirits sagged. He ripped open the envelope to discover that after all of his hard work and despite doing everything the editors had asked for, *Getting It On* was rejected.

"It was a painful blow for me," he later wrote, "because I had been allowed to entertain some degree of hope for an extraordinarily long time."

He licked his wounds for a short time before starting on the next project. After all, Thompson liked his work and told him he would have accepted *Getting It On* long ago if the decision were solely up to him. Plus, Steve didn't feel totally dejected, as he had learned a lot about the editorial process and the nitpicky things that some editors preferred and others detested. Later on, Steve would find out that Bill had actually sent the novel to a few editors he knew at other publishing houses in hopes of placing it elsewhere, something he could have been fired for if the top brass found out.

Bill had asked Steve to keep him in mind for other novels he might be working on, and so Steve took the next novel in the stack and sent it along. *The Long Walk* was about a group of a hundred boys who participate in a yearly punishing walk with myriad rules—no breaks are allowed, walking speed must not drop below four miles an hour—that lasts until only one walker remains. Again, the same pattern commenced: Bill requested a few changes, then the other editors wanted to get their two cents in, followed by the editorial board, which finally turned thumbs-down on the project.

All this was happening while Steve was working full-time at the laundry and writing short stories for the men's magazines, where his track record was better than with Doubleday.

Steve had made his first sale to *Cavalier* over the summer, and "Graveyard Shift" was published in the October 1970 issue. The story was about giant rats in an old factory basement and the men who were sent in to clean out the basement. He'd based it on the stories he'd heard from the July Fourth cleanup crew at Worumbo Mills. Maurice DeWalt was the editor in charge of screening over-the-transom short fiction at *Cavalier,* a hip alternative to *Playboy* that began publishing in the late sixties. Along with contemporary articles and fiction, the primary appeal of the magazine was the photos of sparsely clad female models.

One day DeWalt called his main editor, Nye Willden, to tell him that he had just read an amazing story by a writer named Stephen King. "But," said Willden, "he also told me that it had little or no relevance to the kind of stories we published at the magazine. I told him to bring it over anyway, and when I read it, it truly gave me chills."

He wrote to Steve to accept the story and said he'd pay a hundred bucks. Steve wrote back immediately to accept the offer and enclosed a few more stories for Willden's consideration.

Of course, it was a skin magazine, but Steve knew he had to pay his dues, and he was still optimistic about his future. He continued voraciously reading anything he could get his hands on, the more popular the genre and the trashier the cover art, the better. But occasionally he'd be waylaid when he picked up a book at the library where the covers weren't anywhere in sight. "I'd open it up and in the front I would see something like 'The author would like to thank the Guggenheim Foundation for the money to write this book,' and I'd think, 'You fucking shithead, where do you get off taking that money so you can sit on your ass in some cabin in New Hampshire while I'm trying to write a book at night and I've got bleach burns all over my hands? Who the fuck are you?'

"Steam would come out of my ears, I was so mad and jealous of these guys," Steve said. "And I would think it was all because they would all sit around and sniff each other's underwear in the literary sense. Some English professor says to his grad student, 'You ought to go out and read some Nathaniel Hawthorne,' and the kid comes back and says, 'Gee, chief, Nathaniel Hawthorne's great. Will you sign my application for the Guggenheim scholarship?' It used to make me crazy."

Back on the home front, Steve and Tabby planned to get married, but she had one condition: he get a better job than working at the laundry. So he promised to apply for more teaching jobs in the spring.

"I married her for her body, though she said I married her for her typewriter," he later said. Indeed, her Olivetti was a vast improvement over the ancient Underwood that he'd been banging away on since the late fifties. But the typewriter was a nice added attraction. "Hers had a rather square typeface, a Nazi-salute kind of typeface."

Steve and Tabby were married on January 2, 1971, in Old Town, where Tabby grew up. Steve paid $15.95 for two matching wedding rings from Day's Jewelers in Bangor. The ceremony was at the Catholic church—Tabby's religion—while the reception was held at the Methodist church, the denomination of Steve's youth.

Though Steve had looked for other jobs, they were scarce so he was still working at the laundry at the time of their wedding. They specifically set the date so there would be no conflict with Steve's schedule at the New Franklin Laundry. "We got married on a Saturday because the place was closed on Saturday afternoons," he said. "Everyone wished me well, but I still was docked for not being in that Saturday evening."

Tabby graduated from the University of Maine in June 1971 with a degree in history. It had been a long, hard slog, as she had continued to attend classes while pregnant, and then while dealing with a newborn.

Once she graduated from college, she encountered the same problems that Steve did: she couldn't find a job that fit her qualifications, and for the rest she was vastly overqualified. She applied for a job at Dunkin' Donuts. At first the manager didn't want to hire her because of her bachelor's degree, but he eventually took her on.

In time, Steve and Tabby viewed the smell of doughnuts the same way they viewed lobster. "It was a nice aroma at first, you know, all fresh and sugary," said Steve, "but it got pretty goddamned cloying after a while. I haven't been able to look a doughnut in the face ever since."

Tabby only intended to work as long as it took them to get caught up on the bills. "As soon as we were paid up, I'd stop working because otherwise it was Steve working the day shift, me working the night, not seeing Naomi, not seeing each other, it wasn't good," she said.

"I think that my wife and I had a lot of traditional values from the start," Steve said. "We were old fogyish by the standards of a lot of our friends. We had our kids, and we were raising them in this traditional family home life."

King realized that his dream of becoming a full-time writer wasn't going to happen anytime soon, so when a teaching position opened up at Hampden Academy—the school where he had student-taught in his senior year of college—starting in the fall of 1971, he accepted the job at a starting salary of $6,400, a step up from the job at the laundry.

At the time, Tabby, Steve, and Naomi were living in a rented trailer off Route 2 in Hermon, about seven miles from the school. Steve commuted in a 1965 Buick Special. Before he turned the key in the morning, he crossed his fingers that the car would start; the car was held together with little more than chicken wire and duct tape.

As a high school English teacher, he was finally putting his college education to good use, though he quickly discovered that teaching wasn't what he had expected. "I thought by teaching school I was insuring myself a middle-class life, I didn't think it meant poverty," he said. "Teaching school is like having jumper cables hooked to your ears, draining all the juice out of you. You come home, you have papers to correct, and you don't feel like writing. We were planning to have a car, we were supposed to have a real life, and we were worse off than when I was in the laundry."

He tempered the frustrations of the job by watching how the students acted. He came away with a lot of stories and ideas from studying them and by tormenting them in class, albeit always in a fun way.

He occasionally threatened students who offered little during a class discussion with a novel punishment. "When I was a student teacher, my supervisor had a surefire cure for the Class of the Living Dead," he said to his students." 'Does anyone have any idea why Willy Loman's depression seems so deep in *Death of a Salesman*?' she'd ask. 'If no one answers in fifteen seconds, I'll take off a shoe. If no one answers in thirty seconds, I'll take off another shoe.' And so on. By the time she began to unzip her dress, someone usually came up with an opinion on Willy Loman's depression."

In between teaching, correcting papers, and spending time with Tabby and his daughter, Steve continued to summon up the time and focus to crank away at a couple of novels, but discovered that writing short stories was more lucrative and certain, at least in the short run. He was still in touch with Bill Thompson at Doubleday, but after extensively revising two novels that were still rejected, he decided to concentrate on writing short stories for the men's magazines, which he could crank out in a few hours and sell for at least a couple of hundred dollars.

Besides *Cavalier* and *Adam,* he also wrote for magazines with the titles *Dude, Gent, Juggs, Swank,* and *Gallery.* When he told his mother that he was selling his stories regularly, she was thrilled and understandably wanted to see them in print. Even though the stories were mysteries and not the pornography that appeared elsewhere in the magazines, he still didn't want her to know which magazines they had appeared in. So Tabby would make copies of the printed stories but first block out the ads for X-rated films, lotions, and sex toys that filled the margins of the pages where his stories appeared.

In fact, the editors thought so highly of his work that they asked him to try writing some of the porn stories; after all, they paid better than the horror stories. He made a valiant attempt, but writing about sex just wasn't in his emotional toolbox. He wrote about fifty pages before giving up. "The words were there, but I couldn't handle it. It was so weird, I just collapsed laughing," he said. "I got as far as twins having sex in a birdbath."

He said that it wasn't due to being uncomfortable with sex, but rather from a discomfort in writing about sex outside of a monogamous relationship. "Without such strong relationships to build on, it's tough to create sexual scenes that have credibility and impact or advance the plot, and I'd just be dragging sex in arbitrarily and perfunctorily," he said. "You know, like it's been two chapters without a fuck scene, so I better slap one together."

Steve's decision to concentrate on writing short fiction was right on the mark. In 1972, *Cavalier* published four of his stories: "Suffer the Little Children," "The Fifth Quarter," "Battleground," and "The Mangler." It was sure money and regular bylines, and once Nye Willden had told him that readers were actually starting to ask for his stories, Steve was thrilled. He hadn't completely abandoned his dream of writing a novel that a publisher would want to buy, and he still occasionally corresponded with Bill Thompson, but Steve had nothing to send to him, and he was gun-shy after his extensive revisions were in vain.

Steve had written "The Fifth Quarter," about a common criminal who wants to avenge the death of a friend during a botched robbery, under the pseudonym of John Swithen. He chose another name because this story was different from the others he'd written for the magazine. It was more a hard-boiled crime story than a supernatural horror story, and he used the pulp writers from the fifties as his model. "They used a lot of different names back then because they poured that stuff out," he explained. "This was my time to pour the stuff out too, so I used the John Swithen name, but I never used it again because I didn't really like it."

When school let out for the summer, Steve returned to working full-time at the New Franklin Laundry, and though it was a hot, thankless, exhausting job, it had an upside. As was the case when he worked in the Worumbo Mills right after high school, the laundry environment and its workers would occasionally offer up an idea for a story.

At the laundry, one of King's coworkers was missing his hands and forearms and had to wear prosthetic devices with a hook on the end. He'd been working there for almost three decades and had one day been working on the ironing and folding machine. The employees had nicknamed the machine the Mangler, because that's what happened if anyone got too close. On this unfortunate day, the guy's tie was accidentally pulled into the machine. He went to pull it out and his left hand was sucked into the machine. Instinctively he tried to pull his arm with his other hand and that got pulled in as well.

When Steve worked there in the early seventies, the guy with the hooks introduced himself to new employees by first running hot and cold water over the hooks and then sneaking up on an unsuspecting coworker and setting the hooks on the back of his neck. After Steve had observed this prank more than a few times and been an unwilling participant on the business end of the hooks himself, he thought it would make a good story. "The Mangler" was the result.

One day in the summer of 1972, one of Steve's friends, Flip Thompson, stopped by the Kings' trailer in Hermon for a visit. He read some of the stories Steve was writing and some of the published ones from the men's magazines and started to chew him out. In the early seventies, women's liberation was in full swing, and any enlightened man who expected to win over the modern woman was supposed to be sensitive to women's issues.

Flip asked why Steve continued to write this macho crap for the titty magazines.

"Because the stories don't sell too well to *Cosmopolitan*" was Steve's retort.

Flip accused Steve of not having any feminine sensibility at all, and Steve replied that he could write with that in mind if he wanted to, but that's not what *Cavalier* and the other magazines buying his stories were looking for.

"If you're a writer and a realist about what you're doing, you can do nearly anything you want," Flip countered. "In fact, the more of a pragmatist and carpetbagger you are, the better you can do it."

He bet Steve ten bucks that he couldn't write a story from a woman's point of view, and they shook on it. Steve had been kicking around an idea that he thought might work for *Cavalier*, about an outcast girl with supernatural powers who strikes back at the kids who have teased her for most of her life. He thought back to his school days and his outcast classmates: one girl who had only one outfit to wear for the entire school year, and the other who had grown up with a life-size crucifix in her house.

Since he'd gone back to work at the New Franklin Laundry, he'd noticed an older female employee who was a religious fanatic, and he thought he might use her to develop the mother of the outcast girl in the story.

He had the germ of his story. Now he just had to sit down and write it.

He set the first scene in a girls' locker room. He wrote the first few pages about a high school girl who started menstruating while she was in the shower and started screaming because she thought she was bleeding to death. She didn't know the facts of life because her ultrareligious parents didn't believe in discussing sex with their children.

Her classmates responded by throwing tampons at her, and that's when he ran into a brick wall. How did the girls get all those tampons? Weren't they in coin-operated machines? He didn't know. After all, he'd only been in a girls' locker room once before when he worked alongside his brother, David, at his part-time summer job as a janitor at Brunswick High School.

So he asked Tabby about the coin-op machines. She laughed and told him they were free.

"It was a tough story," he said. "It was about girls and it was about girls' locker rooms and it was about menstruation, a lot of things that I didn't know anything about. The iceberg was a lot bigger. It was women! It was girls! Women are bad enough! Girls are even more mysterious."

He continued to slog away on the story, but after he'd written fifteen single-spaced pages, he gave up and tossed it in the trash. Not only was he having problems with the female part of the story—maybe Flip was right after all—but the story also couldn't be contained in only three thousand words, the limit of his stories for *Cavalier*. He'd only sold one story to the magazine that was longer.

"A short story is like a stick of dynamite with a tiny fuse," he explained. "You light it and that's the end. It suddenly occurred to me that I wanted a longer fuse. I wanted the reader to see that this girl was really being put upon, that what she did was not really evil and not even revenge, but it was the way you strike out at somebody when you're badly hurt."

After he threw away the pages, he needed to relax. Back then, Steve's idea of heaven—besides spending all day at the typewriter—was taking a bath while he smoked a cigarette, drank a beer, and listened to a Red Sox game on the transistor radio propped up on the sink. That was how Tabby found him when she entered the bathroom, snapped off the radio, and wagged the crumpled pages in his face. "You ought to go on with this," she said, "it's good."

"But I don't know anything about girls," he protested.

"I'll help you."

Perhaps Flip was right, but he didn't realize Steve had another source to help him understand the female psyche.

Tabby also told him that the story deserved more than three thousand words, and that it could be a full-fledged novel. Back in college, Steve was attracted to Tabby partly because she was his ideal first reader. "She's an avid reader and a terrific critic," he said. "She'll say, 'This part doesn't work,' she'll say why, and then she'll suggest a few different ways to fix it."

So he uncrumpled the pages and returned to the story. He got stuck when he got to the prom scene once Carrie had unleashed her telekinesis. "I really wanted to reap destruction on these people but couldn't think of how it was going to happen," he said. "Tabby suggested using the amplifiers and electrical equipment from the rock band."

He also drew on his own experience teaching high school students. "There's a little bit of Carrie White in me," he admitted. "I've seen high school society from two perspectives, as has any high school teacher. You see it once from the classroom where the rubber bands fly around, and you see it again from behind the desk."

He followed Tabby's advice, expanded the story, and in only three months he wrote what turned out to be a seventy-thousand-word manuscript. He was encouraged by his progress and how the novel had turned out, but not all was well. Not only did he have to work in the laundry Monday through Friday, handling restaurant tablecloths loaded with bits of lobster and clam and bloody bed linens from hospitals, infested with maggots, but the family had also moved around a lot. Since Naomi was born, the family had lived in two apartments in Bangor—one on Pond Street and another on Grove Street—and in a trailer on Klatt Road in Hermon.

Though Steve enjoyed teaching and looked forward to returning to the classroom in September, he was beginning to have nightmares that he'd get stuck as an English teacher with a bunch of manuscripts tucked away in his desk drawer or hall closet. "There were times when I was writing *Carrie* when I felt depressed and really down," he said.

After he finished the manuscript, he thought about sending it to Bill Thompson, but refrained. After all, Doubleday had already rejected two of Steve's novels, why should this one be any different? So he stuck it in a drawer instead and started to think about an idea for his next novel.

In the freshman English classes he taught at Hampden Academy, Steve was teaching *Dracula* along with Thornton Wilder's *Our Town*. Of course, he loved talking about vampires with his students, but he also explored Wilder's descriptions of how people interact with each other in a small town and how a town doesn't usually change. Being from a small town, Steve could readily associate with the characters.

After a long day in the classroom, but before he retreated to the laundry room that served as his office in the trailer, he discussed the two works with Tabby at dinner.

"Can you imagine if Dracula came to Hermon?" she asked.

Steve's brain shifted into overdrive and he came up with the idea for a novel about a small Maine town that is invaded by vampires with the working title *Second Coming*.

He loved writing the novels, but again knew that the short fiction he sold to the men's magazines was his bread and butter. And so he continued to send stories to Nye Willden. And at the time, he needed more sure things, because Tabby was pregnant again. The Kings' second child, Joseph Hillstrom King, was born on June 4, 1972.

Tabby named him after Joe Hillstrom, better known as Joe Hill, a union organizer and songwriter from the early twentieth century. Hill was executed in 1915 for a murder he may or may not have committed and inspired several writers to pen songs and poems about his life. One of the poems, written by poet Alfred Hayes in 1930, was turned into the song "I Dreamed I Saw Joe Hill Last Night" by Depression-era songwriter Earl Robinson, which sixties icon Joan Baez then sang at Woodstock.

Steve returned to Hampden Academy to teach in the fall of 1972. He was a good teacher, but others often noticed that his attention was elsewhere.

"King was a promising teacher," said Robert Rowe, the principal at Hampden. "It was hard to catch him without a book under his arm, and if he had any spare time, he'd be reading a book. But he always took the time to write."

Brenda Willey had King as a teacher at Hampden. "He was a good teacher who had seven classes a day and a study hall," she said. "He told us that he liked to write, and I think he wanted us to write. He was fun and had a pretty good sense of humor."

During the fall he taught all day, came home and marked papers, then prepared lessons before retiring to the trailer's laundry room to write. For at least several hours a night he sat in the cramped space banging out stories.

One day, Steve and Tabby gathered up the kids and headed down to Durham to visit his family. Naomi had a history of developing ear infections, and on the drive back north, she was showing clear signs of getting sick, howling and crying the entire time. From past experience, Steve knew they needed amoxicillin—what they called the pink stuff—but it was expensive, and on that day they were flat broke. Steve felt his rage and helplessness float up into his throat like bile.

When they got back to Hermon, Tabby unloaded the car and gathered up the kids while Steve checked the mailbox to find a letter and a check for $500 for a story he'd mailed off to *Cavalier* a few weeks earlier. When Tabby reached the door with two squawling kids, he told her not to worry, that they could get the pink stuff.

"There were other, much bigger checks that came along later," he said years later, "but that was the best. To be able to say to my wife, 'We can take care of this. And the reason we can take care of it is because we wrote our way out.'"

Despite the occasional checks that seemed to fall from the sky like pennies from heaven, there was never enough money for the first few years of their married life. Every few months, they'd call the phone company to disconnect the phone because they just didn't have enough money left at the end of each month to pay the bill. He knew that many spouses wouldn't be as understanding as Tabby. "It was a time when she might have been expected to say, 'Why don't you quit spending three hours a night in the laundry room, smoking cigarettes and drinking beer we can't afford? Why don't you get an actual job?'"

Things were so bad that if she'd asked him to take on a second job at night, he would have done it. At the time, the prospect of a part-time job was a real possibility for Steve. The debate club at Hampden needed a new faculty adviser, and Steve's name was offered as a candidate. The job paid $300 over the school year, a good chunk of money that would definitely help—but it would require him to work evenings.

When he told Tabby about the debate club adviser job, she asked him if the additional work would leave him time to write, and he replied that he would have a lot less.

"Well then," she said, "you can't take it."

He was grateful for his wife's blessing, but Steve still felt as if he were walking a tightrope. The stress from working a job he didn't like and never having enough money to pay the bills was building. The only two things that helped were writing and, increasingly, drinking.

"I started drinking far too much and frittering money away on poker and bumper pool. You know the scene: it's Friday night and you cash your paycheck in the bar and start knocking them down, and before you know what's happened, you've pissed away half the food budget for that week. There was never a time for me when the goal wasn't to get as hammered as I could possibly afford to. I never understood social drinking, that always seemed to me like kissing your sister. To this day I can't imagine why anyone wants to be a social drinker.

"I saw myself at fifty, my hair graying, my jowls thickening, a network of whiskey-ruptured capillaries spiderwebbing across my nose—drinker's tattoos, we call them in Maine—with a dusty trunkful of unpublished novels rotting in the basement, teaching high school English for the rest of my life and getting off what few literary rocks I had left by advising the student newspaper or maybe by teaching a creative-writing course."

He obviously loved his family. "On the one hand, I wanted nothing more than to provide for them and protect them, but at the same time, I was also experiencing a range of nasty emotions from resentment to anger to occasional outright hate. It was a vicious circle: the more miserable and inadequate I felt about what I saw as my failure as a writer, the more I'd try to escape into the bottle, which would only exacerbate the domestic stress and make me even more depressed. Tabby was steamed about the booze, of course, but she told me she understood."

"I was more angry at the five bucks that went out every week for the carton of cigarettes than I was anything else," she said. "It was the literal burning of money that drove me nuts."

"The only thing that kept our heads above water were these stories for men's magazines," he admitted. "I've autographed a few of those over the years, and it always gives me a cold shudder to think about where I was when I wrote those stories. My underwear had holes in it in those days."

One day, Steve came home from work and Tabby was standing at the door with her hand out. "Give me your wallet," she said. He handed it over and she emptied the wallet of all the credit cards, the gas cards, the store cards. Then she took an enormous pair of scissors and cut them in half.

"But we're paying our bills," Steve protested.

She said, "No, we're paying the interest. We can't afford to anymore, we've got to pay as we go."

Tabitha listened to a fair amount of her husband's pissing and moaning and finally told him it was time to stop. "She said to save my self-pity and turn my energy to the typewriter," he said. "I did because she was right and my anger played much better when channeled into about a dozen stories."

George MacLeod, his old college roommate, would occasionally visit when Steve and Tabby were living in Bangor. "It was a crap apartment, the kids would be running all over the place, and there would be Steve over in the corner typing away," MacLeod said. "The noise just didn't bother him. He could be in the middle of a crowded room and throw a cloak over himself and disappear into his safe cocoon world of fiction and connect with the story line and the characters. Mentally, his fingers were on the keyboard all the time."

Steve was still focused on cranking out short stories for the men's magazines since they were almost certain to bring in a couple of hundred bucks or more, though of course he still thought about his novels, those he had already written, those in progress, and those for which ideas were still swimming around in his mind. Though he and Bill Thompson at Doubleday still kept in touch, it had been months since the editor had heard from him, so Bill decided to contact Steve. He asked why Steve hadn't sent him anything lately, adding that he didn't want to discover that Steve had signed up with another publishing house.

Figuring he had nothing to lose, Steve dug the manuscript for *Carrie* out of the drawer and sent it to Bill, though Steve held out little hope that this book would turn the tide. Indeed, he thought that of all of his novels, *Carrie* was the least marketable.

"As I worked on it, I kept saying to myself this is all very fine, but nobody is going to want to read a make-believe story about this little girl in a Maine town," he said. "It's downbeat, it's depressing, and it's fantasy."

When Thompson read it, however, he liked it and thought that this time he could really sell it. But as before, it needed some tweaking. Though he was reluctant to ask Steve for another rewrite, he knew this one had the best chance of all to fly. He promised his unpublished author that if he made the changes, he would do everything in his power to get the book published.

After all, ghost stories and horror were hot. *The Exorcist* was published in hardcover in June 1971 with the hotly anticipated movie based on the book due out in December of 1973, and *The Other,* a movie about identical twin brothers, one good and one evil, had come out in 1972 to top box office. And *Rosemary's Baby* was still being talked about since first appearing on movie screens in 1968. Publishers and movie producers were clamoring for the next big thing in horror, and Bill Thompson had an inkling that *Carrie* would strike gold. The novels Steve had previously sent to Bill didn't fall into the category of horror. *Carrie* did.

Despite his doubts, Steve dutifully revised the manuscript and sent it back to Bill within a few weeks and promptly forgot about it to return to writing a few stories he could send to Nye Willden at *Cavalier* for some quick cash. He also resumed work on *Second Coming,* which he had renamed *Salem's Lot* in the meantime.

On this cold, gray late-winter day in March of 1973, Steve's foul mood reflected the weather. He was back in the classroom, teaching reluctant students, and the Kings were once again without a phone.

An announcement came over the PA system, telling Steve that his wife was on the phone—she used a neighbor's phone if there was an emergency—and could he please come to the office. He rushed over with two thoughts in his head: either one of the kids was really sick or Doubleday wanted to buy *Carrie.*

When he picked up the phone, Tabby told him that Bill Thompson had sent a telegram to say the book would be published and offering an advance of $2,500. The couple were ecstatic.

Bill later told Steve that not only did he love the novel, but once it started to make the rounds of the office, it all but caught fire, specifically because of the opening scene in which Carrie gets her period for the first time in the locker room and is pelted with tampons. Female editors made copies of the manuscript and handed them out to secretaries at the company, who then snuck them to friends.

The manuscript required little in the way of changes or revision, but Steve wanted to make one crucial change. When he wrote *Carrie,* he set it in Massachusetts, in the towns of Boxford and Andover, because he never imagined it would see print. When Bill accepted it, Steve said he wanted to change the setting to Maine.

Once *Carrie* sold, Steve bought a blue Pinto, the Kings' first new car, for just over $2,000 and they moved to a four-room apartment at 14 Sanford Street in Bangor for $90 a month.

Best of all, the stress Steve had felt because he thought he was failing at his primary role as breadwinner of the family had disappeared. "I don't know what would have happened to my marriage and my sanity if Doubleday didn't accept *Carrie,*" he said.

Once they had moved into their new apartment, they ordered another phone. Which turned out to be a good thing.

After Doubleday bought the hardcover rights, Bill Thompson had told Steve that the publisher planned to sell the paperback rights, and that they could expect $5,000 or $10,000 dollars from the sale, which would evenly be split between publisher and author as spelled out in the contract.

Though Steve was tempted to quit his teaching job to write full-time after the hardcover rights sold, he knew he couldn't afford it. He was resigned to teaching freshman English to sullen teenagers for a third year starting in the fall.

But on Mother's Day in 1973, all that changed. Tabby had taken the kids to visit her family in Old Town while Steve spent the afternoon in the apartment relishing the time alone to tinker with *Salem's Lot*.

The phone rang. Bill Thompson was on the other end, and Steve thought it was an odd thing for him to call on a Sunday. He asked if Steve was sitting down.

"Should I be?"

Thompson then told him that the paperback rights to *Carrie* had been sold to New American Library.

"For how much?"

"Four hundred thousand."

Steve thought he'd said $40,000, which was still a hell lot more money than he'd ever seen before.

"Forty thousand is great!"

That's when Thompson corrected him. "No, Steve, four hundred thousand. Six figures."

Half of that—$200,000—would be Steve's.

Steve hadn't heeded his editor's advice to sit down. The phone was attached to the wall in the kitchen, and when the numbers sank in, he suddenly lost all the strength in his legs. "I just kinda slid down the wall until the shirttail came out of my pants and my butt was on the linoleum," he said. They continued talking for about twenty minutes, but when they hung up, Steve couldn't remember a word of the conversation except for the $400,000 part.

He couldn't wait for Tabby to get home. He paced back and forth across the kitchen floor for a while until he suddenly decided he wanted to buy Tabby a present. Of course, a litany of worries immediately began to overwhelm his overactive imagination.

"As I crossed the street, I thought that was the time when a drunk would come along in a car and he would kill me, and things would be put back in perspective," he said. He made a beeline to LaVerdiere's drugstore a couple of blocks away and spent $29 on a hairdryer for his wife, who had stuck by his side and believed in his writing even when he didn't. "I scuttled across those streets, looking both ways."

When she came home with the kids a few hours later, Steve handed her the hairdryer with a big grin on his face. She got angry, saying they couldn't afford it. He told her they could and then explained why. Then they both started crying.

Thompson later told Steve that NAL's first offer for the paperback rights was $200,000, which caught everyone at Doubleday off guard. According to Thompson, Bob Bankford, the publisher's subsidiary rights manager in charge of selling paperback rights, was a great poker player, and when NAL's initial offer came in, he hesitated, then drawled that they were expecting a bit more. The publisher then raised the offer.

The money bought Steve his freedom. Now he could definitely quit teaching and do what he was born to do: write novels.

Best of all, Bill Thompson was now clamoring for Steve's next novel. He turned his full attention to finishing *Salem's Lot.*

Steve and Tabby could hardly believe their luck. "It was like someone opened a prison door," he said. "Our lives changed so quickly that for more than a year afterward, we walked around with big, sappy grins on our faces, barely daring to believe that we were out of that trap for good."

Before the paperback rights sold, Steve had only bought one hardcover book in his life: William Manchester's *Death of a President,* which he bought as a gift. Now he could buy hardcovers with a vengeance, as many as he wanted.

At the time, his mother was working at Pineland Training Center, a home for the mentally retarded in New Gloucester, Maine, twenty miles north of Portland. "She served meals, cleaned up shit, and wore a green uniform," said Steve. He went to Pineland to tell her about the paperback sale. "She was pulling a truck of dishes," he remembered. "She looked so strung out; she'd lost forty pounds and was dying of cancer but it hadn't even been diagnosed. I said, 'Mom, you're done,' and that was her last day working. I didn't have the paperback money yet, but I borrowed from a bank and she went to live with my brother in Mexico, Maine."

News of such a large paperback sale for a novel by a first-time author meant that it didn't take long for Hollywood to come sniffing around. The movie rights sold to Twentieth Century–Fox, which were then passed to United Artists.

Despite the sudden influx of more money than he'd ever hoped to see in his lifetime, Steve discovered it was difficult to spend the money. Tabby said he was being ridiculous; after all those years of poverty, he was a success and he should spend some of it and have some fun with it.

"Tabby and I argued more about money after *Carrie* than we ever had before," he said. "She wanted to get a house and I would say no, I don't feel secure. She got very exasperated with me."

After years of scraping by, and after so many false starts with revised novels that didn't sell, he didn't entirely trust what was happening. "My idea was the success would never happen again, so I should trickle the money out," he said. "Maybe the kids would be eating Cheerios and peanut butter for dinner, but that's okay, let 'em! I'll be writing."

With only a month left to teach, he finished out the school year at Hampden, and after spending the first few years of married life living in and around Bangor, he and Tabby decided to move to southern Maine, so they could be closer to Steve's mother. They rented a house on Sebago Lake in North Windham, about sixteen miles northwest of Portland and 130 miles from Bangor, and moved at the end of the summer of 1973.

Steve called on his college buddy George MacLeod to help out, who was surprised to learn that Steve literally didn't know how to move, even though he'd moved from one ramshackle apartment to another several times over.

MacLeod borrowed a friend's old panel truck, an International Travelall, hooked up a trailer behind it, and loaded up all of Steve's stuff. MacLeod drove with the Kings loaded into the front, and he couldn't help thinking he was in a Maine version of *The Beverly Hillbillies*. "We headed down Interstate 95 and delivered the meager stuff he had into this palatial house in the pouring rain," said MacLeod. "It was a huge estate and it was totally empty."

Once they moved in, Steve settled into a routine of writing several hours a day while visiting his mother in between.

He finished writing *Salem's Lot* and sent it to Bill Thompson, along with *Roadwork,* another novel he had written during college about a man who is forced from his home when the city decides to build a new highway running through his house and his workplace, a laundry. When Steve asked his editor which one he wanted to publish first, Bill told him he wouldn't like the answer. "He said that *Roadwork* was a more honestly dealt novel, a novelist's novel, but that he wanted to do *Salem's Lot* because he thought it would have greater commercial success," said Steve. Bill warned that Steve would get stereotyped as a horror writer. "Like Edgar Allan Poe and Mary Shelley? I didn't care. They did type me as a horror writer, but I've been able to do all sorts of things within that framework."

But first, as usual, Bill asked Steve to make a few changes. "He suggested that I rewrite the book a little bit in the beginning to try and keep the reader in the dark for a certain period of time, and I told him that anybody who reads this sort of thing is going to know that it's vampires from the first," said Steve.

His editor politely disagreed. "You're not writing for an audience of forty thousand people," he said. "We want to break you out so you'll appeal to an audience of millions of people, and they don't read *Weird Tales.*" Steve made the changes and later agreed that Thompson was on the mark.

He also asked Steve to rewrite one of the scenes where Jimmy Cody, the local doctor, is eaten alive by a horde of rats. "I had them swarming all over him like a writhing, furry carpet, biting and chewing, and when he tries to scream a warning to his companion upstairs, one of them scurries into his open mouth and squirms as it gnaws out his tongue," Steve said. "I loved the scene, but Bill made it clear that *no way* would Doubleday publish something like that, and I came around eventually and impaled poor Jimmy on knives. But, shit, that just wasn't the same."

While Steve was writing *Salem's Lot,* he visualized Ben Mears as the actor Ben Gazzara, though in his writing he left the physical characteristics deliberately vague. "I don't usually describe the characters that I write about because I don't think I have to," he said. "If they seem like real people to the readers, they'll put their own faces on them. All I really said about Ben Mears is that his hair was black and sort of greasy. Then somebody told me that Gazzara was too old for the role Steve envisioned for Ben Mears, and I saw him in some gangster picture a while later and thought, by God, he *is* too old."

Bill Thompson made an offer for *Salem's Lot* before *Carrie* had even been published and signed Steve to a multibook contract. In the meantime, Ruth's condition was worsening and she didn't have much time left. Steve felt cheated. After all his mother had done for him, supporting his writing, going without food so he could have a little pocket money in college, and now she wouldn't live long enough to see his first published book, though she had seen the galleys for *Carrie,* which Steve had read to her.

On December 18, 1973, Ruth King died of uterine cancer, and something right out of the books Steve had grown up with happened that night. "The night my mother died of cancer—practically the same minute—my son had a terrible choking fit in his bed at home," he said. "He was turning blue when Tabby finally forced out the obstruction." Steve had never had a fear of choking before, but resigned, he added it to the list.

RIDING THE BULLET

Carrie was published in April 1974 in hardcover with a cover price of $5.95. Steve was thrilled that his first novel was finally available in bookstores, but his satisfaction was greatly tempered by his mother's death. Novels on the *New York Times* bestseller list that month were *Jaws*, by Peter Benchley, and *The First Deadly Sin*, by Lawrence Sanders. But *Carrie* wasn't one of them. The book's first printing was thirty thousand copies, but only thirteen thousand sold.

Though Steve was already a heavy drinker, the depression that set in after his mother's death caused him to drink even more. He also plunged into his writing: shortly after his mother died, he wrote "The Woman in the Room," the story of a grown son who helps his terminally ill mother end her life.

Tabby and Steve thought they needed a change of scenery and decided to move to another part of the country, at least temporarily. After all, they could afford to live almost anywhere now. They got a copy of the *Rand McNally Road Atlas* and opened it to a map of the United States. Steve closed his eyes and stabbed his finger on the page; it landed in Colorado.

With the movie rights to *Carrie* sold and a multibook contract from Doubleday, Steve finally loosened up enough to spend a little bit of his windfall and bought a brand-new red, white, and blue Cadillac convertible. But he felt uncomfortable when he visited his friends back in Durham and instead took a rusty 1964 Dodge Dart for his trips home.

In August 1974, the family climbed into their new Cadillac and drove to Boulder, Colorado. They rented a house at 330 South Forty-second Street, and Steve set out to find ideas for new books and stories.

In Boulder, Steve had a hard time focusing on work. He started one story after another, but nothing clicked. Thinking a few days off might help, he asked a couple of neighbors where he and Tabby could spend a quiet weekend. They recommended the Stanley Hotel in Estes Park.

The night before Halloween, Steve and Tabby left Naomi and Joe with a babysitter and headed for Estes Park, about forty miles away. It didn't take long for Steve's imagination to go into overdrive. On the way to the hotel, they passed a sign that read ROAD MAY BE CLOSED AFTER OCTOBER. His antenna perked up. When he and Tabby entered the hotel, he noticed that three nuns were leaving, as if the place were about to become godless, and when he and Tabby checked in, they learned it was the last day of the season before the hotel closed for the winter.

As the bellman was showing them to their room, number 217, they passed a fire extinguisher with a long hose coiled up tightly hanging on a wall. Immediately Steve thought, "That could be a snake."

Further adding to his glee, they discovered they were the only guests in the hotel that night. At dinner, the orchestra played even though they were the sole diners. All the other tables in the restaurant had the chairs turned upside down and placed on top. It was windy and a shutter outside had loosened and banged against the window, a regular thumping rhythm that didn't let up the whole night.

After dinner, Steve's excitement continued to build once they returned to their room. "I almost drowned in the bathtub that should have had scratch marks on the side, it was so deep," he said.

A few weeks before their trip to Estes Park, Steve had been playing around with the idea for a story about a child with ESP at an amusement park. But once he saw all the marvelous props and the spooky setting at the hotel, the idea came to him in a flash, and he changed the story's location from the park to the Stanley. "By the time I went to bed that night I had the whole book in my mind," he said. He immediately began writing the story of a little boy with ESP who is acutely sensitive to the evil in the haunted Overlook Hotel and has to deal with his alcoholic father, who wants to kill him.

Admittedly, the money helped ease their lifestyle considerably, but Steve was still surprised at the anger and rage he felt, particularly toward his kids. It especially surfaced while they were living in Colorado; it was the first time he had lived outside his native Maine, and away from familiar territory he felt unsettled. "I felt very hostile to my kids there," he said. "I wanted to grab them and hit them. Even though I didn't do it, I felt guilty feelings because of my brutal impulses."

After he became a father, Steve discovered that when it came to the rule-book on fatherhood, he had to make it up as he went along. The fifties sitcoms *Father Knows Best* and *Leave It to Beaver* were his role models: "I thought I'd come in the door at night and yell, 'Honey, I'm home!' and the kids would sit around the table and eat their peas and share their interesting little adventures. I wasn't prepared for the realities of fatherhood."

Naomi was born when Steve was twenty-two, and Joe came along a couple of years later. Without planning on it, he began to write several books about fatherhood so that he could at least understand it better. "I had feelings of anger about my kids that I never expected," he admitted.

One day when Joe was three years old, the boy got hold of one of Steve's manuscripts and thought he'd write like Daddy. So he took his crayons and drew little cartoons all over one of Steve's novels-in-progress. When Steve saw it, he thought, "The little son of a bitch, I could kill him."

Steve's mother's words echoed in his ears while he worked on the story that would become *The Shining*. Just as she had told him to say something three times in a row to prevent it from happening, Steve held a hope that if he wrote about something bad—particularly a rage that dwelled deep inside him—he'd never feel compelled to act it out.

"I never wrote anything about children out of a sense of sadism or anger or anything; it was more like, if I write this, it won't happen, like I'm trying to keep the hex off," he explained.

But he was surprised that the rage remained, because although sudden financial success had already smoothed over a lot of things, it didn't necessarily eradicate the demons that had lived within him for most of his life: the shame over his father's leaving.

He wrote most of *The Shining* blazingly fast, but when it came time to write one particular scene, he hit a brick wall. Try as he might, he was petrified of writing a scene where a long-dead woman in a bathtub suddenly sits up and heads straight for the boy. "I didn't want to have to face that unspeakable thing in the tub any more than the boy did," he said. For several nights before he wrote the scene, he had a nightmare about a nuclear explosion. "The mushroom cloud turned into a huge red bird that was coming for me, but when I finished with the scene, it was gone."

On the surface, he knew he was writing *The Shining* to keep his violent urges toward his kids at bay. However, even though he didn't realize it at the time, he was also writing about his drinking and alcoholism, which by the midseventies had become crucial to his daily life.

"I had written *The Shining* without realizing that I was writing about myself," he said. "I've never been the most self-analytical person in the world. People often ask me to parse out meaning from my stories, to relate them back to my life. While I've never denied that they . . . have some relationship to my life, I'm always puzzled to realize years later that in some ways I was delineating my own problems, and performing a kind of self-psychoanalysis."

At one point, *The Shining* became too close for comfort and he took a break from it to start work on another novel that was sparked by the Patricia Hearst kidnapping. "I was convinced that the only way anybody ever could really understand the whole Hearst case was to lie about it," he said. His working title was *The House on Value Street*, and as was usual with Steve, the story unwittingly grew when another news item crossed his path: he'd heard about a chemical spill in Utah that killed some livestock and that inspired a Midwestern preacher to spread the word that the world was about to end as a result.

He had already been working on the novel, which would become *The Stand*, on and off for a couple of years alongside his other projects when he was suddenly stopped dead in his tracks, and it looked like he might not continue. One day he was browsing in a bookstore when he picked up a new book called *Survivors*, written by Welsh author Terry Nation, who had also written *Doctor Who*. "It was about a virus decimating the world and the survivors that were left, and I thought, 'Great, this guy has just written my book,'" he said.

He returned to finish writing *The Shining*, then completed *The Stand* despite the competing book. "I felt like my blood was really flowing out of my stomach, and if I didn't finish the book and stanch the flow, I'd just die," he said.

The family lived in Boulder for about a year before returning home to Maine in the summer of 1975, where they bought their first house for $150,000 on Kansas Road in Bridgton, a town about forty miles from Portland. "We didn't feel comfortable in Colorado," Steve said. When he looked back on the books he wrote in Colorado—*The Shining* and *The Stand*—he saw that the characters still carried the sensibility of the working-class people that he grew up with. "We were in Colorado, but I really took my Maine with me," he said. "You carry your place with you wherever you go."

Salem's Lot was published in hardcover in October 1975; the paperback rights sold for $500,000. Again, Stephen got half. His first two novels had made him almost half a million dollars, which was phenomenal for a new writer, and there was the promise of more money from the sale of the movie rights. However, Doubleday published only twenty thousand copies of *Salem's Lot*, since the thirteen-thousand-copy sell-through on *Carrie* had not met the publisher's projections. To help boost sales, just before the book went to the printer the sales department decided to lower the price of the book by a dollar, changing the price on the dust jackets to $7.95 from $8.95. *Salem's Lot* did not hit any bestseller lists, but Steve didn't really care. He was a full-time novelist and no longer had to worry about providing for his family. He was living his dream.

In the winter of 1976, Steve went to a publishing party in New York where he met an agent who primarily worked with fantasy and horror writers. Kirby McCauley, who had recently moved to New York from the Midwest, had read only one of King's two books when they met, *Salem's Lot,* but after chatting with Steve discovered they shared many of the same interests in obscure authors from the 1940s and '50s. As they spoke about such authors as Frank Belknap Long and Clifford Simak, McCauley saw out of the corner of his eye that most of the other writers were queuing up to talk with author James Baldwin, who was holding court in a corner of the room. But Steve was happy to stay with McCauley, and he was impressed when the agent mentioned some of his other clients, including Frank Herbert, Piers Anthony, Robert Silverberg, and Peter Straub. When Steve told him he didn't have an agent, McCauley told Steve to keep him in mind.

"One of the jobs of an agent is to look ahead at what's down the road so the writer's career is protected," he told King. At the time, a long-term career wasn't even on Steve's radar, since his sole purpose up to that point was to write as many books and stories as he could churn out. However, Steve filed it away for the future.

Once the family was back in Maine, Steve was just as productive as ever, and he was grateful that the books continued to sell and that readers were clamoring for more of his work. "Money makes you a little saner," he said. "You don't have to do things you don't want to do."

He bought himself a Wang word processor so he wouldn't have to retype his manuscripts, which would give him more time to create stories. He gave Tabby's gray Olivetti typewriter—the machine he wrote *Carrie* and *Salem's Lot* on—to Naomi, who was exhibiting an interest in writing stories. As he was beginning to enjoy his success, a few nagging, little health problems started to surface, even though he was just shy of thirty years old.

He took medication for high blood pressure, and he occasionally complained of insomnia. Plus, he began to experience migraine headaches, which he referred to as a "work symptom." And he was still drinking heavily.

In November, *Carrie,* the first movie based on one of Steve's books, was released. Brian De Palma, who had directed a few low-budget thrillers, was the director, and Paul Monash produced the film. The production designer was Jim Fish, who was married to actress Sissy Spacek. She was invited to audition for the roles of Sue Snell and Chris Hargensen, but De Palma thought she'd be better cast as Carrie and asked her to read for the part.

The film was a box-office smash. *Carrie* was made for less than $2 million dollars but ended up grossing $30 million in the United States alone. And it exposed Steve to an entirely new audience. "*Carrie* the movie put King on the map in a way that a book just won't," said George Beahm, author of several books on King. "It got people who don't normally go into bookstores through the doors." Once there, they bought *Carrie* and *Salem's Lot,* and they knew to buy *The Shining* when it was published two short months later.

Steve loved how Brian De Palma interpreted the book into film. "He handled the material deftly and artistically and got a fine performance out of Sissy Spacek," Steve said. "In many ways, the movie is more stylish than my book, which I still think is a gripping read but is impeded by a certain heaviness, a Sturm und Drang quality that's absent from the film."

Some things had to be changed in the movie. In the book, as she wandered back home in shock after the prom, Carrie blew up a few gas stations, which sent the entire town into flames. De Palma struck it from the movie because the special effects would cost too much.

More good news followed in January when Sissy Spacek was nominated for an Oscar for Best Actress in a Leading Role, and Piper Laurie, who played Carrie's mother, received a nomination for Best Actress in a Supporting Role.

The movie sold more of Steve's books and attracted a larger audience who wanted to know more about his motivations as well as his background. "A question started to appear in their eyes, sort of like, 'Where are all the bodies buried, Steve?'" he recalled. "Or else they'd casually ask me about my childhood and if I was ever beaten or burned with cigarettes. And I'd say, 'Really, I'm just like you are,' and they'd step back."

Whenever interviewers broached the question, he'd crack a joke and then begin his rote explanation: "Basically, all I'm doing is saying things that other people are afraid to say. The job's not much different than being a comedy writer. What's the one thing that nobody wants to talk about, the literary equivalent of taking a fork and scraping it across a blackboard, or making somebody bite on a lemon? And when I find those things, generally the reaction from readers or moviegoers is 'Thank you for saying that, for articulating that thought.'"

High sales and increasing name recognition gave Steve the confidence to ask Doubleday to publish books that had been rejected before *Carrie* was released. Stephen was keen to have *Getting It On,* the first novel he wrote back in college, published. The story was about a student who takes over a school and holds his classmates hostage, but Doubleday didn't want to saturate the market with his name.

He had several first drafts of completed novels and others he had written before he had written *Carrie.* While some writers may have considered these novels to be just apprenticeship books, learning opportunities and unpublishable, Steve wanted them to be given a chance to see the light of day as finished books. Back then, editors and publishers didn't want to publish more than one book a year by one author, believing that each new book would cut into the sales of the others. But Steve was annoyed with the publishing industry's attitude of "We do it this way because this is the way it's always been done."

So instead of sending it to Doubleday, Steve sent *Getting It On* to Elaine Koster, his editor at his paperback publisher, New American Library. The single-book credo wasn't an issue because, from the start, Steve maintained, he wanted the book to be published under a pseudonym, to see if it could find an audience on its own without the growing star attraction of his name.

"I was emphatic about not wanting the book to be publicized," he said. "I wanted it to go out there and either find an audience or just disappear quietly. The idea was not to just publish a book that I thought was good, but to honestly try to create another name that wouldn't be associated with my name, like having a Swiss bank account."

The pen name he originally chose for the book was Guy Pillsbury, the name of his late grandfather. Koster passed the manuscript around to other editors and the marketing department for their opinions, but word soon traveled that King was the author. He was so incensed that he took back the book and decided to make a few changes so the same thing wouldn't happen again.

First, he changed the title to *Rage,* then he looked around his office for inspiration for his pen name. He spotted a book by Richard Stark on the shelf—the pseudonym of mystery writer Donald Westlake, whose work Steve greatly admired—and a record by Bachman-Turner Overdrive, one of his favorite bands, was playing on his stereo.

Richard Bachman it would be.

Koster accepted the novel with the caveat that no one at the publisher would know who the real author was.

The Shining, published in January 1977 with a first printing of fifty thousand hardcover copies, was Steve's first hardback bestseller. He was in a whole new league. Book reviewers from the *New York Times* to *Cosmopolitan* lauded King's ability to hook the reader into one of the first novels to really explore in depth the actions of an abusive parent.

He based the title on a song by John Lennon and the Plastic Ono Band called "Instant Karma," with a refrain that went "We all shine on." But he had to change the title to *The Shining* after the publisher said that *shine* was a negative term for African-American.

But it was too scary for others. Because of the book's visibility and popularity, it was the first of King's books to be banned from school libraries, most often instigated by parents, and some teachers, for portraying a father as being truly evil. A few school librarians called Steve—this was at a time when he was still answering his own phone—and asked for his opinion.

He replied that it was okay if some parents felt that way, since they're the ones who paid the taxes for the library, and since the school was legally responsible for the kids during school hours, they were within their rights to remove the book. He then added a caveat: "But I think that every kid in the school should know it's been banned and should immediately get to the nearest bookstore or public library to find out what it was that their parents didn't want them to know. Those are the things kids really ought to know, what people don't want them to know."

Readers and reviewers criticized the murderous Jack Torrance and questioned why Steve felt compelled to write about such things. He explained his motivation for writing the book by describing the impulses that dwell inside every human being, giving the example of a typical headline from the *National Enquirer* or the *Weekly World News* in the late seventies: "Baby Nailed to Wall." "You could say you never did that to your kids even though you had the impulse a couple of times, and that's where the horror is born," he said matter-of-factly. "Not in the fact that somebody nailed a baby to the wall, but that you can remember times when you felt like knocking your kid's head right off his shoulders because he wouldn't shut up."

Though Steve was notorious for telling interviewers that he just wrote his stories, he didn't stop to analyze them, *The Shining* was one of the first stories where he came right out and said the main character Jack Torrance was tormented by his father, though he stopped short of adding that he'd suffered the same fate.

"People ask if the book is a ghost story or is it just in this guy's mind. Of course it's a ghost story, because Jack Torrance himself is a haunted house. He's haunted by his father. It pops up again, and again, and again."

However, Steve failed to mention anything about the theme of alcoholism in the book, as he wasn't ready to admit—to himself or others—that he shared something else in common with Jack Torrance.

As expected, Hollywood came knocking, especially given the success of the movie *Carrie,* which had been released two months earlier.

Despite his runaway success and his now having enough money to live on for the rest of his life, Steve continued to write stories for the men's magazines, which had helped him buy medicine for his kids when he and Tabby were living in virtual poverty just a few short years earlier. Partly it was a way to thank the magazines and editors that had helped give him his start, but he also appreciated that the magazines provided an outlet for the stories that continued to pour from him.

Since his first publication in *Cavalier* in October 1970, Steve had continued to submit stories to his editor Nye Willden. Since the first story, "Graveyard Shift," had been published, almost a dozen of King's stories had appeared in the magazine. One day, Willden thought it might be a great idea to have a short-story contest in *Cavalier.* Steve would write the first half of a horror story and readers would be invited to finish the story, with prizes awarded to those who finished the story the best, according to King.

Willden found a facial close-up photograph of a strange, insane-looking cat, and he thought the image would spark a great first half-story from Steve, who loved the idea, and the editor sent him a copy of the photo.

A couple of weeks later, back came a manuscript entitled "The Cat from Hell," with a note: "There was no way I could write just a half of a story," Steve wrote, "so I wrote a complete story. Cut it where you wish for your contestants and maybe, after you award the winner you might want to publish my complete story to show what I did to it."

The first five hundred words of "The Cat from Hell" appeared in the

March 1977 issue of *Cavalier,* with Steve's full-length version appearing in the June issue along with those of some of the winners and runners-up.

After the success of *The Shining,* Doubleday wanted another novel from King to be published the following year. But King had already started to work on *The Stand,* and he knew it wouldn't be ready in time. So instead he offered Doubleday a short-story collection of the pieces he had sold to *Cavalier* and other men's magazines over the last seven years and called it *Night Shift.* The book contained the stories "The Mangler," "Battleground," "Trucks," and "Children of the Corn," among others.

He would have offered Doubleday one of the Richard Bachman novels, except that King felt his pseudonymous books were of a different flavor, and besides, he had already promised his earlier novels—*The Long Walk, Rage,* and *Roadwork*—to New American Library, the publisher of his paperback novels and the Bachman books.

Doubleday agreed to the short-story collection, though the publisher believed interest in such a book would be limited, and so in February 1978 fifteen thousand copies of *Night Shift* were published. The first printing was less than that for *Salem's Lot.*

To everyone's surprise, *Night Shift* went into a second printing shortly after publication, and Doubleday was caught off guard by the demand. They had to raid the stash of books they supplied to the book clubs—including their own in-house book club, the Literary Guild—and sent books made with cheaper paper out into the marketplace to satisfy bookstore and distributor demand.

Though Steve loved his work and was thrilled whenever he saw a book with his name on it on a bookstore shelf, he realized he was starting to burn out a little, and he started talking about taking a break.

"I keep telling myself I'll take it easy for a while after I finish a book, but after a few days I think it would be fun to work up one of the ideas I've stowed away while I worked on the previous book," he said. "Sure, writing is fun. After all, you're entertaining yourself too, you know."

But he had an added incentive to cut back on his workload, because on February 21, 1977, a third child was born to Steve and Tabby: Owen Phillip King.

From the beginning, they suspected that their third child was not going to be as smooth sailing as the first two. Owen's head at birth was extremely large in proportion to his body, and Steve and Tabby thought he might have hydrocephalus, a congenital condition where fluid builds up in brain tissue to create pressure that can lead to hemorrhage, coma, and brain damage.

Over several weeks, they brought Owen to the hospital for a battery of medical tests. Though the tests proved inconclusive, Steve's fear over having one of his children die obsessed him.

"I always wondered how parents coped with a handicapped child," he said. "It was stunning to discover that I not only loved Owen in spite of his big, mushroom-shaped head, but because of it. It's a shock to look back at our home movies and see what an odd little duck of a baby he was, this long, skinny, pale person, with his little face under his bumper of a forehead. He wasn't hydrocephalic, just a kid with a monster head, but we went through a terrifying period in which we feared for both Owen's death and his life."

Despite now being able to publish two novels a year—one under his real name with Doubleday and one with NAL under his pseudonym, Richard Bachman—Steve was becoming increasingly perturbed at Doubleday, his hardcover publisher, particularly at the way the publisher's executives were treating their number one author. Other top authors at the publisher were Alex Haley, author of *Roots,* and Leon Uris, who wrote *Trinity,* who both seemed to be given more respect.

"Every time he came to New York to meet with me or go over manuscripts, some of the top brass would walk by and they never once recognized him. I would have to introduce him all over again," said Bill Thompson.

In September of 1978, *The Stand* was published with a first printing of thirty-five thousand copies. Steve considered the book to be his first masterpiece, an apocalyptic novel about a superflu that kills most of the population. The survivors are then engaged in a battle of good against evil. He viewed it as his version of *Lord of the Rings* set in the American landscape. He pegged good guy Stu Redman against Randall Flagg—stand-in for the devil—and tossed the sixteen-year-old Harold Lauder into the mix to see which side he would pick.

"I wrote the line 'A dark man with no face,' and then combined it with that grisly little motto, 'Once in every generation a plague will fall among them,' and that was that," he said. "I spent the next two years writing an apparently endless book called *The Stand*. It got to the point where I began describing it to friends as my own little Vietnam, because I kept telling myself that in another hundred pages or so I would begin to see the light at the end of the tunnel.

"To a large extent, Harold Lauder is based on me. With any character that a writer creates, you try to look at people and get a feel for them and understand the way they think. But Harold is a terrible loner, and he is somebody who feels totally rejected by everybody around him, and he feels fat and ugly and unpleasant most of the time."

Steve also said that the destructive side of his personality had a particularly good time when he was writing *The Stand*. "I love to burn things up, at least on paper, and I don't think arson would be half as much fun in real life as it is in fiction," he said, citing one of his favorite scenes, when the Trashcan Man set the tanks at an oil refinery on fire. "I *love* fire, I love destruction. It's great, it's black, and it's exciting. *The Stand* was particularly fulfilling because there I got a chance to scrub the whole human race and, man, it was fun! Much of the compulsive, driven feeling I had while I worked on *The Stand* came from the vicarious thrill of imagining an entire entrenched social order destroyed in one stroke. That's the mad-bomber side of my character, I suppose."

Steve noted, "Although many people still regard *The Stand* as an anthology of the AIDS epidemic, the disease had not even been identified when the book was first published. When the AIDS thing started to happen, I couldn't believe how much it was like *The Stand*. It was almost as though I'd invented it myself."

When King first handed in the manuscript for *The Stand,* at twelve hundred pages and weighing in at twelve and a half pounds, Doubleday said it was too long. Doubleday's press at that time could only bind a book that was so thick—around eight hundred pages—and that was it. They told Steve they needed to cut four hundred pages, saying he could do it or they could do it.

He said he would do it, though he was becoming increasingly incensed at his publisher. Given the millions of dollars his books had generated for Doubleday, he felt he had the right to call his own shots. But they insisted on cutting the book by one-third, or else they refused to publish the book. To make matters worse, because of the first contract he had signed, which doled out money in small yearly increments, he wasn't even seeing his share of the profits. The original contract specified that the publisher would invest the author's royalty income, paying him up to $50,000 a year. Most authors, then and now, came nowhere near generating that amount of income each year. But

Steve did. And he asked Doubleday to alter the clause. They refused, even though he was making hundreds of thousands of dollars a year from the movie rights as well as the foreign editions. He felt Doubleday was deliberately ripping him off. He was reaching his limit with the publisher who had thrilled him in 1973 when they told him they would publish *Carrie*. Based on the income the publisher was generating just on the paperback sales of his books, King felt he not only deserved more respect but more money. *The Stand* was the last book that King contractually owed the publisher, so he threw a deal on the table.

Doubleday would get his next three novels if they paid an advance of $3.5 million.

Thompson, always an advocate for his star author, pressed his bosses to meet Steve's demand, but they refused. The publisher offered $3 million.

Steve thought back to the literary agent Kirby McCauley, whom he'd met the previous year, and asked him what he should do. McCauley suggested they turn to the most logical publisher next, one who was familiar with the revenue his books could generate: his paperback publisher, New American Library. They met Steve's demand, and even though they only published paperbacks, NAL became Steve's publisher, selling the hardcover rights to Viking.

Steve severed his relationship with Doubleday, hired McCauley to be his literary agent, and Thompson ended up a casualty of the cross fire. "When I left Doubleday, they canned him," said Steve. "It was almost like a taunt: we'll kill the messenger that brought the bad news."

Steve thought the instant change of publishers and news of the million-dollar deal would float all boats, including his first Richard Bachman book, *Rage,* published in mass-market paperback in September of 1977 by NAL. While it was a great story, King forgot that his name wasn't on it, but his pseudonym.

The book disappeared without a trace a month or two later. After all, the world was not looking for a Richard Bachman book, but it *was* looking for a Stephen King book. While he was obviously pleased that some of his early work was appearing in print, because his name wasn't on the cover, obviously the sales didn't come close to those of *The Shining.* Steve was clearly frustrated, even though he had made it clear that he wanted *Rage* to sink or swim on its own.

In the aftermath of the Doubleday difficulties, Steve and Tabby thought it was time for a change of scenery. "I thought that people would get tired of everything being set in Maine," he said. "England was the land of the ghost story, so I thought I'd go over there and write a ghost story. So we took the kids and put them in school for a year abroad." They rented a house with the name of Mourlands at 87 Aldershot Road, Fleet, in Hampshire. Author George Beahm said that the Kings had advertised for a home as follows: "Wanted, a draughty Victorian house in the country with dark attic and creaking floorboards, preferably haunted."

Almost immediately, Steve discovered the move was a big mistake: his work suffered: "I was totally flat while overseas. It was like my umbilical cord had been cut."

One good thing that came out of the trip was that he met Peter Straub, an American writer who lived in London at the time. Straub had written several well-received novels including *Julia, Under Venus,* and *If You Could See Me Now,* and his novel *Ghost Story* was just about to be published when he and King met. One night the writers and their wives, Tabby and Susie, got together for dinner at the Straubs' house on Hillfield Avenue in London, and the men stayed up drinking and gabbing long after their wives had gone to bed. "We ought to write a book together," said Steve, and Peter immediately agreed. However, when they compared their schedules, they discovered that both writers were so booked up that the first chance they would have to start was four years into the future. They shook hands on the deal and wrote the date into their appointment books.

During the year they lived in the U.K., the Kings couldn't get warm. The rented house they were living in was cold and damp, and they could never heat it properly. After Steve and Tabby moved back to the United States, Susie Straub wrote in a letter, "It really does take time to get used to the English notion of heating, I swear to you, they don't like being warm."

The Kings had intended to stay a full year in England, but after only three months, they decided to return home in mid-December and purchased a new lakefront home in Center Lovell, Maine, where the majority of residents only lived in town for the summer.

In 1978, Steve was on a roll, cranking out novels and short stories, though with the success of *The Stand,* he was getting a quick lesson in what it meant to be a celebrity author in America.

Some fans were starting to follow him into the men's room at restaurants and pushing books under the stall for him to sign, though he admitted that people at home in Maine basically left him alone. "It's different in Maine, you know the people you sign for, but I go some places and people can't even believe that I exist," he said. "There's no way to explain it, you feel like a freak."

Although by 1978 Steve had made enough money from his first three novels, a collection of short stories, and selling the movie rights to two books to make for a comfortable future, it didn't mean that he was just going to throw it around. He couldn't escape the frugality of his childhood. And even more than before, he didn't like to feel he was being taken advantage of.

His high school classmate Pete Higgins remembers one evening they went out barhopping. "Though he had his Cadillac by that point, he was still driving his old Dodge Dart around," said Higgins. Together they hit a dive bar in Lisbon, sat down, and ordered a couple of beers. The waitress told them if they wanted to get on the dance floor, they'd have to pay a cover charge of a couple bucks. They had no intention of dancing, but it was the principle of the thing, Steve thought. So they finished their beers and headed for a bar in Lewiston, a twenty-minute drive away.

"The cover charge there was five dollars," said Higgins. "I looked at him and he looked at me and he said, 'I'm not paying that,' and I said, 'Neither am I.' So we left and ended up at another place with no cover charge. We sat down and we had a good night talking about old times and sipping down a few. But the point was he was into some money at this point and could have easily paid the cover charge for everyone in the room. But he refused."

In 1978, he decided to give back to his alma mater, the University of Maine at Orono, by teaching for a year. It was his way of thanking the university and, in particular, the English Department, for all that they had done for him as a young student who was trying to find his way to understand more about literature and become a writer.

Samuel Schuman, now chancellor emeritus at the University of Minnesota, was on the faculty of the English Department at UMO when Steve returned. He says that Steve's main responsibilities were teaching a couple of classes to freshman, including Introduction to Creative Writing. "He didn't do a lot of the kind of star literary turns you'd expect from a novelist of his stature, like readings and signings," said Schuman. "He carried his share of the academic responsibilities that went along with the job, like serving on department committees and helping to plan curricular matters."

According to Schuman, students initially were a bit in awe of him, but that wore off once they began to work with him and see his demeanor in the classroom, and from all appearances, the students treated him pretty much like any other professor.

"He was not, by any stretch of the imagination, a daunting figure, and at that point he was still fairly young, casually dressed, and very informal in his manner," said Schuman, adding that Steve would show up to teach a class and his shirt would sometimes not be buttoned right and his socks didn't match. "He looked like the kind of guy who just jumped into his clothes when he got up in the morning." Which probably made him less threatening to the students he was teaching.

"I found it interesting to see him come back as a famous person relating to people who had been his teachers," Schuman continued. "He was still more deferential to his former teachers than they were to him. He treated them the same way that any college graduate treats his old professors, and the faculty treated him like a former student."

One of the committees Steve served on was in charge of deciding which students were to receive a slate of departmental awards such as Best New Writer and Best Paper of the Year. "It was not a committee that people were fighting to get on, so they assigned it to Steve, who didn't know any better," said Schuman. "But the other professors were happy that he was willing to dig in and do that kind of work like everyone else."

Schuman was impressed that King appeared to be remarkably unspoiled by his rapidly growing success and fame. "He really seemed like he had his head screwed on right in terms of his values and his sense of who he was."

Of course, Steve drew on his experience teaching high school students during his tenure back at UMO, but he immediately noticed the difference in college students:

"The thing about high school is that the students look at school in a different way because they're forced to go there, and a lot of times their attitude was that they might as well enjoy it and get what they could out of it. In college, a lot of my creative-writing students really wanted to be writers, so their egos were mortally involved in this. After a while I did the worst thing a creative-writing teacher can do, especially with a poetry class. I started to get very timid with all of my criticism because I was afraid that some student would go home and perform the equivalent of hara-kiri. I didn't want to be responsible for destroying anybody's ego completely."

Despite the change in venue and his day being taken up with teaching responsibilities, he continued to work on his own writing steadily. All he had to do was follow the same routine he had for years.

"There are certain things I do if I sit down to write," he said. "I have a glass of water or a cup of tea. There's a certain time I sit down, from eight to eight thirty, somewhere within that half hour every morning. I have my vitamin pill and my music, sit in the same seat, and the papers are all arranged in the same places. The cumulative purpose of doing these things the same way every day seems to be a way of saying to the mind, 'You're going to be dreaming soon.'

"It's not any different than a bedtime routine. Do you go to bed a different way every night? Is there a certain side you sleep on? I mean, I brush my teeth, I wash my hands. Why would anybody wash their hands before they go to bed? I don't know. And the pillows are supposed to be pointed a certain way. The open side of the pillowcase is supposed to be pointed in toward the other side of the bed. I don't know why."

While Steve was teaching at the university, the Kings lived in a rented house on Route 15 in Orrington on the outskirts of Bangor. The house was on a busy road that they soon discovered was treacherous. So many animals were killed by speeding trucks that the neighborhood children had created their own burial ground in the woods behind the property.

"Our son John and a little neighbor girl named Bethany Stanchfield started the pet graveyard," said Noreen Levesque, who still lives in the neighborhood. "It started out with a little dead bird or squirrel they found out on the road, and in the beginning they would bury them in the sandbox in our backyard." However, before long, cats and dogs joined the list of casualties, and they moved the whole thing up the hill.

"One of the kids would have his wagon, put the body in the wagon, and wheel it to the cemetery," said neighbor Alma Dosen. "They'd hold a ceremony, dig the little graves, bury them, and make the markers. Then they'd have a little after-burial party." At least thirty kids maintained the cemetery.

Like most things he saw or heard that were out of the ordinary, Steve thought he'd be able to use it in a story or novel someday. In the meantime, he and Tabby dragged a few lawn chairs to the burial ground, and he'd often head up there for some quiet time when he wanted to write. Whenever they were out on the front lawn playing with their kids, however, it was a different story.

"Like most toddlers, Owen thought that running away from Mommy and

Daddy was a total scream," said Tabby. "Just after we moved to Orrington, Owen made a serious break for freedom, heading across the lawn for Route 15, a truly terrifying stretch of road. We got him, but it left us both wrecks. Owen just laughed to see Mommy and Daddy collapsed on the lawn."

Despite a laundry list of fears of all varieties, the incident confirmed that Steve's greatest fear was of losing one of his kids.

Naomi's cat Smucky was hit by a truck on the highway one afternoon when she and Tabby were out shopping. When they got home, Steve pulled Tabby aside to tell her what had happened, and that he had already buried the cat in the pet cemetery. "He wanted to tell Naomi the cat had run away, but I insisted on frankness," said Tabby. The family held a funeral, made a grave-marker, and placed flowers on the cat's grave. "And that was the end of it," Tabby said wryly. *"Almost."*

Steve used the experience to begin writing the novel he'd call his most terrifying. *Pet Sematary* was the story of a father who brings his child back from the dead. He was terrified by what he had written.

He gave it to Tabby to read, and she hated it. "When the two-year-old was killed on the road in the book, I found that very, very hard to read and deal with," she said. Even his friend Peter Straub thought it was a horrible book and that Steve should stick it in a drawer and forget about it.

That's exactly what Steve did. As usual, it didn't take long for him to become distracted. On October 1, 1978, *The Shining* was published in mass-market paperback. With the release of the movie two years later, the paperback would eventually sell 2.5 million copies.

After he put *Pet Sematary* away, Steve started writing *The Dead Zone*, which he termed a love story, but was really a response to his increasing concern about the problems that fame was beginning to bring into his life, as well as into his family's, and all because of his rare gift for storytelling and scaring the pants off people. Fans were beginning to knock on his door and ask for autographs and money, and they were becoming more aggressive. Steve wasn't sure how to ensure his privacy but still wanted to live as a regular guy.

During this time, a manuscript resurfaced from several years earlier that he had written and also tucked away. But unlike *Pet Sematary,* he was quite fond of this manuscript: *The Gunslinger.* He found it by accident in the basement after a flood. "The pages were all swelled up but they were still readable, and I thought maybe I could sell these to a magazine of short stories." He retyped it, sent it out, and *The Magazine of Fantasy and Science Fiction* published "The Gunslinger" in its October 1978 issue.

For Steve and Tabby, life was comfortable beyond their wildest dreams. But they had struggled for so long that it was still hard to get used to their new-found security.

"The money's never been real," said Tabby. "I have a kayak, Steve has guitars. Nevertheless, there it is, like an elephant in the living room. We grew up poor and people did for us. So we do for others."

"The idea is to take care of your family and have enough left over to buy books and go to the movies once a week," said King. "As a goal in life, getting rich strikes me as fairly ludicrous. The goal is to do what God made you for and not hurt anyone if you can help it."

He was driven, to be sure. But it wasn't clear how obsessive he could be until one day in 1979.

After Owen, their last child, was born, Steve decided to get a vasectomy. He went to the doctor's office for the thirty-minute procedure, the doctor told him to take it easy for the next couple of days, and Steve headed home. All was fine until the next day when he was in the midst of a furious writing session and he started bleeding from the incision. He was finishing up a chapter in his new novel *Firestarter* when he realized he was bleeding, but he didn't want to stop until he finished the chapter since the work was going so well.

When Tabby came into the office and saw him sitting in a pool of blood, she panicked. "Anyone else would have been screaming, but he said, 'Hold on, let me finish this paragraph!'" she said. He continued to write until he finished the chapter. *Then* Tabby took him to the hospital.

THE RUNNING MAN

Though he spent most of his time in Maine, publishers, movie producers, and reporters began to demand more of Steve's time. Though he considered himself shy and preferred to hole up at home with his family and his word processor, Steve started to travel a bit more. He was still tickled that after all the difficult years, people were clamoring for his work.

In the movie and media world of the late seventies, drugs were as much as part of doing business as alcohol, and it wasn't unusual to see Valium, quaaludes, and cocaine presented in abundance at cocktail parties and industry functions. As Steve began to spend more time in this world—and given his experimentation with drugs back in college—it was inevitable that he would try out these drugs as well, and so around this time he used cocaine for the first time. After all, it seemed as if the rest of the world were doing it back then too. But with Steve's built-in addictive and obsessive personality, it wasn't a good thing.

"With cocaine, one snort, and it owned me body and soul," he said. "It was like the missing link. Cocaine was my *on* switch, and it seemed like a really good energizing drug. You try some and think, 'Wow, why haven't I been taking this for years?' So you take a bit more and write a novel and decorate the house and mow the lawn and then you're ready to start a new novel again. I just wanted to refine the moment I was in. I didn't feel that happiness was enough: that there had to be a way to improve on nature."

While he had no qualms about drinking in front of other people even when they knew he had a problem with booze, Steve was always careful to conceal the coke from his friends and family. As is the case in any good alcoholic family, each member had long ago perfected his or her role of codependency and denial. From time to time through the years, Tabby would tell him to clean up his act, but she usually let up after it was clear she was wasting her breath. And while she had stuck by him through thick and thin, she was also pretty good at keeping up the public façade as well. "He is not now and never has been an alcoholic," she said in 1979, the same year he got hooked on cocaine.

But cocaine didn't replace the beer; if anything, he used it along with the several six-packs of beer he already downed each night, to dull the high from the cocaine enough so he could fall asleep.

While he had smoked pot in college, he'd lost his taste for the drug because he was fearful of the additives. "Anybody can squirt anything into it if they want to, and that scares me.

"My idea of what dope is supposed to be is to just get mellow," he said. "And what I do, if I smoke it anymore, is when I'm driving to the movies, is to smoke a couple real quick so I can sit there in the first row. It's kind of interesting and they have all the good munchie food too."

After college, Rick Hautala, Steve's classmate from the University of Maine, was working at a local bookstore and writing fiction in his spare time. Steve often visited the bookstore and they ended up shooting the breeze. One day, Steve asked Rick if he was still writing, and he said he was working on a novel. Steve said he'd like to take a look, and he liked what he saw enough to pass it along to McCauley. As a result, Hautala signed with Kirby, who promptly sold Rick's horror novel *Moondeath* to Zebra, which published it in 1981. King wrote a blurb for that book and Hautala's second, *Moonbog*, which came out the following year.

They also renewed their friendship by visiting bars in and around Bangor. "It scared me how fast he could drink a beer," said Hautala. "I liked having a couple of beers, but he would put down six or eight in the same time I had two. At first, I actually thought he was dumping it onto the floor."

Chuck Verrill, an editor who started working with King at Putnam around this time, noticed the same thing: "Whenever we went to a bar, I'd order a beer and Steve would order three."

What bothered Rick even more is that Steve would drink during book signings. "Public drinking in the Maine Mall with hundreds of fans milling around," said Hautala. "You know the old expression, 'instant asshole, just add alcohol'? Once Steve got into his cups, he could be pretty obnoxious."

King mostly remained sober whenever he had to teach a class at the university. Students liked him because of his informal teaching style—they were also being taught by a bona fide celebrity—and because he still considered himself to be one of them. He could have dressed in the finest designer clothes, but, of course, you didn't do that in Maine, at least not where he came from. So his jeans jacket looked as if it were pulled from a Salvation Army reject bin, and with his Levi's and flannel shirt—the official dress code of the state of Maine—he fit right in.

He also didn't look any older than his students, who were at least ten years his junior, and he had a finely honed theory about this.

"There are a lot of writers who look like children," he said. "Ray Bradbury, he . . . has the face of a child. Same thing with Isaac Singer, he has the eyes of a child in that old face." Steve theorized that it was because writers and other artists use their imaginations the way that children do, and always have, and that's why their faces retain a youthful look.

He readily acknowledged, however, that he had no other marketable or useful talent to use in the world: "I have no skill that improves the quality of life in a physical sense at all. I can't even fix a pipe in my house when it freezes. The only thing I can do is say here's a way to look at something in a new way. It may be just a cloud to you, but really, doesn't it look like an elephant? And people will pay for me to point it out to them because they've lost all of it themselves. That's why people pay writers and artists, that's the only reason we're around. We're excess baggage. I am a dickey bird on the back of civilization."

Steve continued to write short stories and submit them to the same magazines that had published him in his poverty-stricken pre-*Carrie* days. He held on to the rights to reprint them in a collection of short stories, especially since his first collection, *Night Shift,* had sold well. And he still relished the challenge of the short form, as compared with the novel.

"The Crate" was first published in the July 1979 issue of *Gallery.* As usual, the initial idea for the story came to Steve in passing when he heard a news story on the radio about some old artifacts that had been stored under a heavily traveled stairway in a chemistry building for at least a century, including an old wooden crate. The story mentioned a few of the other items, but Steve's imagination was already off and running.

"What got to me was the idea of a hundred years' worth of students going up and down those stairs with that crate right underneath," he said. "It probably had nothing in it but old magazines, but it kind of tripped over in my mind that there could have been something really sinister in there." So that's where the story went, and when it came time for Steve to describe the creature that comes alive once the crate was pried open, all he could think of was the Tasmanian Devil in the Bugs Bunny cartoons. "All teeth!" he said. "One day my kids were watching one of those cartoons, and I thought, 'shit, that's not funny, that's horrible!'"

His second Richard Bachman novel, *The Long Walk,* was also published in

July. Like *Rage,* the first Bachman book, it pretty much disappeared from view in a couple of months. In contrast, *The Dead Zone,* the first novel with his new publisher, Viking, would be published the following month, with fifty thousand copies printed in hardcover.

"That's the first real novel I wrote," he said. "Up until then, the others were just exercises. That's a real novel with real characters, a real big plot and subplots."

The Dead Zone was his first book set in Castle Rock, a town in Maine that he's said he's patterned after Durham and Lisbon Falls. He borrowed the name from William Golding's *Lord of the Flies,* one of his favorite books as a kid. Castle Rock is the rocky part of the island where Golding's story occurs.

To promote his book, King went out on his first major book tour that fall, hitting seven cities in six days. When it was over, he said, "It feels like you've been in a pillow fight where all the pillows have been treated with low-grade poison gas." Stephen King was quickly becoming a household name, five short years after his first novel was published. He often felt overwhelmed, but was happy. This is what he had worked so hard for, this is what he wanted, he thought.

Next up he'd hit television for the first time. *Salem's Lot* was a four-hour miniseries that aired on CBS in two parts on November 17 and 24, 1979. Steve could have chosen to be involved with the picture, but decided to concentrate on writing books. Possibly he opted out because he sensed that the story would have a hard time getting past the network censors, or else he anticipated that he'd be frustrated by their cuts. Producer Richard Kobritz said the crew worked at a breakneck pace because another miniseries dropped out of the fall schedule shortly after filming finished, and they had eight weeks to prepare the film for air.

"We worked seven days a week just to edit the thing and then dub it and add the score," said Kobritz. "Steve never came to the set of either picture, so we sent a videotape of a rough cut so he could get an idea what we did. I think he enjoyed not being involved and looking at it as a finished product."

Kobritz said that one of the biggest challenges he faced was how to cast the lead vampire, and the lead role of Richard Straker. Earlier that same year, two vampire movies were box-office hits, and both the stars were handsome, sexy, and eloquent middle-aged men: George Hamilton starred in the comedy *Love at First Bite,* released in April, while Frank Langella played the lead in *Dracula,* a near-faithful adaptation of the Bram Stoker novel, which appeared in July.

To make Kurt Barlow, the vampire character in *Salem's Lot,* stand out, Kobritz decided that Barlow would not speak a word in the entire movie and that all of his dialogue would go to Straker, his human go-between, played by James Mason. He also tried to delay the vampire's first appearance as long as possible to draw people into the story; Kobritz said that the vampire first appeared almost halfway into the movie, at the 90-minute mark. The entire uncut version is 184 minutes without commercials.

Before the airdate, the miniseries was previewed at a large theater in Beverly Hills, and Kobritz's hunch was correct. "The first time the vampire appeared, the audience started screaming, and again when the little boy who was dead and buried pops out of the coffin," he said. When the vampire was staked in the heart, the network censors dealt with the violence by darkening the image on the screen. The following year, the miniseries was repeated during a mayoral election in Los Angeles, so the movie was cut into occasionally for news updates and election news. "The network received a record number of calls to complain about the interruptions," Kobritz said.

Salem's Lot was nominated for three Emmys and nominated for an Edgar for best television feature or miniseries. Best of all, Steve was happy with the way the miniseries turned out.

As a result of his increasing visibility, Steve was also getting well acquainted with the part of the life that many bestselling authors loved, and some, such as him, loathed: the media interviews, publicity, and kissing up to reporters, all to sell books.

"As a kid, I didn't talk much, I wrote," he said. "A day of interviews with reporters is hard for me because, generally speaking, I'm not a very good talker. I'm not used to externalizing my thoughts other than on paper, which is typical of writers. When someone tries to make a thing out of being a writer, that's bad enough. What's even worse is if people call you an author and you let them do that."

Yet, there was a definite upside. He said it felt beyond surreal when he was in New York for a meeting at the Waldorf-Astoria with the producers of *The Shining* to discuss who would make a better lead, Jack Nicholson or Robert De Niro.

Getting back to Maine was a reality check—and a relief.

"I come back home and pick up the toys and see if the kids are brushing in the back of their mouths, and I'm smoking too many cigarettes and chewing aspirin alone in this office, and the glamour people aren't here," he said. "There is a curious loneliness to my life. I have to produce day after day and deal with my doubts that what I'm producing is trivial and maybe not even that good. So, in a way, when I go to New York City, I feel like I've earned it."

Plus, the nice thing about Maine was that for the most part people left him alone. Back home, he didn't have books thrust in his face constantly and people sucking up to him. And while he tried to write every day when he was traveling, no matter how busy he was, the ideas just didn't come to him the same way they did back in Maine, especially in rural Maine. "It really does feel as though reality is thinner in the country. There is a sense of the infinite that's very, very close, and I just try to convey some of that in my fiction," he said.

He was also getting a little tired of moving around so much; he was uneasy with it, the constant relocation was beginning to remind him of his peripatetic childhood. He wanted to find one place and settle down, preferably never to move again.

Once Steve finished up his teaching responsibilities at the university, the Kings spent a few months at their lake house in Center Lovell before figuring out their next move.

He and Tabby had batted around the idea of living elsewhere, maybe somewhere a little more glamorous than Maine, but they had found that Colorado didn't fit and neither did Great Britain. They were native Mainers, they still lived like it, and it's where they felt most comfortable. So they decided to buy another house instead of living year-round at the summer house in Center Lovell, which was in an area mostly populated by summer people and therefore virtually deserted nine months out of the year. Tabby wanted Naomi, Owen, and Joe to live near other kids, where they could run out the door and play kickball or tag by just crossing the front lawn.

The choice came down to Bangor or Portland.

"Tabby wanted to go to Portland and I wanted to go to Bangor because it was a hard-ass working-class town—there's no such thing as nouvelle cuisine once you are north of Freeport," Steve said. He also thought an important story was hidden somewhere in the city that he didn't yet know about. He had an idea about bringing together everything he'd ever learned about monsters, and he knew he wouldn't find it in Portland because it was the same kind of place as Boulder, filled mostly with white-collar types.

So once they chose Bangor, they started to look for a house where they could feel at home. It didn't take long to find it.

As many a craggy-faced, old Yankee has said when asked for directions from an out-of-towner, when it comes to Bangor, Maine, "You can't get they-ah from he-yah."

Well, you can, but it's going to take a lot longer than you think. Bangor, an old, stagnant mill town, is an oasis unto itself. Many visitors think that those who live there either feel trapped, almost as if there were nowhere to go because anywhere else is so far away, or else it's a perfect hideaway for the reclusive.

Stephen King undoubtedly fits into the latter category. Once you enter Maine on I-95, it's an hour to Portland, the largest city in the state, and then another hour on into Augusta, the state capital. The drive so far is interesting, not boring, punctuated by smallish cities and invitations to nearby shoreline attractions. Between Augusta and Bangor, however, the story changes, and rapidly.

The view for the last eighty miles is not much more than trees, an occasional fellow motorist, and moose-crossing signs.

As Steve himself has put it, you either want to get to Bangor so badly that you'll withstand the trip there or you'll stay far away. If you fly, there are only two daily flights, from Boston. And if you want to fly from Portland to Bangor, you really can't get there from here, because there are no direct flights between the two cities.

"One of the reasons that I live in Bangor is because if somebody wants to get to me, they have to be really dedicated," Steve said. "They have to really want to come here. It isn't like I lived in New York or L.A. and somebody could pull my chain whenever they wanted to. So I stay here because there are no distractions whatsoever."

Bangor, long referred to as the Queen City, was once a thriving lumber town, its primary commodity white pine from the forests that surround it for hundreds of miles in every direction. The city hit its industrial peak in 1872, when twenty-two hundred ships entered the harbor that year, carrying out almost 250 million board feet of lumber for export worldwide. During that time Bangor was referred to as the Lumber Capital of the World, but as people began to migrate west and harvest the rich stands of forests in the Midwest and the Rocky Mountains, there was less call for the hearty white pine of down-east Maine. In 1870 the population of Bangor was 18,289, which dropped to 16,857 only a decade later. It has rebounded since then. In 2000, the population was recorded at 31,473.

In 1980 the Kings bought the William Arnold House at 47 West Broadway, the only Italianate-style villa, built between 1854 and 1856, in Bangor. The square tower on the right that faces the street was original to the house; the octagonal tower on the left side was added sometime in the late 1880s. The mansion contains twenty-four rooms and sits on seven acres.

When she was in her teens, Tabby would stand outside the house while on a walk with a girlfriend and imagine the house was hers. But for a girl from Old Town, one of eight children whose family ran the general store, she knew it would remain a dream. But when Steve and Tabby started to look for a house in Bangor and discovered the red house with the two oddly shaped towers was for sale, they jumped at it.

"I thought it was destiny," said Tabby.

Once the house was theirs, the Kings got busy turning it into their dream house. It took a small team of carpenters, plumbers, electricians, and wrought-iron artists three years to renovate the house from top to bottom, and from the front of the property line to the back.

For the kitchen, six smaller rooms were combined to create a massive open space with a custom-made counter a bit taller than the norm so Steve could chop vegetables and knead bread without strain. There's a brick oven made from Royal River bricks, which were kiln-fired near Durham. A mammoth sink is the color of fresh blood, with massive butcher-block counters, and an electric dumbwaiter sends soiled towels and kitchen linen up to the second-floor laundry.

Steve, still grateful that Tabby stood by him during the scathingly tough years of the early seventies when most spouses would have been long gone, asked what she wanted more than anything else in the world.

She had learned how to swim a few years earlier, and she said all she wanted was a pool.

"Consider it done," said Steve, and a forty-seven-foot-long pool, twelve feet at its deepest end, was built in the barn that was perpendicularly attached to the house out back. During the renovation, the tiny square windows that had lit the inside of the horse stalls stayed, and a new, larger stained-glass window—with an image of a flying bat—was added to a room overlooking the pool that serves as Steve's office in the barn, accessible through a hidden passageway. From the inside of his office, there appears to be no way out; the door is actually a thick chunk of the bookcase that leads out. The boy who had grown up with no indoor plumbing now had a forty-seven-foot indoor swimming pool.

In true Stephen King style there are bats outside and inside the house—both real and fake. He leaves Tabby to take care of the real ones. "We get bats in the house because it's an old house," she said. "I'm the one who is in charge of bat control. I capture the bat and put it out while he just screams."

Then there's the fence. Yes, *that* fence.

Architectural blacksmith Terry Steel designed and built the elaborate wrought-iron fence around the house. "It was important for the fence and gates to work with the architecture of the house, to be graceful and attractive, and yet to reflect the personalities of the occupants as well," Steel said. "While Steve wanted bats for the fence, Tabby wanted spiders and webs." The Kings also wanted the fence to convey an even more important message: "Look all you want, but don't even think of trespassing."

When Steel met with the Kings at their house for design consultations, he saw numerous *Superman* and *Batman* comic books scattered around the house. He decided to use the bat symbol from *Batman* for the shape of his bat. "I wanted superhero characters, not demonic characters," Steel explained.

From start to finish, the fence was eighteen months in the making, and in the end it contained 270 lineal feet of hand-forged iron that weighed in at just over eleven thousand pounds. In addition to the bats, spiders, and webs requested by the occupants, Steel threw in a couple of goat heads as well.

Once the family had moved into the house, besides the secret passageways Steve and Tabby noticed another unexpected feature of the house: a resident ghost. While Steve said he's never seen the presence—apparently that of a General Webber, who died in the house a hundred years before the Kings moved in—he does say that occasionally when he's writing late at night after everyone else has gone to bed, he starts to feel spooked and gets the sense that he isn't the only one in the room.

Tabby, however, has noticed the ghost's presence in sudden sounds that aren't just the noises an old house makes, and in a strong cigar smell she'll suddenly encounter when walking through the house.

A few other spooky things have been noted about the house on West Broadway. It was the third place in a row the Kings lived where someone had killed himself. When Tabby went shopping for furniture for the house, she bought a bedroom set from a used-furniture store, and when the shopkeeper wrote up the order, he told her it was the third time that he'd sold the same exact set; the first two times, the husbands had died in the bed and the widows couldn't bear to have the furniture around. When she told Steve the story, he wasn't bothered by it, figuring the third time's a charm. And it has been . . . *so far*.

Though Steve has never seen General Webber, he did witness a strange apparition in another old house on Grove Street in Bangor where a political fund-raiser for former U.S. senator George Mitchell was held, shortly after the Kings moved into the West Broadway mansion.

Steve had put his and Tabby's coats in an upstairs bedroom on a bed designated for that purpose. They stayed for about a half hour before deciding to go for dinner at Sing's Polynesian Restaurant, their favorite Chinese joint. He went back upstairs for the coats—the stack on the bed had grown exponentially in the short time they were there—and started to paw through the pile. Just then, out of his peripheral vision, he saw a man in a chair across the room sitting with his hands crossed.

"He wore glasses and a blue pinstripe suit, and he was bald," said Steve, who immediately became nervous because he thought the man thought Steve was rummaging through the coats to steal something. "I started to say something to him about how hard it was to find your coat at these things, and suddenly there was nobody there. The chair was empty."

While Steve believed in ghosts, he had his limits: "I would not participate in a séance under any circumstances, not even if my wife died and a medium said she had a message from her." He also believes in psychics and ESP: "We have enough documentation so that anyone that doubts the psychic experience is on the level with a person who continues to smoke two or three packs of cigarettes a day and denies that there is a link between smoking and lung cancer."

When Stanley Kubrick first expressed interest in directing *The Shining*, Steve didn't believe it.

"I was standing in the bathroom in my underwear, shaving, and my wife comes in and her eyes are bugging out. I thought one of the kids must be choking in the kitchen. She said, 'Stanley Kubrick is on the phone!' I didn't even take the shaving cream off my face."

Steve had already heard a story about the legendary director that made the rounds of Hollywood. At the time, Kubrick was actively searching for a book to turn into a movie, and his secretary became accustomed to hearing a loud thump from inside his office every half hour or so. Kubrick would pick up a book and start to read, but after forty or fifty pages he'd give up and throw it against the wall before picking up the next, only to repeat himself a short time later. One morning the thumps ceased, and the secretary contacted him on the intercom. When he didn't respond, she rushed into the room because she thought he'd had a heart attack. She found him reading *The Shining*. He held it up and said, "This is the book."

Kubrick was known for his perfectionistic ways in his previous vocation as a photographer for *Look* magazine. He brought his obsessive tendencies with him when he first started to direct movies in the 1960s, including *A Clockwork Orange, 2001: A Space Odyssey,* and *Dr. Strangelove*. He was adamant that he control every aspect of his later films and would often shoot hundreds of takes of one scene before moving on to the next.

With a budget of $22 million and Kubrick writing the screenplay with novelist Diane Johnson, Steve expected the movie would turn out to be as good as *Carrie* and *Salem's Lot*. While *The Shining* would eventually gross over $64 million, he was greatly disappointed at Kubrick's execution of his story: "It's a Cadillac with no engine in it. You can't do anything with it except admire it as sculpture."

His primary issue was with the casting of Jack Nicholson as Jack Torrance. He preferred Michael Moriarty—today best known for his role as Assistant District Attorney Ben Stone on *Law & Order* in the early nineties, but who also played a major role in the 1978 film *Who'll Stop the Rain*—or Jon Voight, who appeared in such major seventies films as *Coming Home, Deliverance,* and *Catch-22*. "Nicholson was too dark right from the outset of the film," said Steve. "The horror in the novel came from the fact that Jack Torrance is a nice guy, not someone who's just flown out from the cuckoo's nest. There was no moral struggle at all."

Parts of the film were shot at the Timberline Lodge in Mount Hood, Oregon. Kubrick changed the all-important room number from 217 in the book to 237 in the film. The Timberline had a room 217 and the owners thought that guests would refrain from booking the room after the movie came out, but there was no room number 237, so Kubrick changed it.

After *The Shining* was released, the questions about Steve's background increased exponentially. "People always want to know what happened in my childhood," he complained. "They have to find some way of differentiating, they think there has to be some reason why I'm writing all of these terrible things. But I think of myself as a fairly cheerful person. My memories are that my childhood was quite happy, in a solitary way."

He tried to put his disappointment over *The Shining* behind him as he worked on more novels, stories, and screenplays. In September 1980, *Firestarter* was published, the first of King's books to be published in a limited edition, which he would later come to rue for their preciousness and unaffordability. Limited-edition books are typically produced by small publishers in print runs as small as a hundred copies, and they are usually designed in graphically beautiful formats. They are more expensive than their mass-produced counterparts, and in many cases after publication their prices can rise, sometimes several times over, as they are bought and sold by fans of the author. *Firestarter* is a novel about Charlie McGee, a girl who is pyrokinetic, or can start fires merely by wishing it, and the novel did nothing to reduce the questions from readers and reporters who wanted to know what had happened to Steve when he was growing up. Whereas before he would politely explain to the curious that he led a pretty normal childhood and wasn't beaten by his mother or locked in a closet, this time he started to deflect the questions by talking about his own kids and his experiences being a parent, in the hopes of coming across as the regular guy that he perceived himself to be.

"To me the real purpose of having kids has nothing to do with perpetuating the race or the survival imperative, rather, it's a way to finish off your own childhood," he explained. "By having children you're able to reexperience everything you experienced as a child, only from a more mature perspective." Only at that point, he felt, could he finally leave his childhood behind.

"Charlie McGee was very consciously patterned on my daughter, because I know how she looks, I know how she walks, I know what makes her mad. I was able to use that, but only to a certain degree. Beyond that, if you tie yourself to your own children, you limit your range. So I took Naomi, used her as the frame, and then went where I wanted."

He was also coming under fire by critics for using brand names in his work, such as when the character Royal Snow drinks a Pepsi in *Salem's Lot* and Miss Macaferty drove a Volkswagen in *Carrie*. He defended it, saying, "Every time I did it, I felt like I nailed it dead square. Sometimes the brand name is the perfect word, it will crystallize a scene for me."

Reporters quickly learned that one way to break the ice with King was to start talking about his beloved Red Sox and his obsessive devotion to the team. Fans were fascinated to learn the details of King's dedication, such as that he stops shaving in the fall after the last game of the World Series and doesn't take a razor to his face until spring training starts. "A part of me dies when the World Series is over," he said.

He explained away his undying loyalty to the Red Sox by way of his race: "I'm a white guy. I don't want to sound like a racist, but Boston has always had a white team. The Red Sox give klutzy white guys something to root for. It shows that maybe white guys can do something in sports." Despite some obvious racial changes to the team in recent years, Steve has remained a steadfast fan.

Though most fans were content to read about the details of his life and enjoy his books, Steve was starting to see that fans could be just as obsessive about him as he was about baseball, and in some cases, a lot more so.

"Sometimes I look in their eyes, and it's like looking into vacant houses," he said. "They don't know why they want autographs, they just want them. Then I realize, not only is this house vacant but it's haunted."

He described one occasion when he was late for an appointment and ran into a fan begging for his autograph, yelling that he was Steve's biggest fan and had read all his books. Steve apologized and got in the car, and the fan suddenly switched gears and called him a stupid son of a bitch. "The aggregate weight of fanship is overwhelming. They want stuff from you. They want boxes of it," he said. "The line is so thin between I love you and I hate you. They love you, but part of them wants to see you fall as far as you can."

Perhaps how far a fan could go hit home for King on December 8, 1980, when John Lennon was assassinated. When he heard the news, Steve thought back to May of that year when he had been in New York on a promotional tour for *The Shining*. As he was leaving Rockefeller Center after a TV interview, a fan who introduced himself as his number one fan rushed up to him and asked for an autograph. King signed a slip of paper, then the fan handed his Polaroid camera to a bystander and asked him to take shot of them together. *Then* the fan asked for an autograph on the photo too, giving Steve a special marker to write on the photograph. "The fan had obviously done this often," said Steve, with a vague recollection that he had scrawled on that photograph, "Best wishes to Mark Chapman from Stephen King." But later on, Steve realized it couldn't have been him.

"I could never have met Chapman, the dates just don't fit," he said, explaining after doing a little digging that Chapman was in Hawaii when King was in New York in late May. At the time, however, he did have an overly obsessive fan "who was always making me sign things," he recalled. "And he had little round glasses, like the ones Lennon used to wear."

From this maelstrom of fan obsession, an idea began to bubble up. Something that the-man-who-could-have-been-Chapman had said started to swirl around in Steve's mind: "I'm your number one fan."

Tabby was starting to worry: "It makes me nervous, I worry about his security. There's always the possibility that someone might try to do to him what was done to John Lennon. He's very well-known, and there are real crazy people out there."

Sometimes she felt she was a prisoner of his success.

Steve told her she had nothing to worry about.

Spurred on by her husband's success, Tabby's urge to write had returned with a vengeance. However, with three children to care for, ranging from four to eleven, she found it hard to carve out time for herself. She'd start stories and never finish them and complain to Steve about the lack of time. After hearing Tabby grumble once too often, Steve presented her with a brand-new typewriter and told her to rent an office outside the house where she could work without interruption. After they moved to the West Broadway house, she began going to an office regularly and worked on the story that would turn out to be *Small World,* her first published novel.

Tabby was never shy about admitting that she was riding on her husband's coattails, at least in terms of getting a quick look from an editor, whereas the manuscripts of other first novelists would end up in a publisher's slush pile, lucky to get read at all. "Being Steve's wife helped, either in providing me with a decent agent, or perhaps some publisher thought they would make sales on the novelty," she said. Steve passed *Small World* to his editor, George Walsh, at Viking, who later told Tabby that he grudgingly decided to read it as a favor to her husband and that he wasn't expecting it to be anything more than a first good effort, albeit unpublishable. But he liked it, accepted it, and scheduled it for publication in 1981.

Though Steve was indeed proud of his wife, he did admit that he felt a tiny bit threatened when Tabby returned to the writing she had all but neglected since college.

"I felt jealous as hell," he said. "My reaction was like a kid's. I felt like saying, 'Hey, these are *my* toys, you can't play with them.' But that soon changed to pride when I read the final manuscript and found that she had turned out a damned fine piece of work."

As usual, Tabby had a more prosaic view: "I think we're both willing to say that I put ten years into helping him advance in every way that I could, from socializing to reading the manuscripts and making suggestions, as he did with mine. It was quite a trick to write when the children were small. Fortunately, they got used to being ignored. Kids need a modicum of being ignored, just as they need a soupçon of boredom. Being ignored is how you find out you're small potatoes, and boredom often leads to actual thought, exploration, and discovery."

That it was now her turn to shine had as much to do with her approach toward writing as with raising the kids. Whereas Steve could write in the middle of a tornado and would go through withdrawal if he couldn't write, Tabby was never that obsessed. "For me, the problem has always been getting started," she said. "I am one of the world's greatest avoiders. But once I start, I'm hard to turn off."

Along with differing in their drives, their work styles varied as well. Tabby loved nothing more than to bury herself in the research before writing a word. "I have my compulsions, but they're not in the direction of working every day," she said. "They're more in the direction of researching the living crap out of it and then entering the story."

Steve, on the other hand, loathed research. "If I read a few case histories, I tend to get a kind of feel for it," he said. "I'll sit down and write the book and do the research after, because when I'm writing a book, my attitude is 'Don't confuse me with facts. Just let me go ahead and get on with the work.'"

Tabby was an inveterate outliner, but Steve rarely sketched out anything in advance. "I start with an idea and I know where I'm going, but I don't outline," he said. "I usually have an idea of what's going to happen ten pages ahead, but I never write any of it down because that sort of closes you off from an interesting side trip that might come along. Theodore Sturgeon told me once that he thinks the only time the reader doesn't know what's going to happen next is when the writer didn't know what was going to happen. That's the situation I've always written in. I'm never sure where the story's going or what's going to happen with it."

In the original Doubleday hardcover edition of *The Stand,* Harold Lauder left a chocolate fingerprint on a diary after eating a PayDay candy bar. However, PayDays didn't contain any chocolate back then, and many fans sent Steve irate letters and PayDay bars to prove it. In the subsequent paperback editions he changed the candy bar to a Milky Way, but later on, PayDays did come in chocolate. Fans write to him in droves after each new book is published to point out errors, and he always fixes them. Some suspect he deliberately inserts an error to make sure fans are paying attention.

After Steve's first editor, Bill Thompson, left Doubleday, he took a job at a small publisher called Everest House. He asked Steve to write a book that would be partially a memoir of King's early horror influences and partially a history of Americans' fascination with the horror genre. Steve loved the idea and began working on *Danse Macabre*, his first nonfiction book.

As he started to write the book, an idea that he had kicked around for years—and had successfully ignored—was knocking on the door again. In the summer of 1981, Steve realized he finally had to face it head-on and start writing.

"I had to write about the troll under the bridge or leave him—*IT*—forever," he said. "I remember sitting on the porch, smoking, asking myself if I had really gotten old enough to be afraid to *try,* to just jump in and drive fast. I got up off the porch, went into my study, cranked up some rock and roll, and started to write the book. I knew it would be long, but I didn't know *how* long."

Cujo was published a few months after Steve started writing *IT*.

He got the idea for *Cujo* by continuing his habit of connecting two seemingly unrelated subjects. With *Carrie,* it was "adolescent cruelty and telekinesis."

With *Cujo,* it was two incidents a couple of weeks apart. While bringing his motorcycle in for service to a mechanic located on a remote back road, his bike gave out in the yard. He called out, but instead of a human, a mammoth Saint Bernard galloped out of the garage heading straight toward him, growling all the way. The mechanic followed, but the dog continued to charge. When the dog lunged at King, the mechanic hit the dog on the butt with a massive socket wrench.

"He must not like your face," he said, then asked Steve about the motorcycle.

Even though they were now flush, Steve and Tabby were still driving the Ford Pinto they had bought new with the $2,500 advance from *Carrie,* even though the car had been plagued with problems from the beginning. A couple of weeks after Steve's run-in with the Saint Bernard, the car acted up and Steve's wild imagination thought back to what if Tabby had driven the car to the mechanic and the dog had lunged toward her? And what if there no humans were around? Worse yet, what if the dog was rabid?

Steve didn't come up with the idea of making the dog the main character until later. At first, he was just chewing on the idea of a mother and son who were confined to a small space. One angle that he started to pursue was that the mother would be rabid, and the suspense in the book would revolve around her fighting herself not to injure her son as the rabies engulfed her.

However, Steve had to backtrack a bit after he did a bit of research about rabies and discovered that the gestation period took a bit longer. "Then the game became to see if I could put them in a place where nobody will find them for the length of time that it takes for them to work out their problem."

Steve was off and running, and before he knew it, he had churned out close to a hundred pages of the story with his motto of never let the facts get in the way of telling a good story. This shows how a story starts as a seed in Stephen King's mind: "You see something, then it clicks with something else, and it makes a story," he explained. "But you never know when it's going to happen."

Cujo was an experiment for King, the first book he had written where the story was told all within the confines of a single chapter. It didn't start out that way; he had initially envisioned the story in terms of traditional chapters. But as the story developed, along with the sense of horror, he altered his approach: "I love *Cujo* because it does what I want a book to do. It feels like a brick thrown through somebody's window, like a really invasive piece of work. It feels anarchic, like a punk-rock record: it's short and it's mean."

Readers gave him an earful about it, and he received letters by the truckload that criticized him for letting a child die in a book, albeit one who was innocent and simply in the wrong place at the wrong time, unlike the dozens of teenagers who were killed in *Carrie,* who seemingly deserved it because of their actions.

But the characters in *Cujo* felt as if they were light-years away from Steve's own existence for another reason: the subplot showed a woman having an affair and what happened when her husband found out. Just as Steve had procrastinated about writing the difficult scene of the woman in the bathtub in *The Shining,* Steve put off writing a scene in *Cujo.*

"The hardest scene I ever had to write in my life was when the husband goes home and confronts her," he said. "I've never faced that situation, not even with a girlfriend, but I wanted to work it out in a way that would be fair to both of them, and I didn't want to turn one of them into a villain." He wrestled with the characters, the dialogue, the action. "It was easy enough to react to the man because I know how I'd feel. It was tougher to react sympathetically to the woman."

It took him two days to hammer it out when he would normally have banged out a scene of similar length in ninety minutes. "It was a lot of sitting and looking at the typewriter and looking at the page," he remembered. "But it wasn't where I'm trying to frame a sentence, it was more like, 'Why did she do that?' And the answers are not perfect in the book as to why she did that. But what's there is honest enough."

Six years of cocaine and alcohol addiction was taking its toll. He was such a heavy user that to continue his late-night marathon writing sessions, he was snorting coke through the night, having occasionally to remove the blood-soaked cotton balls he stuck up both nostrils to keep the blood from dripping onto his shirt and the typewriter.

He would later admit that when he did the revisions for *Cujo* in early 1981, he had no recollection of doing so.

With his growing success and international acclaim, Steve was still sending his short stories to magazines because they all knew that running his name on the cover would give them the boost so many of them desperately needed. Sometimes it even meant the difference between continuing to publish or shutting the doors. When *Cujo* was scheduled for publication, Steve contacted Otto Penzler, a mystery editor and publisher who was running a small publishing company called Mysterious Press, and offered to let him print a limited edition of *Cujo*. He accepted Steve's generous offer and printed 750 copies with a cover price of $65 in 1981.

"The income from that one book covered the printing bill for *Cujo* as well as our previous book, and there was enough money left over to have another book printed," said Penzler. "I probably would have gone out of business if it hadn't been for *Cujo*." He'd heard similar stories from several other small presses, all of whom had no money and were constantly struggling. When Steve offered the limited-edition rights to a book, they were soon not just back on their feet but prospering and growing. Penzler's press became partners with Warner Books in 1984, who bought him out five years later.

Steve and Tabby also made a new friend and kindred spirit. Penzler ran the Mysterious Bookshop in Manhattan, and the Kings would often visit the store together to buy books and ask Penzler's advice on what to read next. He found their respective tastes a bit curious. "I always thought it a bit bizarre that she tended to like really tough, violent, serial-killer books while he liked P. D. James," Penzler said.

One of the unexpected benefits of working at home was that Steve was able to spend a lot of time playing and reading with his kids.

When he heard that the average father spends an average of twenty-two minutes with each of his kids in a week, Steve thought that was pathetic. "Mine are in my hip pocket all the time," he said. "And I like it that way."

It almost sounded as if he were in his second childhood, or perhaps the first real one that he'd had, where now he had the control and power, not to mention the money, that he lacked as a kid. "It's like being in a time machine. If you don't have kids, there are a lot of things you never have a chance to reexperience: taking kids to Disney pictures, and watching *Bambi* and saying, 'Jeez, what schlocky shit this is.' And then you start to cry, because it pushes the old buttons."

Joe, nine years old at the time, was turning into a miniature version of his father. They loved to go to horror movies together, and Joe said that when he grew up, he wanted to be a writer like his dad. Said Tabby, "The kid can write a story, he's really got the bones down." Owen, five years younger, wasn't far behind. The walls of his room were plastered with superhero and space-adventure posters while a toy Loch Ness monster presided over his bed. Even at his tender age, like his brother, he also seemed to have a natural affinity for horror movies, the gorier the better. "You know what parts I like best? The bl-o-o-d-y parts!"

While their parents clearly benefited from the sheer abundance of time they were able to spend together as a family, it was impossible to avoid thinking about the downside for too long, specifically their father's fame and notoriety.

"They're going to realize someday that there are people who will want their acquaintance only because their father's famous," said Tabby in 1982. "They haven't gotten to the hard part, the moment they have to decide whether they're going to rebel against us or imitate us. We all come up against this, but it's a little more difficult when your parents are well-known. It'll be interesting to see what happens."

It wasn't likely that Steve's fame was going to diminish anytime soon. In August 1981, he made publishing history as the first writer to have three titles on the *Publishers Weekly* list simultaneously: *Firestarter* in hardcover, and *The Dead Zone* and *The Shining* in paperback.

The pressure was continuing to build around him, not only from his fans, but from his publisher. Michael Pietsch today is the publisher at Little, Brown and the editor for James Patterson's books. With his words about Patterson, Pietsch could have been speaking about King's early blockbuster years.

Pietsch said that the hardest part of editing a star author is the pressure that comes from the publishing and business side: "When an author gets to a very high level of success, they become part of the company's financial planning, basically, for the budgeting part of the month-by-month planning. So the time pressures can become much more urgent because those books are really counted on to be published at a particular moment as part of the company's highest-level strategy."

King knew he was extraordinarily fortunate to have built a successful career in such a short time. In 1982, he decided to extend a helping hand to struggling artists and writers by letting them use the star power of his name. He supplied blurbs to novelists for the covers of their books and granted film rights to his short stories to amateur filmmakers in exchange for a dollar, as long as they were not shown for profit in movie theaters and he received a copy of the final film. He referred to the movies as Dollar Babies, and the first, *The Boogeyman*, was directed by Jeffrey C. Schiro and released in 1982, based on a short story that appeared in *Night Shift*.

In addition to Mysterious Press, Steve was also helping a few other small publishers keep their heads above water. Donald M. Grant was running a small press called Donald M. Grant, Publisher, when he read Steve's story "The Gunslinger" in the *Magazine of Fantasy and Science Fiction* in October 1978. He told Steve he wanted to turn the story into a limited-edition book. King agreed, but first he wanted to polish the story and convert it into chapters of a novel as he had originally intended. The book appeared four years later with a printing of ten thousand with a limited edition of one thousand signed copies, and they all sold out quickly. Everyone was pleased with the final product, and no one thought anything more of it. Though Steve knew he wanted *The Gunslinger* to be the first of seven books in a projected series, he had enough on his plate and knew he couldn't return to Roland Deschain's world anytime soon.

Plus, it was very different from his bestsellers. "I didn't think anybody would want to read it," he said. "It was more like a Tolkien fantasy of some other world. And it wasn't complete. There was all this stuff to be resolved, including what is this tower and why does this guy need to get there?"

In May of 1982, *The Running Man,* the fourth book written under the Bachman pseudonym, was published and met with the same fate as the previous three: published to little fanfare, it disappeared from paperback racks within two months.

That fall, the movie *Creepshow* came out. The legendary horror director George Romero, one of King's childhood heroes, who directed *The Night of the Living Dead,* teamed up with Steve. The movie consisted of five of his short stories: "The Crate," "Father's Day," "Something to Tide You Over," "They're Creeping Up on You," and "The Lonesome Death of Jordy Verrill," which featured King in the leading role. The movie paid homage to the beloved E.C. Comics of his youth.

The pair first met in the summer of 1979, when Romero headed to Maine with producer Richard Rubinstein to discuss *The Stand* with Steve, to which they held the rights. Steve was eager to start on the film version of *The Stand,* but all three agreed to first prove themselves with a smaller low-budget project first, which they could then present to the studio as a success and therefore justify the cost for the big-budget *The Stand*. However, once they started brainstorming and decided the cast needed well-known actors such as Leslie Nielsen, Adrienne Barbeau, and Ted Danson, the budget ballooned from less than $2 million to more than $8 million.

Romero and King found in each other kindred spirits. "I think we automatically got along because we're both guys who live somewhere in the middle, avoiding New York and L.A.," said Romero, who started out in the business directing commercials but went on to direct the classic cult horror movie *Night of the Living Dead* in 1968. "We can both sit and giggle at the most gruesome sights, probably because neither of us can conceal his delight—and his amazement—in the fact that he's not the victim himself. I think we both really do toss out our nightmares for the consumption of others."

And both the writer and the director—seven years older than Steve—have loved horror movies since childhood. "If you love horror movies, you have to have a love of pure *shit*," said Steve. "You turn into the kind of person who would watch *Attack of the Crab Monsters* four times."

Though King always liked to see how a director and actors interpreted his stories, he wasn't crazy about being a part of the process in his starring role as Jordy Verrill, least of all the time he had to spend in makeup and wardrobe. Near the end of filming his segment, he had to spend six hours a day having a green AstroTurf-like substance applied to his body.

In one of the scenes, Steve sticks out his tongue and it's covered with fungus, but first the designer Tom Savini had to make a mold of his tongue. "He slathered this stuff onto my tongue with a stick, and I had to sit there for ten minutes with my tongue out and about ten pounds hanging off it," Steve said. Savini got a perfect cast of the tongue, from which he made four green latex tongues, as thin as surgeon's gloves, that King rolled onto his tongue. Perhaps because of the arduous process, Steve decided to have a little fun with it.

One day he was wandering through a nearby shopping mall between takes and took one of the tongues with him. When a salesgirl asked if he needed any help, he stuck out his tongue. She screamed and called mall security. Steve laughed and explained it was just a prop. "It was worth it, it was so funny."

He liked being on the set, though it was tedious at times. Working cooperatively with other people was light-years away from how he normally spent his working time, by himself in front of a computer. "It isn't that I didn't have fun playing Jordy, but I really think of it as work," he said. "You just try to do it, and you know when you're doing a good job and you know when you're doing a bad job."

At first, not surprisingly, he was doing a poor job of acting compared to the work of the other actors in the *Creepshow* stories, including Adrienne Barbeau, Ted Danson, and Leslie Nielsen. Romero helped Steve get up to speed. "He wanted a caricature of a dirt farmer, not a real one, and I had a little trouble giving it to him," Steve said. After one particularly bad take, Romero pulled him aside and told him to think back to the Roadrunner cartoons. "You know how Wile E. Coyote looks when he falls off a cliff?" Romero asked. Of course, said Steve, and George told him that's how he wanted him to act. From that point on, Steve nailed the part.

Steve wasn't the only member of the family with a starring role in the film. Romero noticed that Joe resembled the sketch of the boy in the promotional poster for the movie, and he asked Steve if he could try him out for the role of Billy, the child of an abusive father who appeared in the prologue and epilogue reading a comic book. Steve said okay, Joe tested for the role, and Romero cast the boy, who was nine at the time.

At first, it was a bit unnerving. "He did get freaked out for a while," said Steve. "For a little boy to be in his pajamas with a whole bunch of people around his bed on a movie set with all the lights and everything was pretty unsettling. But he got to the point where it was either freak out or go to work, so he went to work."

The benefits of being on a set of a horror film were definitely attractive to a little boy. Taking after his dad, Joe had long exhibited a love of creepy things, and people on the set let him play with whatever was at hand. The nine-year-old boy had a field day. "There were all these cool rubber monster parts lying around," Joe said years later. "For a little kid, it was a blast."

One day not long after shooting began, Steve asked his son what he thought of the experience so far.

Joe blithely told him that he had worms crawling out of him in one scene while they hammered a nail into his head in another. Watching the two converse from afar, the scene could have been nothing more than a cozy little father-and-son powwow. They could have been discussing a Little League game.

After another day of shooting, Steve and Joe headed back to the motel where they were staying and stopped to pick up dinner on the way. Joe still had his movie makeup on—complete with bruises, cuts, and scabs—when they went through the McDonald's drive-through window. Steve had a full beard at the time and admittedly looked pretty rough. The girl at the drive-through took one look and called the cops, then stalled Steve for a few minutes. "The next thing you know," said Steve, "the cops have us in the back of the cruiser and Joe's eating his fries saying, 'It's just a movie,' and I'm going, 'That's right, just a movie, officers.' "

In August 1982, *Different Seasons,* King's first book of short stories to be published since *Night Shift* four years earlier, came out. One of the stories in it was "The Body." His old college buddy and roommate George MacLeod bought the book and read it, just as he had bought and read all of Steve's other books. When he got to "The Body," he smiled when he saw Steve had dedicated the story to him. But as he started to read, he froze.

One day back in college at the apartment on North Main Street in Orono, Steve asked what MacLeod was working on, and he told him the plot and details of a short story based on an incident from his own childhood. He and a few of his friends had heard of a dead body near the railroad tracks, and they went off to find it. Though he described the story in great detail and knew exactly how it would end, he never finished writing it.

"He stole it from me," said MacLeod. "I recognized that story as being literature, and Steve recognized it too, though not on a conscious level. He later told me he had borrowed my story to write his. All of those anecdotes were lifted right out of my story, and essentially the difference is that he had a dead body in his and I had a dead dog in mine. Other than that they were pretty much the same."

In interviews, King has described "The Body" as his coming-of-age story. "A lot of 'The Body' is true, but most of it is lies," he said. "As a writer, you tell things the way they should have turned out, not the way they did."

MacLeod has admitted that Steve always has his ear tuned for a good story, whether it comes from a book, a movie, or a friend's story. "If he's near something, he will absorb it like a sponge," said MacLeod. "He's Velcro when it comes to popular culture, he picks it all up. It's his strength, and naturally it's his weakness, too."

Sandy Phippen, author of numerous novels and short stories and a friend of both, witnessed the whole thing: "Steve published it as his own story, and of course, what do you say about that? But Shakespeare did the same thing; I mean, the story belongs to him who tells it best." Phippen added that it wasn't the first time he'd heard of King borrowing another writer's story, whether spoken or already published.

"I don't know if I'd call it plagiarism," Phippen said, but he did hear about an author who had a good track record of selling books, and several of her stories were packaged in one of the *Twilight Zone* anthologies from Rod Serling. One was about a car that was inherently evil and killed anyone that came in its path, the exact plot of Steve's novel *Christine,* which would be published in 1983. Phippen would later mention the story to a friend who was a cousin of Serling's, and Phippen asked if they knew about this. The cousin replied that they did indeed know about it, but that they chose to let sleeping dogs lie.

MacLeod still felt as if he had been kicked in the stomach. He let it slide until a few years later when he saw a TV commercial for *Stand by Me,* the movie based on "The Body."

According to Phippen, MacLeod got in touch with Steve, who asked him what he wanted. MacLeod told him that he wanted his name on the movie and some money. Steve didn't agree, and that was the end of their friendship.

It wasn't the first time that a relationship with an old friend was severed because he expected Steve to bring him along on his coattails, at least a little bit. Steve's childhood friend Chris Chesley also prided himself as a writer, and though Steve had read some of the work Chesley had written as an adult, he declined to pass it along to an editor or agent who could help. Supposedly Chesley became irate and refused any further contact with Steve.

Steve not only attracted a number of overzealous fans but also women who wanted only one thing from him.

"There are a lot of women who want to fuck fame or power or whatever it is," he said. "Sometimes, the idea of an anonymous fuck is appealing when some gal comes up at a bookstore signing and asks me to go to her place when I'm leaving the next morning. And I'm tempted to say, 'Yeah, let's pour Wesson oil over each other and really screw our eyes out.'"

But he says he would never risk his marriage for a one-night stand. "Besides, sexually, I'm not terribly adventurous, there are no orgies in my life," he admitted. "My marriage is too important to me, and anyway, so much of my energy goes into my writing that I don't really need to fool around."

He added that Tabby was not someone he was about to screw around on. "I don't necessarily believe in marriage," he said cryptically, "but I believe in monogamy. She's a rose with thorns, and I've pricked myself on them many times in the past, so I wouldn't *dare* cheat on her!"

"Infidelity is a shooting offense," Tabby concurred.

While he had addressed some of his greatest fears in his work so far, he said he hadn't yet dealt with one sexual fear: "I'd like to write a story about the *vagina dentata,* the vagina with teeth, where you were making love to a woman and it just slammed shut and cut your penis off."

Instead of writing about this he put the finishing touches on another book, this time about a Gypsy curse. At the time he was writing *Thinner,* he was unsure whether to publish it as a King or a Bachman book. Though his earlier Bachman books were edgier and rougher around the edges since they were written in his pre-*Carrie* days, *Thinner* was different.

The idea for the book arose when he was in the doctor's office for his annual exam, and the news wasn't good. He knew he had gained some weight, and when he entered the exam room, the first thing the doctor asked him to do was step on the scale. "I remember being pissed off because he wouldn't let me take off my clothes and take a shit before I got up on the goddamn scales." After the physical exam, the doc handed him the bad news: he was overweight, his cholesterol levels were through the roof, and he needed to lose weight and stop smoking.

King's reaction—possibly because the whole world loved him, he could write a laundry list and it would end up on the *New York Times* bestseller list, and no one dared to say boo to him except for Tabby—was absolute rage. He left the doctor's office and hibernated, fumed, for a few days: "I thought about how shitty the doctor was to make me do all these terrible things to save my life."

After his funk ended, he decided to follow his doctor's advice and lose the weight and stop smoking, or at least cut back. He started to lose a few pounds, and while part of him was happy about it, he was surprised to discover that another part of him was in distress: "Once the weight actually started to come off, I began to realize that I was attached to it somehow, that I didn't really wanted to lose it. Then I began to think about what would happen if somebody started to lose weight and couldn't stop."

Another random experience or stray comment, another book. Just another day in the life of Stephen King.

"I really don't prepare for my novels in any kind of conscious way," he said. "Some of the books have germinated for a long time, the ideas just won't sink. My mind is like this very deep pool: some things sink and others keep bobbing up. Over time I begin to see them in a different way. Sooner or later everything comes up, and I use everything."

When Steve had signed his first contract with Doubleday back in 1974, the contract contained a clause on the company's Author Investment Plan, allowing the publisher to hold on to all but $50,000 of the money due to the writer per year, while investing the rest. Of course, most writers didn't earn that much money in a year back then, or even now, but King's books were selling so well that he and his accountants knew the publisher was making money hand over fist.

This still held true even though Steve had switched publishers in 1977. By the end of 1982, millions of dollars had accrued in the AIP fund, but Steve was still receiving a paltry $50,000 per year. King asked Doubleday to cancel the agreement and remit all the money he was owed. But according to the contract he'd signed nearly a decade ago, the publisher was not legally obligated to do anything.

When King threatened to sue, McCauley had another idea. He suggested that King give Doubleday a novel to publish in exchange for releasing the funds. Since all the Bachman books were already spoken for by NAL, only one remained: *Pet Sematary*. Though Steve was angry with his old publisher, he agreed to give them the one novel he'd written that he had never wanted to see in print.

"I couldn't ever imagine ever publishing *Pet Sematary,* it was so awful," he said. "But the fans loved it. You can't gross out the American public, or the British public for that matter, because they loved it too."

Since his first bestseller in 1977, *The Shining,* a little voice in the back of Steve's head had always whispered that perhaps Donald King, the father he'd never known, would come forward, admit the errors of his ways, and want to be a part of his son's life.

Steve kept writing his stories and never forgot that his father might one day show up, much as his mother had held out hope, although it had all but disappeared by the end of her life.

What would Steve do if Donald King ever showed up? He had numerous ideas about how he'd react, each of which could serve as the germ for a new novel or story.

1. See what I've been able to accomplish on my own even after you ditched us?

2. Maybe Steve's writing would cause his father to come back and beg his forgiveness and Steve would accept him back into his life.

3. Or maybe Donald come back after his son had become a household name, beg to be part of his life, and his son would refuse.

The questions came fast and furious once people discovered the common ground between many of Steve's stories and his early abandonment. In the end, Steve would never know if his father knew that Stephen King was his son.

"There are a lot of fathers in my stories, and some are abusive and some try to be loving and supportive, which is what I had always hoped that I would be myself, as a dad," Steve said. "But my father was just an absence. And you don't miss what's not there. Maybe in some sort of imaginative way I'm searching for him or maybe that's just a lot of horseshit, I don't know. There does seem to be a target that this stuff pours out toward. I am always interested in the idea that a lot of fiction writers write for their fathers because their fathers are gone."

Indeed, after reading just a couple of his early books, from *Salem's Lot* to

The Shining, it's easy to see why a reader would think Steve assumes that buried deep within every man who appears normal on the outside, there's an absolute monster and murderer scratching to come out.

Steve agrees up to a point: "I don't think it's in every man, but I think it's in most. I think that men are wired to perform acts of violence, and I think that we're still very primitive creatures with a real tendency toward violence."

Michael Collings, an acquaintance of King's and a scholar who has written several books analyzing King's work, believes the issue of an abandoned child permeates every word he writes: "The issue of his father's abandonment is in everything, but it's never in any one thing completely," he says. "Very rarely is there a functioning father in his stories. If there is one, he's like Jack Torrance, who's out to get the kid. In every one of his stories is the sense that somehow the father, and occasionally even the mother, has abrogated the crucial role. That's the one thing that's consistent throughout his work."

Steve has admitted that he has thought about trying to find out what happened to Donald, but he always hesitated: "Something always holds me back, like the old saw about letting sleeping dogs lie. To tell the truth, I don't know how I'd react if I did find him and we came face-to-face. But even if I ever did decide to launch an investigation, I don't think anything would come of it, because I'm pretty sure my father's dead."

Maybe Steve already knew from the few ties that still remained to his father's family, and he didn't want to get the media all hot and bothered over the issue. After all, it would call attention to Steve, and not his books, which is where he preferred that the focus remain.

While he was constantly aware of his past, he was also prescient about his legacy. Even in the early eighties, Steve had a sense of how his work would be regarded by future generations, and he was sanguine about all of the critical and negative reviews that had appeared over the first decade of his life as a published author:

"After a while, if you live long enough, by the time you're so old that you've begun to parody yourself, and you and your contemporaries have all had your strokes and your heart attacks, then people start reviewing you well, mostly because you've survived the demolition derby. That's when you get good reviews, after you've done your important work."

Part of the issue may have been that he was cranking out a few more books than people knew about, under his Bachman pseudonym, in addition to writing articles and short stories, and traveling to promote the books that were just published. Be careful what you wish for, because the more he wrote, the more his publisher wanted, which meant that the quality had to suffer somewhere along the way. In his case, it came from accelerated publication schedules.

His habitually wrote three drafts for every book. For the first two drafts, he still followed what his editor John Gould at the *Lisbon Weekly Enterprise* had told him way back in high school: "When you write a story, you're telling yourself the story, and when you rewrite, your main job is taking out all the things that are not the story." Steve's third draft came after he'd received comments from his editor and incorporated those he wanted to keep along with a final polish of the other changes he'd implemented. "As the successes have mushroomed, it's been tougher to get my editors to give me time for the third draft," he said. "I'm really afraid that one will say a manuscript is great just because it fits the publication schedule. Every year I'm on a faster and faster track. I'm supposed to read the proofs in five days, and what if a bunch of dumb errors go through? We'll fuck up real good one of these days and then people can say, 'Steve King writes for money,' and at that point they'll be right."

Christine came out in April of 1983 and hit the top of the bestseller lists the first week it was published. Because it had long been regarded as a forgettable American car, Steve had chosen a 1958 Plymouth Fury to serve as the car that was inherently evil from the time it was still on the assembly line. "They were the most mundane fifties car that I could remember," he said. "I didn't want a car that already had a legend attached to it, like the Thunderbird or the Ford Galaxie. Nobody ever talked about Plymouth cars anymore."

Richard Kobritz had produced *Salem's Lot* the TV miniseries back in 1979, and he had also bought the film rights to *Christine*. The film would be released to theaters in December 1983.

As was the case with *Salem's Lot,* King had no control over the production nor did he write the screenplay. In December 1982, Kobritz received a script from screenwriter Bill Phillips—his sole credit was for *Summer Solstice,* a made-for-TV movie that was silent-film star Myrna Loy's last starring role—and the green light to start production came the following April. John Carpenter, who had directed some of King's favorite movies including *Halloween* and *The Fog,* finished shooting the picture two months later.

The challenges Kobritz faced as producer of *Christine* were different from those on *Salem's Lot,* though there were some similarities. "The hard part of doing a horror movie is that a lot of the suspense is in the imagination of the reader and in the author's description," said Kobritz. "The light that comes through at the bottom of the door, the vibration that the person feels on the other side, and what's behind it in visual terms without making it corny or repetitive has always been the problem. It's not expressed in dialogue, it's expressed in mood, in lighting, and occasionally in special effects. Sometimes it works and sometimes it doesn't."

Kobritz, Carpenter, and Phillips faced a specific problem with *Christine.* "We were working on the script when I asked if the car was born bad or did it become evil later in life, and none of us had an answer," said Kobritz. "I called Steve and asked him. He said he didn't know and that we could do whatever we wanted, so we elected to make the car inherently evil. That's why the car killed a man on the assembly line, which wasn't in the book. But it did show you that the car was born bad."

Kobritz bought twenty-four different 1958 two-door Plymouth Furies, Belvederes, and Savoys—other Plymouth models with similar body styles—and had them shipped to Santa Clarita, California, where most of the movie was filmed. In 1958, just 5,303 Furies came off the assembly line. The techs on the film cannibalized parts of each the twenty-four so they ended up with seventeen working cars, each earmarked for a specific purpose in the script: one was the burning car, one was retooled with a rubberized front hood, and so on. After filming was complete, only two cars were left: one was donated to a public radio station in Santa Cruz, California, for their annual auction, while the other was awarded to the winner of a contest at a new cable channel called MTV.

When Steve saw the rough cuts of *Christine,* he told Kobritz he was happy with the way they told the story. *The Dead Zone* movie had come out a couple months earlier, and Steve was pleased with that one as well.

"I thought Christopher Walken was about as right for Johnny as any mainstream Hollywood actor I could think of," Steve said.

Despite his hands-off approach to the film, he had retained approval for casting, and his first choice was Bill Murray. Dino De Laurentiis, an Italian producer who was involved with such hits from the seventies as *Serpico, Lipstick,* and *King Kong,* was producing the film and thought Murray would work for the starring role too, but the actor had a prior commitment. Then DeLaurentiis suggested Christopher Walken, and Steve thought he was a great choice for the role.

Of his two movies released in 1983, he was batting a thousand, but he was still hedging his bets. After all, he still was skittish about dealing with Hollywood after *The Shining.* For the most part, critics reviewed *The Dead Zone* favorably. Critic Roger Ebert wrote that the movie "does what only a good supernatural thriller can do: it makes us forget it is supernatural."

Although he was talking with Hollywood on the phone and doing deals with some of the biggest names in the entertainment industry, Steve still preferred to hang out with his old friends. He was grateful for his success and was only half-joking when he said he was glad that he had escaped the path he'd feared he would follow for the rest of his life.

He'd joke with his friend Sandy Phippen, who taught English to high school students, that Phippen's life was his worst nightmare. In addition to working as a teacher, Phippen was also the book editor for *Maine Life* magazine. He was four years ahead of Steve at the University of Maine, so their paths never crossed until they'd both been out in the world for some time.

In the early eighties, Steve started making money hand over fist with movie options, paperback deals, foreign deals, audio deals, royalties, and book advances. Steve had loosened up about spending the money by this time, but his first big splurge after buying the Bangor house and a couple of cars was a couple hundred bucks for a really good guitar, which was something he'd always wanted but could never afford. After he bought it, he left the price tag on to remind him how much it cost.

However, when it came to spending money on other people and helping them out, he never hesitated. "He and Tabby were always very generous with everybody," said Phippen. "They'd pay for a new set of tires on a friend's car, they'd cover the rent, you could ask them for anything. Once I needed to borrow a couple hundred dollars, and I saw that Tabby was having a book signing in Bangor. So I drove to the bookstore and stood in line, and when she signed the book, I told her I needed some money. She took out her purse and wrote me a check just like that."

Steve didn't change his lifestyle one bit, at least not around Bangor. In fact, he was often out and about so much that it became a game with some people: how many times did you spot Stephen King *this* week? "I'd go shopping, and there he was," said Phippen. "Or I'd go to a movie and he'd be there. He used to ride the city bus all around Bangor, reading books in the back of the bus. Some of my students would tell me, 'Stephen King was on the bus this morning.' He was the local famous person."

In the meantime, Tabby's notoriety was growing as well, as her second novel, *Caretakers,* was published in the fall of 1983. The story was set in Maine and explored a secret love affair between a man and a woman who belonged to different social classes. Of course, one of the first questions interviewers asked was about her famous husband, and sometimes they'd accidentally snag an interview with him when he wandered into the room. The obvious question was if he felt jealous.

"We work on entirely separate tracks, so it isn't much of a problem," he'd say. "Every now and then she'll accuse me of stealing one of her ideas."

While her novels revolved around personal stories that didn't involve horror, Tabby admitted that she drew on the raw stuff inside the same way her husband did: "Every character I have ever imagined was rooted in some aspect of myself, including the nasty ones. I'm not saying that I'm a rapist or an alcoholic, but it's my job to imagine what it would be like to be such a person."

Another obvious question was if she wanted to be as famous as her husband. Her answer was always an unequivocal *no.*

"Steve published before I did because he's better than I am and more driven and because I was busy having babies," she explained. "He's intensely ambitious and has always had a fantastic sense of priorities. I'm conflicted about ambition, am easily distracted, and don't write anything like he does."

She was also reluctant to pursue her writing more than she did because she feared how the attention would affect her life: "I resist the star-maker machinery because I witness the almost total loss of privacy my husband has had to suffer. I grant interviews, but always with reservations that have deepened over the years. People are inevitably disappointed when they learn that someone they thought they knew and loved is merely another flawed human being."

Her feminist viewpoint was still as strong as it was back in college. "The wife of a successful man is still essentially seen as chattel," she noted. "One of the reasons I rarely give interviews has to do with this assumption that I've taken up his fucking hobby. If I asked if it was okay with him if I wrote a book, it would be as unnatural as if I asked him if it was okay to have breakfast."

When Steve traveled for meetings with his editors or to go on promotional tours, he liked to fly out of Logan Airport in Boston, partly because when he was heading home, the four-hour drive allowed him to decompress enough so that he could gradually cross the boundary from the frenzied life of the public

Stephen King to the much calmer, radically different life of the private Stephen King.

On Halloween 1983, he got off the plane and jumped in a rental car, which was equipped only with AM radio. Steve had always liked hard-core rock and roll, the louder and meaner the better. The drive home that day seemed interminably long since then, as now, AM radio was a veritable wasteland of talk shows, sports, religious stations, news, maybe a few oldies stations, but no rock. Bangor had one rock station, WACZ, and it was on the AM dial. Steve had become friends with Jim Feury, also known as Mighty John Marshall, one of the DJs at the station, and after he returned home, Steve had complained bitterly about his drive back from Boston. Marshall filed this comment away.

One day Marshall asked Steve if he'd be interested in buying the station, which had just been put up for sale. If it was sold to someone else, the only way that WACZ could make a profit would be to run it via remote control, with automatic reel-to-reel machines and programmed Top 40 music.

Steve didn't hesitate. He bought the station because he didn't want Bangor to be without a rock station. It was selfish, but in a way, he did it for the same reason why he gives blurbs to unknown writers whose work he loves: "If no one plays groups like the BoDeans and the Rainmakers, they won't get contracts. If that happened, some of the fun would go out of my life, that sense of liberation only fresh, straight-ahead balls-to-the-wall rock music can provide."

In a way, he viewed the station, given the new call letters of WZON, as another form of expressing himself in addition to writing. "We're going to do some things to make it an interesting station, and I've got to be able to harness some of my own talents to it," he said in 1983, shortly after the purchase, admitting he was a novice when it came to running a radio station. "I'm studying how everything runs, it's like I'm on my student driver's permit." If all went well with radio, he envisioned buying a TV station somewhere down the road; it would play horror movies twenty-four hours a day.

The same month he bought the radio station, the book he never wanted to see in print, *Pet Sematary,* was published. His deal with the devil, Doubleday, was fulfilled.

"That book came out of a real hole in my psyche," he said. "If I had my way about it, I still would not have published *Pet Sematary*. I don't like it. It's a terrible book, not in terms of the writing, but it just spirals down into darkness. It seems to be saying nothing works and nothing is worth it, and I don't really believe that."

In *Pet Sematary,* in the front of the novel where previous books of an author are listed, sharp-eyed fans noticed a book they'd never heard of: *The Gunslinger.* When *Pet Sematary* came out, King's office was flooded with calls and letters from readers who wanted the unheard-of book and became incensed when they were told they couldn't have it, since the publisher Donald Grant had sold out of the limited-run copies through his mail-order business. Grant's office, along with Doubleday, was also inundated with communications from angry readers. Grant asked if he could print ten thousand more copies, and Steve agreed.

Steve learned an important lesson about fans who were so adamant about reading every word he'd ever written that he could indeed publish his grocery list and haul in millions.

MAXIMUM OVERDRIVE

If Steve had even been thinking of cutting back on his increasing cocaine and alcohol consumption, the publication of *Pet Sematary* all but squelched it. He was so upset that the book had been published—and he still fumed at the way Doubleday had essentially blackmailed him into giving them the book—that he cranked his already sizable consumption of beer and cocaine up a few notches. Though Tabby and his kids occasionally tried to intervene, Steve continued to deny that he had a problem.

Cycle of the Werewolf was originally published in 1983 as a limited edition by the small publisher Land of Enchantment. The story of a small Maine town that has to deal with the sudden appearance of a werewolf that starts terrorizing the residents, *Cycle of the Werewolf* is ridiculously short by King's standards, 128 pages, and was published in paperback two years later with a new title, *Silver Bullet*, to tie into the movie based on the book. King wrote the screenplay, and it was the directorial debut for Daniel Attias, who would go on to direct one of Steve's favorite TV series over two decades later, *Lost*.

King spent the first six months of 1984 campaigning for presidential candidate Gary Hart and held a fund-raising dinner at his house that winter. Hart was there and Steve played the proud host, inviting all of his friends to meet with the candidate and donate money to the campaign.

Sandy Phippen noticed that Steve acted differently during the fund-raiser. "The house was packed, there were a lot of people, and he basically shifted into his public Stephen King persona," he said, describing this mode as the opposite of his private one. "He was playing the role. That's what you learn to do after a while, and that's what people want to see."

Even Owen knew there were two Stephen Kings. Whenever Steve would leave Bangor to go on a book tour or to meet with movie producers or bookstore owners, his seven-year-old son would say, "Daddy's going out to be Stephen King again."

A flurry of movies based on his books followed that fall, including *Graveyard Shift* and *IT,* which became a made-for-TV miniseries.

In May of 1984, the movie *Firestarter* came out. A twenty-five-year-old Egyptian producer by the name of Dodi Fayed had acquired the rights to the movie for $1 million. Later, he would become known as the man who died with Princess Diana in her fatal car crash in Paris on August 31, 1997.

Dino De Laurentiis viewed eight-year-old Drew Barrymore as the Shirley Temple of her generation and decided to cast her in the lead role of Charlie McGee. Barrymore was already familiar with the book; when it first came out, her mother saw the book and thought the picture of the girl on the cover resembled her daughter. They bought it and Drew started to read. A few chapters into the book, the little girl told her mother, "I'm the Firestarter, I'm Charlie McGee."

De Laurentiis served as producer and Mark Lester, whose previous credits included *Roller Boogie* and *Truck Stop Women,* directed *Firestarter.* When he first saw the movie, Steve, who didn't write the screenplay, thought the movie was on the same level as *The Shining.* "*Firestarter* was one of my most visual novels and a resounding failure as a film," he said. Steve's dissatisfaction with the movie resulted in a bit of a public feud between writer and director.

"I was appalled at some of the things he said," said Lester, who added that King had earlier said he liked the way the film turned out. "I'm just appalled that a man of his wealth would actually stoop to these slanderous comments that he makes about people, attacking these movies."

"Mark's assertion that I saw the movie and loved it is erroneous," Steve volleyed back. "I saw *part* of an early rough cut. When I saw the final cut months later, I was extremely depressed. The parts were all there, but the total was somehow much less than the sum of those parts."

Although *Firestarter* bombed both with Steve and with the critics—Roger Ebert wrote that despite a roundup of interesting characters, "the most astonishing thing in the movie is how boring it is"—King's name was still held in high regard across the board, and requests for him to star in a variety of sometimes surprising venues began to pour in.

One of the few he agreed to was a TV commercial for American Express. In the early 1980s, the charge-card company had created a campaign featuring famous people whose faces weren't necessarily well-known. Some of the other eighties-era celebrities who would ask viewers, "Do you know me?" in the ads included John Cleese, Tip O'Neill, and Tom Landry. Dressed in a smoking jacket, Steve wandered through the stage set of a haunted house complete with spooky organ music and lots of fog and thunder.

He would later admit that it was a mistake to do the ad. "He felt like he created his own Frankenstein monster with those commercials," said Stanley Wiater, author of several books about King, because his portrayal in the ads clearly played up to the stereotype of how people expected him to act.

Yet, he'd had lots of practice, albeit on a much smaller stage. "The man is a frustrated actor," said Tabby. "Peek in and listen to him read to his children. It might be from Marvel comics, or *The Lord of the Rings*, or something he's written just for them. Or perhaps there's an improvised puppet show with a makeshift stage and a cast of *Sesame Street* puppets, and our own repertory company of dragons, vampires, assorted Things."

After the American Express ad, the offers kept coming. If Steve had wanted to, he could have guest-starred on *The Love Boat* or channeled Rod Serling by hosting an updated weekly version of *The Twilight Zone*. He didn't want to do them for a number of reasons: despite his increasing visibility, he still preferred that people and the media focus on his work, not him. He also knew even from being on the sidelines of *Salem's Lot* that network censors would place unreasonable demands on him to water down his work.

"You can't show someone getting punched in the nose more than once in an hour of prime-time television, and you want to put horror on TV?" he asked rhetorically. "I didn't want to do it because I didn't want to be on TV for six weeks and then be axed because everybody tuned out when they found out there was nothing there to watch."

He continued to be a bit dumbfounded by the way people glommed on to him just because he was famous: "I'm a little bit amazed by the whole thing, and I don't really understand it. Writers are not stars, they're not supposed to be stars. It's a thing that will play itself out in time. It'll pass."

Famous last words. In any case, Steve knew he'd reached a saturation point when he received a call from a producer who asked if he wanted to appear on the game show *Hollywood Squares*. He turned down the opportunity, but not long after he was reading a story in the *Boston Globe* about the Red Sox when the reporter compared a particular game to one of his novels.

"I've sort of become what I was writing about," Steve said. "In a way, it's the ultimate horror and the ultimate comedy at the same time." But he took it in stride. "I think that America needs Santa Claus, and to some extent America needs the Easter Bunny, and America really needs Ronald McDonald, more than Santa Claus now, I think. But America needs a bogeyman too. And Alfred Hitchcock's dead, so I got the job for a while."

Though he continued to live as normal a life as he could, his international exposure meant things had definitely changed when he went out in public. He especially rued going to a mall. If he arrived early to do a book signing, he'd often wander around to do some window-shopping. That's when the whispers started: "That's Stephen King!" He tried his best to ignore it, but people would often follow him around.

The publishers and editors who published him in the early days—and whom Steve continued to help out with an occasional story or introduction here and there—were also not immune from taking advantage of Steve's star power. Not only did the magazines put his name in forty-eight-point type on the cover, but the anthologies such as *Stalking the Nightmare, Tales by Moonlight,* and some of the annual fantasy-story collections were quickly turning into the worst offenders. He couldn't fault them entirely since these collections of stories by many different writers needed a few marquee names to get readers to pick up the book in the first place.

However, he thought they were getting a bit carried away. "My name has been used prominently on enough covers stateside to make me feel a little bit like the come-on girl in the window of a live sex show on Forty-second Street," he said.

He announced that from that point on he would refuse to do "whore duty for some marketing guy" and altered all anthology contracts to dictate that his name appear alphabetically in the list of contributors as well as appear in the same-size font as theirs on the cover.

With so many people grabbing at him, hoping to benefit from his success, he retreated more fully into his life at home. Bangor was one of the few places where he felt he could completely let down his guard and be himself. But he was also ambivalent about the place where he'd grown up and that had nurtured him as a writer.

"I love Maine and I hate it," he said. "There's a bitter feel to the real country of Maine. Most people think of Maine as lobsters and Bar Harbor. But the real country is poor people with no teeth, junked-out cars in front yards, and people who live in pup tents in the woods with great big color TVs inside them."

He saw no reason to go looking far afield for stories when plenty were right under his nose in Bangor: "The small town is a great setting for a story of suspense, because we understand that there's a microcosm. In New York City, there might be one hundred thousand town drunks. We really only need one. And in a small town, you only have one."

As Steve hunkered down in Bangor, he spent more time with Tabby and the kids. One of the family's favorite pastimes was to sit at the dining room table and pass a book around, with each family member reading a passage before giving it to the next in line.

They'd also play a game in which Steve would provide the setting and first few lines of a story before handing it over to one of the kids to continue. Later on, Owen and Joe would play a variation of the game on their own called the Writing Game, with one writing a page of a story before the other would take over.

Joe, in particular, was showing signs of taking after his father. At age twelve, he wrote an essay and sent it to the *Bangor Daily News,* which printed it a few days later. "I thought I was on the verge of major celebrity," he said. His feelings changed, however, when the story came out. "When I read it in the newspaper, I realized it was full of trite ideas and windy writing. At the end, they had added a little postscript that said, 'Joseph King is the son of bestselling novelist Stephen King,' and I knew that was the only reason they published the piece. At that age, the fear of humiliation is probably worse than the fear of death, and not long afterward I started to think I should just write under a different name."

Steve and Tabby never censored their kids' choice of books or movies. In Joe's case, it resulted in a higher-than-usual tolerance for the movies his father liked. For his twelfth birthday, he told his parents he wanted to invite his friends over to watch *Dawn of the Dead.* It was Joe's tenth viewing of the film, but the first for most of his guests. Slowly, his friends left the room, but a couple stayed behind, wordless and white as ghosts.

As Steve discovered with the flap over including *The Gunslinger* in his list of published books in *Pet Sematary,* an increasing number of people wanted to own everything he'd written, whether it was a limited edition of *Cujo* or a copy of one of the men's magazines that contained one of his stories. They were known as completists: collectors who want to own everything he's ever published, and then some.

Even by 1984, the unofficial list of Everything King was long. In addition to first-edition hardcovers, there were first-edition mass-market and trade paperbacks and every foreign translation in all formats. In the limited-edition category were signed-and-numbered and signed-and-lettered books. Then there were audiotapes, video games, scripts, posters, and other promotional materials from Stephen King movies, not to mention the book-club editions, both U.S. and foreign, and lastly, Tabby's novels.

In coming years, the challenge for a completist would only grow and would come to include a signed, limited-edition Stephen King guitar. In 1997, a guitar-manufacturing company bought the black-walnut tree featured in the film version of *Cujo* and made 250 guitars from the wood. Each guitar had a sticker inside with King's signature.

Although he has authorized limited collectors' editions of his own work, mostly to help fledgling publishers who are struggling, he began to have mixed feelings about the trend: "People would bring me books all wrapped up in cellophane and say, 'Oh, please, just be very careful when you lift the cover, that binding has never been broken!' I'd tell them what in the world were they talking about, it's just a book! It's not the fucking *Mona Lisa*."

King was still making public appearances at the horror and fantasy conventions that he had first started to attend back in the late seventies, though by the early eighties he had started to cut back. The fans were becoming scarier, in his opinion: "I've been at a couple of science-fiction conventions, and those people were out in a fucking void. There were people there who were literally separated from reality. Fundamentally, it seemed to me that they all felt alien, and maybe that's why they like science fiction."

He did attend the Fifth International Conference on the Fantastic and the Arts in March 1984, where several scholars and professors studying King's work were scheduled to present papers and talks. Tony Magistrale, then an associate professor of English at the University of Vermont, had written an essay entitled "Stephen King's Viet Nam Allegory: An Interpretation of 'The Children of the Corn,'" about the Vietnam elements in King's short story.

Afterward, Steve went out with several of the presenters, and he zeroed in on Magistrale's paper. "He told me there was no way in hell he intended that story to be an allegory for Vietnam," said Magistrale, who thought that it didn't matter, adding the main criterion of English teachers and professors everywhere: "Literary criticism isn't about what you meant, it's about what I can prove."

Magistrate noted, "To me, there were so many things that stood out in the story: the guy was a medic in Vietnam, kids were getting killed at eighteen, the land had become tainted and polluted, and the high school was named after JFK. Steve didn't concede my point, but we just chalked it up and laughed."

Magistrale included the essay in his first book on King, *Landscape of Fear: Stephen King's American Gothic*.

In November 1984, *Thinner,* the fifth Richard Bachman book, was published.

This, the first Bachman book to appear in hardcover, was heavily promoted with advertising and pushed as a featured title at the American Booksellers Association Convention in May 1984. It was also heavily promoted to booksellers throughout the country.

"As the publisher of some of the finest horror novels ever written, it takes a lot to get me excited about a new horror writer. Such a writer has now appeared," Elaine Koster gushed in a promotional letter sent to booksellers with advance reading copies.

"I wanted to jump up and down and say, 'This is Stephen King!' But I couldn't," said Koster. "We had many questions, but we never led anyone to believe that it was Steve. We stonewalled it, even though it would be to our advantage not to. It became a mission for me to respect Steve's privacy."

The photo on the back of the book was of Richard Manuel, a friend of Kirby McCauley's who lived near St. Paul, Minnesota, and made his living building houses. "We had to find someone who lived a long way from New York," said McCauley. "There was a chance that someone in New York would recognize Manuel walking down the street."

For his part, Manuel was amused. After the book came out, a few friends and relatives called him to let him know of the striking resemblance he bore to the author of the hot new thriller.

Soon after publication, readers began to send irate letters to Bachman, accusing him of deliberately copying Stephen King. "A lot of them were angry with me for that," said Steve, who read the letters addressed to Bachman. "'You *can't* copy him,' they said."

Thinner brought renewed interest to Bachman's previous books. All but one, *The Long Walk,* were still in print after six years, highly unusual for a mass-market paperback by a supposedly no-name thriller writer, given the brief shelf life of most mass-market paperbacks.

After *Thinner* came out, however, the questions about whether King was really Bachman started to come fast and furious. Each time King denied it, though he admitted he knew Bachman informally and that he was a chicken farmer, was shy, and disdained publicity. "The poor guy was one ugly son of a bitch," he'd tell reporters.

King and his publisher continued their denial for a couple of months in the face of a barrage of calls from all the major network TV shows from *Good Morning America* to *Entertainment Tonight.* Even a buyer at B. Dalton's, then a major bookstore chain, called NAL with their suspicions and committed to purchasing thirty thousand copies if they would just fess up. One of the major book clubs, the Literary Guild, accepted *Thinner,* and King was amused when one of the club's early readers remarked, "This is what Stephen King would write like if Stephen King could really write."

The cover was blown by Stephen P. Brown, who worked in a bookstore in Washington, D.C. Brown was a big King fan who had also read all of Richard Bachman's books. After reading one of the advance reading copies of *Thinner* that came to the store a few months before publication, he suspected that Bachman and King were the same. "I was about eighty percent convinced Bachman was Stephen King," said Brown.

He looked at the copyright pages on each of the first four novels, and *Rage* listed Kirby McCauley as the copyright holder. He sent a letter to King telling him of his discovery, thoroughly expecting to receive a letter of outraged denial. Instead he picked up the phone one day at the bookstore to hear the following on the other end:

"Steve Brown? This is Steve King. Okay, you know I'm Bachman, I know I'm Bachman, what are we going to do about it? Let's talk."

"All the Bachman books are sad books, they all have downbeat endings," said Brown, which runs counter to King's general philosophy about his books, that they should end on an up note. *Pet Sematary* and *Cujo* were the exceptions, while *Thinner* more closely resembled a King book with its upbeat ending, which is perhaps why so many people suspected Bachman of being King.

"The Bachman books didn't fit into his career very well," said McCauley. "He was known for his supernatural horror novels, and his fear was that he would lead his audiences astray."

King officially came out as Bachman in the *Bangor Daily News* on February, 9, 1985, under the headline "Pseudonym Kept Five King Novels a Mystery."

Once the cat was out of the bag, the number of copies of *Thinner* in print jumped tenfold, from 28,000 copies to 280,000. Regarding his unveiling as Richard Bachman, "I never meant that to come out," said King. "I thought I could get away with it." Bachman "died of cancer of the pseudonym."

He said, "When I write as Richard Bachman, it opens up that part of my mind. It's like a hypnotic suggestion that frees me to be somebody who is a little bit different. I think that all novelists are inveterate role players, and it was fun to be someone else for a while, in this case, Richard Bachman."

Even though he wrote the book as Bachman, some of King's habits stuck. In several places in the story the characters talk among themselves in Romany, the Gypsy language. "I yanked some Czechoslovakian editions of my books off the shelves and just took stuff out at random, and I got caught," he admitted. "I got nailed for it by the readers, and I deserved to be because it was lazy."

The Talisman, his first joint venture with Peter Straub, was published the same month as *Thinner,* with a first printing of 600,000 copies. The novel is the story of a twelve-year-old boy named Jack Sawyer who sets off on a coast-to-coast walk from New Hampshire to California in search of a talisman that will save the life of his mother, who is dying. Along the way, he finds himself in the Territories, a parallel universe set in medieval times. As before, attaching King's name to anything resulted in a veritable gold rush.

"The book is full of little tricks between us where we're trying to fool the reader into thinking that the other guy wrote it," said Peter Straub. "If you come along something you think is a dead giveaway, it's a trick."

"One of the biggest practical jokes they played was to imitate each other," said Bev Vincent, a friend of King's and author of *The Road to the Dark Tower.* "If you read a section of *The Talisman* that has something to do with jazz, the natural assumption is that Peter wrote it, while in reality Steve did. And if there's a rock-and-roll section, it's probably Peter pretending to be Steve."

"We both agreed that it would be nice to make the book seamless," said King. "It shouldn't seem like a game to readers to try to figure out who wrote what. When I worked on my half of the copyediting, I went through large chunks of the manuscript unsure myself who had written what."

Once *The Talisman* came out, Straub was taken aback at his increased visibility, especially among the fans. "He got a taste of Steve's life when the hard-core Stephen King fans started to follow him around trying to find out what Steve was really like," said Stanley Wiater. "Things got pretty wild there for a while with people knocking on his door and calling him to pick his brain. He wasn't sure he could handle it."

Nineteen eighty-five was another breakneck year of accomplishment and accolades. *Skeleton Crew,* another collection of short stories, appeared in June. Given his unveiling as Richard Bachman earlier in the year, a collection of his first four pseudonymous works was published in October with the title of *The Bachman Books,* including *Rage, Roadwork, The Long Walk,* and *The Running Man.*

The only downside was the growing number of fans who traveled to Bangor every year to see the famous mansion and hopefully catch a glimpse of their idol, as well as a corresponding increase in mail. Steve had to hire a couple of assistants to help out not only with the deluge—more than five hundred fan letters were coming into the office each week by the mideighties—but also to assist with the contracts, agreements, and business correspondence Steve had to respond to. At one point, Shirley Sonderegger, one of his assistants, suggested that King launch a monthly newsletter, *Castle Rock,* in the hopes that this would satisfy his more rabid fans and cut down on the amount of fan mail that he and his staff had to answer. He agreed, though he wanted nothing to do with the publication beyond contributing an occasional article.

He never forgot that his success was due not only to his talent but also to being in the right place at the right time. "I think if I started publishing in the midsixties, I would have become a fairly popular writer," he said. "If I started in the midfifties, I would have been John D. MacDonald, somebody that twenty million workingmen knew about, that they carried in their back pockets to work." He just wouldn't have been Stephen King, household name.

For years, Hollywood—and Dino De Laurentiis in particular—had been bugging Steve to direct a movie based on one of his stories, but he kept turning the idea down. Things came to a head when he handed in the screenplay for a film based on his short story "Trucks," where trucks, tractors, and machinery of all kinds turn on humans, killing anyone in their path.

In his screenplay, which he wrote with no thought of directing, Steve included hundreds of specific camera shots, which suggested to De Laurentiis that Steve would be a competent director. Steve turned him down, but Dino wouldn't take no for an answer. Steve reluctantly accepted, with one condition: if at any point in the project De Laurentiis felt that Steve was dropping the ball, Dino would not hesitate to replace him. They agreed, and production started in July at the De Laurentiis Studios in Wilmington, North Carolina.

Once Steve warmed up to the idea, he was happy that his virgin attempt at directing would be *Maximum Overdrive,* the name they chose for the film. "I did *Maximum Overdrive* because I thought I wouldn't have an actor walk off and have a tantrum if the actor happens to be a Mack truck," he said. "Or that the electric knife won't say it couldn't do the nude scene because it was having its period. I thought that working mostly with machines would be easier than working with actors."

It turned out to be totally different. "The trucks and the machinery were the real prima donnas!" he complained. "They fucked up without fail, while my actors always gave me more than I expected."

Everything that could go wrong did, and not just due to King's inexperience. Trucks refused to start, an electric knife got broken, and Armando Nannuzzi, the director of photography, lost an eye when a possessed lawn mower ran over a pile of wood chips and threw a splinter. But there were funny moments as well. The truck-stop set constructed for the movie looked so authentic that at least once a day a real truck would wander onto the set and the driver would hop out expecting to get some grub.

In one scene, a beer truck was supposed to get blown up and send hundreds of cases flying through the air. However, beer cans—which Miller donated to the movie for a plug—fly through the air a lot better when they're empty. The cast and crew were all but ordered to take mass quantities of beer home and return the empty cans the next day. But even they couldn't polish off enough beer. Steve postponed the scene as long as he could, but when the fateful day arrived, the crew poured the rest of the beer down the drain.

Despite his admonishments to both De Laurentiis and the crew to treat him like any other first-time director, for the most part they left him alone. "Once you get successful enough, there's a perception of power that goes along with that so that people who know you're messing up will stand back and sort of allow you to mess up," he said, describing it as "the emperor's new clothes" syndrome.

"I wish someone had told me how little I knew and how grueling it was going to be. I didn't know how little I knew about the mechanics and the politics of filmmaking. People walk around the director with this 'don't wake the baby' attitude. Nobody wants to tell you this, that, or the other thing if it's bad news."

What made matters even worse was that the mostly Italian crew spoke little English—De Laurentiis had brought the crew over from Italy—and Steve didn't speak Italian, which meant that comments and direction that would normally have run a minute or two easily snowballed into ten or twenty minutes.

Later, he said that he hated the experience: "It was too much like real work. It took too much time and I was away too much. It made things difficult for

Tabby and for the kids, and I just can't see going through that kind of thing again."

When the movie came out a year later, Steve was invited to be a guest VJ on MTV for an entire week, to coincide with its release. Among his favorite videos he introduced that week were "Who Made Who" by AC/DC, "Come On Feel the Noise" by Quiet Riot, and "Addicted to Love" from Robert Palmer.

While he was making the movie, an antipornography law went into effect in North Carolina. A lifelong proponent of free speech—after all, censorship is a direct threat to his livelihood—he saw the effects of the obscenity law firsthand: "When their antiporn statute became law, between Tuesday evening and Wednesday morning, all the *Playboys* and *Penthouses* disappeared from the convenience store where I stopped for my morning paper and evening six-pack. They went so fast it was as if the Porn Fairy had visited in the middle of the night."

Of course, another little issue on the set was Steve's escalating drug use. "The problem with that film is that I was coked out of my mind all through its production, and I really didn't know what I was doing," he said. During postproduction on *Maximum Overdrive,* his editor Chuck Verrill visited him, and he was appalled at the change in his author. "He was gargling Listerine and popping pills," said Verrill. "He was still a nice guy and coherent, but he did seem to be strung out."

Sandy Phippen saw the trouble brewing, describing how Steve ended up in the drunk tank at the Bangor police station one night. Steve also lived in an apartment in Brewer for a time after Tabby had reached the limits of her patience and kicked him out of the house.

Just as Steve liked to drink beer at book signings, he brought along a couple of six-packs when doing readings for local fund-raisers. Phippen was the librarian in Hancock Point, a summer colony about forty miles from Bangor. In 1982, he invited Steve to speak at an event at the local chapel to raise money for a new roof for the library. Sandy poured beer into an old white pitcher so members of the audience would think Steve was drinking water. But it was obvious, and some of the ladies were so appalled that he would be drinking beer in the church that they walked out.

The same thing happened during a talk he gave at the Virginia Beach Library Pavilion in 1986. Fifteen minutes into his talk, he pulled out a beer from an inside pocket and yelled, "Who's going to be at the Silver Bullet tonight?" to the crowd. When the first can was gone, he popped open a second and lit a cigarette. The next day, some people called the library to complain.

Twelve years into his career, King was seemingly indestructible, and nothing and no one could stop him. Certainly the booze and the cocaine weren't interfering with his output.

Steve continued to insist that he didn't have a problem with drugs and alcohol, that he could quit anytime he wanted. But a part of him still needed to get high. He didn't see a reason to stop. And until he was forced to, he wouldn't.

In October 1985, King broke his previous record by having four books hit the *New York Times* bestseller list at the same time: *Skeleton Crew* in hardcover, and *Thinner, The Talisman,* and *The Bachman Books* in paperback.

His literary agent, Kirby McCauley, also made headlines when he negotiated a $10 million, two-book contract with New American Library—with a twist. Instead of the standard deal, assigning rights to a publisher for the life of the copyright, King decided to license books to a publisher for fifteen years. If he was happy with how the publisher marketed and promoted the books at the end of that time, he'd renew the deal for another fifteen years. If not, he'd look for another publisher.

"We're not selling the books anymore, we're renting them," said Steve.

This was a novel arrangement even among bestselling authors, and many publishers were not happy since they expected that other internationally famous writers would insist on the same kind of deal in the future.

With all the money, however, Steve's wealth still felt surreal. "Basically, I'd like to be like Scrooge McDuck and put all of my money in Shop 'n Save bags and keep it in a vault to play around with," he said. "Then it might seem real."

He also spoke about retiring from writing: "I want to clear everything off, get this stuff out of the way, and not take on any more commitments. Then I'm just going to sit around." He described his perfect day: "When I get up in the morning, I'll just grab hold of a book and go somewhere and sit in the corner and read all day long—except I'll take a walk in the morning, and I'll break at lunch for some hamburgers at McDonald's, and take another walk in the afternoon."

But he knew it was just a pipe dream. "I'd be bored shitless. I would be real unhappy if I were doing that. But that is the sort of goal that I always have in mind."

In fact, in 1986, he moved his office out of the house and into a former National Guard barracks on Florida Avenue in Bangor, out near the airport behind a General Electric plant and next to a tuna-processing plant. To his friend Tony Magistrale, his choice of location was entirely appropriate: "That's the heart of Bangor, which is perfect for Steve, who came from poverty and has strong blue-collar roots." When Magistrale visited King in Bangor, he wanted to meet him at his office, not his house, because he felt it provided a clearer picture of the real Stephen King.

"There are two Stephen Kings," Magistrate explained. "There's the Stephen King who's the Horatio Alger story of America, and the other Stephen King, the working-class hero who can create salt-of-the-earth characters like Stu Redman and Dolores Claiborne."

Steve had repeatedly said, in interviews and to anyone who would listen, that he used his writing as an outlet for his fears in the hopes they would dissipate somewhat, if not disappear entirely. The funny thing was, with every book and screenplay he churned out, his fears not only didn't go away, but they burned brighter in some cases. He even developed a few entirely new fears.

"I can still find fear. I can find more fear than I used to be able to find," he said. "I can't go to sleep in a hotel without thinking who's in the room underneath me, dead drunk and smoking a cigarette and about to fall asleep so that the room catches fire, and when was the last time that they changed the batteries in the smoke detector?"

His biggest fears concerned his kids. "Because I have some money, I worry about whether bad guys are going to come and kidnap my kids and hold them for ransom. I'm afraid of what it's doing to their lives, I'm afraid of what it's doing to my life."

Of course, the kids thought their parents' fears were overblown. The thing that bugged Naomi most when she was a teenager was when teachers singled her out and strangers would gush over her because she had a famous father. "It's sort of like somebody recognizing Robin because he's Batman's sidekick," she said. "It impresses the hell out of some people, but it puts you on a pedestal."

It appeared that the Kings' desire to raise their family as normally as possible and out of the glare of the spotlight by living in Bangor had been the right choice, for both kids and adults. "There are a lot of people who don't know who I am, and that's what I love about western Maine," said Tabby. "And if they do, they don't care. To them, I'm just another woman driving around with a dog in her car."

Steve seemed to be particularly protective of Owen, yet also calmer. After all, Steve was closing in on forty, his success seemed pretty much entrenched, and his three kids were turning out fine so far. Given his vasectomy, there wouldn't be any more, so a certain tenderness came over him when it came to his youngest child.

"Lately my smallest son has got this horror of going to school on rainy days," he said. "I don't know what it is, maybe they wouldn't let him into the building. He's only six and it's in his brain but he can't get it out of his mouth, it's too big. So I keep him in the car on rainy days until the bell rings and it's time for him to go in. A psychiatrist would say that I'm treating the symptom but not the cause, but I couldn't give a shit about the cause. If keeping him in the car until the bell rings makes him feel better, then okay."

One day Owen was complaining that whenever he needed to go to the bathroom, he had to raise his hand. "Everybody knows that I have to go pee-pee," he told his father. Steve started to tell him he shouldn't feel that way, but suddenly stopped because he'd felt the same way when he was in elementary school decades earlier. He comforted his son as best he could and immediately began to think how he could use the experience in a story, using the idea of "mean old teachers who make you raise your hand in front of all these little kids, and they all laugh when you're walking out of the room because they *know* what you're going to do."

The result was "Here There Be Tygers," published in *Skeleton Crew* in June of 1985. Steve dedicated the book to Owen.

As he began to treat his youngest with more compassion, Steve began to remember back to his own childhood more. "None of us adults remember childhood," he said. "We *think* we remember it, which is even more dangerous. Colors are brighter, the sky looks bigger. Kids live in a constant state of shock. The input is so fresh and strong that it's bound to be frightening. They look at an escalator, and they really think that if they don't take a big step, they'll get sucked in."

Nineteen eighty-six was the first year since 1980 that King published only one novel. But given the size and scope of *IT,* published in September, it's understandable. The book was mammoth, a 1,138-page tome with more than half a million words, King's longest to date, although *The Stand* should have been just as long, or longer.

"As far as I'm concerned, it's my final exam," he said. "I don't *have* anything else to say about monsters. I put all the monsters in that book."

The idea for *IT* came from a couple of different places. First, one of his favorite cartoon segments as a kid was when the entire cast of the *Bugs Bunny Show* came on-screen at the beginning of the opening credits. He wanted to write a book where all the monsters he came to love during his childhood—Dracula, Frankenstein's creature, the werewolf, and others—could all be in one place as well.

Then he thought back to a fairy tale called "The Three Billy Goats Gruff" and the bridge the characters crossed. "What would I do if a troll called out from beneath me, 'Who is trip-trapping over my bridge?'" he said. "All of a sudden I wanted to write about a real troll under a real bridge."

Once he started to work on *IT,* some surprising things began to happen. For one, as he began to explore the stories of the kids in the book, memories from his own childhood began to surface, so he incorporated some of them into the book. But to his distress, though he usually knew where a story was heading a few writing sessions in advance, he drew a blank when it came to *IT* and didn't know what was coming next.

He had written about eight hundred pages of the manuscript and needed to write a scene about the body of a young girl that was going to be found. As he wrote the preceding scenes, he still didn't come any closer to knowing her fate, and he became increasingly anxious. The night before he was due to write the scene, he still had no clue, so when he went to bed, he willed himself to have the idea by the time he woke up the next morning.

He fell asleep and began to dream that he was the girl he was writing about, and he was standing in a junkyard filled with discarded refrigerators. He opened the door to one and saw what looked like pieces of macaroni hanging from the shelves. One of them suddenly grew wings and flew onto his hand. "All of a sudden, this thing turned from white to red, and the rest of the shells flew out and covered my body. They were leeches. When I woke up, I was very frightened, but also very happy, because then I knew what was going to happen. I took the dream, dropped it into the book, and didn't change a thing."

He knew he needed some outside feedback, so he turned to Michael Collings, the author of several books about King, and a retired professor of English and director of creative writing at Pepperdine University. They had been corresponding for a while, and Steve felt comfortable with how Collings viewed his work from an academic standpoint, so he sent along the manuscript for *IT* in the spring of 1986 with a warning: "Never write a book whose manuscript is bigger than your own head."

"He told me *IT* was his magnum opus and that the novel would not only be the culmination of his exploration of the theme of the child in jeopardy, but would also be the last monster-oriented novel he would write," said Collings, who read the manuscript, suggested a few changes, and sent it back. When the book was published six months later, he was pleased to see that King had incorporated his advice.

"I have a sense of injustice that came from my mother," said Steve. "We were the little people dragged from pillar to post. We were latchkey kids before there were latchkey kids, and she worked when women basically cleaned up other people's messes. She never complained about it much, but I wasn't dumb and I wasn't blind, and I got a sense of who was being taken advantage of and who was lording it over the other people. A lot of that injustice has stuck with me, and it's still in the books today."

"All of his works are rooted in childhood trauma, or a violation of childhood in some way," said Collings. Maybe Steve kept revisiting this theme in his books in an effort to eradicate it—after all, he forgot about the bad things in his life when he was writing—but also in a way to try on different personae and to live vicariously through the lives of other kids, who ultimately found a way to be powerful, as opposed to Steve's real life, in which he was always reminded about the lack of power that he and his poverty-stricken family had as compared with the rest of the world.

When he first started writing *IT*, he deliberately put himself in a frame of mind where he could return to childhood. At first, he struggled to remember anything. "But little by little, I was able to regress, and the more I wrote, the brighter the images became," he said. "I started to remember things that I'd forgotten. I put myself into a semidreaming state and I started to get a lot of that stuff back."

After writing more than a dozen novels, one thing hadn't changed: Steve rarely provided detailed physical descriptions for the characters he created. "For me, the characters' physical being is just not there. If I'm inside a character, I don't see myself because I'm inside that person," he explained. "If a character goes by a mirror or if there's a situation where his or her physical looks become important, then I provide a description."

And after he finished writing *IT*, he announced he was done with writing stories of traumatized children. "When I wrote the books that people remember so clearly, like *The Shining, Salem's Lot,* and *Firestarter,* I had kids in rubber pants and diapers all those years," he said. "And now, my youngest kid is nine, and I don't seem to have so much to say about kids anymore."

If King seemed inclined to rest on the laurels of his magnum opus, the next fourteen months changed all that as four more books followed in quick succession: *The Eyes of the Dragon* (February 1987), *The Dark Tower: The Drawing of the Three* (May 1987), *Misery* (June 1987)—with a first printing of nine hundred thousand copies, it was the fourth-bestselling hardcover novel for the year, according to the *New York Times* bestseller list—and *The Tommyknockers* (November 1987), whose initial print run was 1.2 million. He continued his frantic pace of public appearances and fund-raisers and contributed to small magazines. *Time* magazine made him its cover story in October 1986, calling him "The Master of Pop Dread."

But it seemed that the more the world encroached on his life, the more he would pull back. Occasionally, the stress from everybody wanting a piece of him would become too much to bear, and Steve would simply disappear for a while. Stanley Wiater recalled a few such occasions when he was trying to get in touch for some follow-up questions for an interview, and he contacted Peter Straub, whom most of Steve's cohorts considered to be his best friend.

"Where's Steve?" Wiater asked.

Straub didn't know, adding that Steve wasn't even responding to his calls. "He's in one of his reclusive states," Straub told him.

Wiater said that King once told him that every so often the fame got to him and he had to drop out. "He's a driven man, compulsive and obsessive. If he doesn't write every day, he gets cranky," said Wiater. "I've known other writers who are like that, but I'm not one of them. Steve lives with a book for months, sometimes years. Basically, he just has to get out of his own way and occasionally shut down."

King continued to use his name to benefit others, especially when it came to education.

He and Tabby had given away hundreds of thousands of dollars to friends, strangers, and charitable organizations since *Carrie* was published, and in 1987 they decided to create their own foundation—The Stephen and Tabitha King Foundation—to make it official, not to mention to simplify bookkeeping for tax purposes. This way, nonprofits could apply directly for grants instead of a friend of a friend asking if the Kings could help out with fund-raising for a particular charity.

Steve funded an endowment to award four college scholarships of $2,000 a year to graduates of Hampden Academy. When a high school student in California wrote telling him that she was unable to go to college due to recent cuts in federal education funds, King obtained her high school academic records and decided to pay for her to attend the University of Southern California for four years.

Influenced by the effects of the antipornography statute he had witnessed in North Carolina the previous year, King began to use his fame for political clout in his home state. In the spring of 1986, the Maine Christian Civic League issued a referendum to prohibit the sale of pornographic material in the state. Steve spoke out against the bill as well as other forms of censorship, and voters turned it down in the June 10 primary.

Perhaps with *IT* finished, and Steve vowing not to write any more books about the lives of disenfranchised, abused kids, he turned to helping his own children with their writing. It was clear the writing gene had taken hold of all three of his offspring.

At sixteen, Naomi was already writing feature articles for *Castle Rock,* King's fan newspaper. Just as her father was regularly deluged with unintelligent questions from his fans, so were his kids. Steve taught them to regard the inquiries in the same light that he did: with as much sarcasm and over-the-head irony as possible.

In response to the number one question, "What's it like being the daughter of Stephen King?" Naomi replied, "He is thoughtful, considerate, and kind. He doesn't beat or molest us, and we don't get locked in dark closets."

Instead of the fishbowl the family has lived in all their lives, Naomi not-so-secretly wished that her father tended more toward the J. D. Salinger mold. "There are people out there who think my father can walk on water," she said. "I'm sorry to disappoint you, but he can't, and that's the honest truth."

Joe was pursuing a writing career of his own. When he was twelve years old, he sent a story to Marvel Comics for the company's *Try-Out Book,* which provided aspiring comic-strip writers with the beginning of a story and let them write their own ending, which was reminiscent of Steve's 1977 story "The Cat from Hell." Joe worked on his story and sent it off, only to receive a form rejection letter a short time later. But again, like his father, who had thrilled when an editor had taken the time to scrawl a brief note on the slip, Joe was ecstatic that the editor in chief, Jim Shooter, had written on his note. "I felt great euphoria at the idea that he had read some of my script, and felt like I was on my way," Joe said. "It definitely motivated me to write more."

Even Owen got into the act. An avid collector of everything G.I. Joe, he wrote to Hasbro suggesting they introduce a new doll that could see into the future and name it Crystal Ball G.I. Joe. The toy company accepted his idea and brought out the Sneak Peek G.I. Joe the following year. As payment for his suggestion, Owen received several boxes of G.I. Joe dolls and assorted accessories.

The kids were also turning out to be a chip off the old block when it came to another of their father's obsessions: baseball, and the Red Sox in particular.

One of King's loneliest memories of childhood was when he was nine years old and the family were living in Stratford, Connecticut. Steve was sitting alone in front of the TV on October 8, 1956, when he watched Don Larsen of the New York Yankees pitch a perfect game against the Brooklyn Dodgers in the fifth game of the 1956 World Series. He was ecstatic at the conclusion of the game, but lamented that he had nobody with whom to celebrate the momentous occasion. He felt not only his brother's absence, but more painfully, the acute lack of his father—after all, Steve knew his friends' fathers celebrated with them—and it became all too much for the young boy to bear. He switched off the TV and waited in the silent apartment until his mother and brother came home.

Exactly three decades later, King took Owen, who was nine years old, to Fenway Park in Boston to see a World Series game, where the Red Sox took on the New York Mets. Steve studied his son closely. "His eyes are everywhere, trying to take in everything at once," said King. He was painfully aware of the "almost ceremonial way in which the joy of the game is handed down from generation to generation. Plus," he said, not bothering to try to hide the giddiness in his voice, "there was a dad in the picture this time around."

Unfortunately, the Red Sox lost to the Mets 7–1.

Owen was caught unaware by his disappointment over the loss, and as father and son left Fenway, both were taken aback by Owen's tears. King told him about that lonely day thirty years ago when he watched Don Larsen's perfect game. Twenty minutes later, the Red Sox's loss didn't seem so bad. And quite possibly, the edge had been smoothed over on that still painful memory.

THE LONG WALK

Though Steve had already resolved that he would no longer write *about* kids, he decided to write *for* kids, specifically, for his daughter.

While Joe eagerly read *The Stand* and *Salem's Lot* when he was eleven years old, Naomi had no desire to read her father's work. "My daughter is a more gentle soul," he said. "She has very little interest in my vampires, ghoulies, and slushy crawling things." Naomi instead preferred fantasy novels by Piers Anthony and works by John Steinbeck, Kurt Vonnegut, and Shakespeare.

"She never read anything that I had written, and in a way that hurt. So I thought, all right, if she won't come to me, I'll go to her." He sat down to write a story of sibling rivalry set in a faraway mythical kingdom, originally calling it *The Napkins,* in 1983 and gave it to Naomi to read. She liked it, and he was so pleased with it that he decided to send out the story for his annual Christmas missive in 1984. He renamed it *The Eyes of the Dragon* and published it himself through his own small press, Philtrum. He had started Philtrum, in 1982, to publish the first installment of *The Plant*. One edition of 1,000 signed copies numbered in black pen had been sold via lottery to fans, and a second edition of 250 signed copies were numbered in red, which he sent to his Christmas-card list. Philtrum later expanded to publish limited editions of stories and novellas that Steve deemed to be either too short or too far away from his typical style for his New York publishers.

Though he never intended *The Eyes of the Dragon* to be published for the general public, in 1987 Steve decided that the story deserved to be read by a wider audience, and so he granted permission to Viking to publish a trade edition of the book for distribution to bookstores. Deborah Brodie, a freelance book editor who had worked with noted children's authors Jane Yolen and Patricia Reilly Giff, was brought on to edit the book, and she was impressed at how well King took her editorial direction.

She asked him to introduce Peter's best friend, Ben, earlier in the story; in the original, Ben showed up at the halfway point. "Steve wove several references into various scenes early in the book, and then he created a whole new scene with a three-legged sack race to explain the genesis of their friendship," she said. "That's a very exciting moment for an editor, to ask the right questions and have the author do more than just answer it."

She was initially concerned that she'd feel intimidated working with King, but her fears were dissipated when he told her, "The book is the boss."

In March 1987, Stephanie Leonard—Tabby's sister and the editor of *Castle Rock*—dropped a bomb on Stephen King fans. Though he'd previously hinted at retiring from writing, it now looked as if he would finally do it.

In her editor's column, Leonard announced that Steve would be taking some time off from writing. "We've heard him say he'll take five years," she wrote.

The reaction was fast and furious. Fans flooded the office with phone calls and letters to protest and beg him to reconsider, and the story made headlines around the world. To pacify the fans, Steve backtracked a bit.

"I think it would be a good idea," he said, laughing, "but I don't know if I can. Tabby says that I can't. She says that I couldn't stop writing any more than I could stop breathing."

The backlash and outrage forced Stephanie Leonard to amend her editor's letter a few issues later: "Stephen is not really retiring, he is hoping to cut back on work so he can spend more time with his family. There will not be any more five-book years anytime soon. He plans to continue writing but publish less."

His fans were somewhat mollified a few months later when *Misery* was published . . . at least those readers who didn't take his novel about a nightmare fan personally.

As usual, King had ripped the headlines from his own life to create a novel. He'd been thinking about branching out from his usual oeuvre of horror—*Eyes of the Dragon* was the first real step in this direction—and he realized that some of his fans would fight him tooth and nail, which was particularly evident in the wake of his most recent retirement announcement. *Misery* is the story of a romance novelist who wants to work in a genre totally different from the one he has long been pigeonholed in, and one obsessed fan who kidnaps him and demands that he write another novel in the old genre.

Some fans reacted with anger as they interpreted the message of the novel—originally written as a Bachman book—to be King thumbing his nose at them. Because the character of Annie Wilkes was written as an over-the-top caricature, some of Steve's fans believed that he held nothing but contempt for them.

During media interviews for the book, he was careful to say that he still loved his fans, and that he wouldn't be where he was if it not for them. However, he had experienced firsthand a dark side to some fans that he spoke about publicly for the first time:

"Fans still buy the food I put on my table. On one level it still knocks me out that people get off on what I'm doing that I can't help but love them. But if you buy the book and spend two or three days reading it and really get off on it, then that's all you deserve. That's all your $17.95 should buy. It isn't like a ticket into my house or my life or my bedroom or anything else.

"I've been a lightning rod for a certain number of crazy people. We keep files on them. The people who are the most devoted fans have a churning need to identify emotionally with the object of their worship." Where it got really scary, he said, was when the adulation spilled over into actual resentment. "They feel that what I have achieved was really meant for them."

As usual, Tabby didn't mince words when she gave a pointed warning to his fans in the pages of *Castle Rock* two months after *Misery* was published: "In some very real way, you, the readers, know this man very well. I would like to suggest that you do *not* know him at all. In seventeen years of marriage, I am still discovering things I did not know about Steve, and I hope he's still discovering the unknown in me."

Steve said the same thing about Tabby: "I think of my wife as holding a deck of fifty-two cards. If you ask me how many she is showing me, I wouldn't know. We are as close to each other as two people can be, but one can never be sure how much you do and do not know about another person."

His original idea for *Misery* was a lot more graphic: Annie Wilkes had planned to kill Paul Sheldon, feed him to Annie's pig—named Misery after the heroine in Paul's books—and take his skin to bind the book he'd written for her. The original title? *The Annie Wilkes First Edition.*

Even though Annie was based on an amalgam of King's scariest fans, he did grow quite fond of her while writing the book. "Of the characters I've created that readers know about, Annie Wilkes is my favorite. She always surprised me, she never did exactly what I thought she would do, and that's why I liked her," he explained. "She had a lot more depth and she actually generated a lot more sympathy in my heart than I expected."

In truth, however, Annie Wilkes was a stand-in for Steve's addictions. "I was writing about my alcoholism and didn't have a clue."

King's next book was *The Tommyknockers,* published in November of 1987, the story of a female writer who discovers an alien spaceship buried in her yard, and how the inherent evil in the spaceship affects the people in her town. Even his loyal fans said it wasn't among his best—and critics lambasted it.

The response to *The Tommyknockers* underscored a criticism of his writing that he'd been getting for some time. King's books had become bloated from his typical overwriting, and his work badly needed an editor. Steve once joked that he suffered from a permanent case of *literary elephantiasis.* "I have a real problem with bloat. I write like fat ladies diet."

"The guy is a machine," said Stephen Spignesi, the author of numerous books about King, including *The Essential Stephen King.* "He is a very prolific creator, and he sometimes tends to overwrite. He doesn't look at his work and say this could be shorter and he would be more effective. For instance, he'll go on for two pages describing a room or something when the reader just wants some action." But Spignesi admits some buried treasures are in the bloated pages: "Very often the excess description is often where King excels in literary imagery."

"Nobody can make me change anything," Steve once said in regard to his writing style. "Where does a ten-thousand-pound gorilla sit? The answer is, any place he wants. It's too easy to hang myself. I have all this freedom, and it can lead to self-indulgence." He was well aware of the criticism. "I think that I'm a little more sloppy than I was. I'm forty-four, my editor's thirty-five, and I think, 'What the fuck does he know? Don't tell me how to make this hat, boy, I've been making these hats since from when you were in your mother's womb.'

"But the fucking hat doesn't have any brim or the thing's inside out, and in fact he knows quite a lot. I try to listen and figure, if you're the biggest ape in the jungle, you better be pretty careful."

Even Steve was unhappy with the way *The Tommyknockers* turned out. "It just went on and on. It was a hard one to write, to keep track of all those people in the story. When I finished the first draft, it looked like the Bataan Death March, with lots of cross-outs and stuff. I locked myself in the bathroom and I laughed hysterically and cried and then laughed again. I never did that with a book."

Of course, the trouble could have come because Steve had hit bottom in his drug addiction and alcoholism. After dealing with his drinking and blackouts for years, Tabby was starting to hint at an ultimatum. Steve recognized he was on thin ice, admitting that he didn't trust himself, and that was why he continued to push himself, crank out the books, push people past the gross-out point they'd become accustomed to in his previous novels.

His writing life started to look especially bleak after he handed in the manuscript for *The Tommyknockers* early in 1987, when he came down with a severe case of writer's block. "It was *terrible*," he said. "Everything I wrote for the next year fell apart like tissue paper."

In the fall of 1987, Stephen King should have been on top of the world. Despite the negative reaction to *The Tommyknockers, Misery* had met with wider acclaim than his books usually did. The *New York Times,* a newspaper not previously known to look favorably on Steve's novels, called it "an intriguing work," while *USA Today* crowned it "King's best." *The Running Man,* with Arnold Schwarzenegger in the starring role, pulled in just over $8 million on opening weekend in mid-November. But perhaps the thrill of Steve's entire year came in October at a Johnny Cash concert at the Bangor Auditorium, when he was invited onstage by the Man in Black to join him on "Johnny B. Goode."

He was tickled by the chance to play with Cash, but Stephen King was not in a good place. While he was thinking about what new horrors to inflict upon the lives of the characters in his work-in-progress, he was trying to forget about the horrors in his own life, specifically his overwhelming addictions. When he took the stage with Cash, no one in the audience or in the band could have imagined that the internationally famous horror writer who stood at the mike belting it out was only sober for about three hours a day, and he spent most of that time thinking of blowing his brains out.

"I love my life and my wife and kids, but I've always been somewhat quasi-suicidal most of the time, constantly wanting to push things past the edge," he said.

His blackouts from cocaine and alcohol had become more frequent in the last few years, as he drank and drugged more not only to keep up the pace but also to keep the demons at bay: "You think the world loves you? We really know what's going on, and we're not going to let you forget we're here."

He said, "My kind of success does not lead you humbly to say, 'Yeah, I guess you're right. I'm an asshole.' Rather, it leads you to say, 'Who the fuck are you to tell me to settle down? Don't you know I'm the king of the fucking universe?'"

He tells a story his mother had told him during his childhood. When Ruth was pregnant with him, she'd pull up a piece of tar from the road in front of the house and chew it. She didn't know why she was compelled to do it, but she absolutely craved something in that tar, and if she couldn't have it, she'd do nothing but think about it until she gave up and ran out into the middle of the road, where she fell on her hands and knees and clawed a hunk of asphalt out with her fingernails. She waited until she was heading back to the house before she popped it into her mouth and began mindlessly chewing as if it were a piece of taffy. She instantly felt better. Her husband, Donald, Steve's father, was thoroughly disgusted and ordered her to stop, but she couldn't. "There was something in that tar that she, that I, needed," Steve would say years later.

Her son would later joke that something in that tar spawned his craving for drugs and alcohol, or else he had inherited the addiction gene from Ruth and it got rewired somewhere along the way. Or maybe it was responsible for the gene that compelled him to write, which he was thoroughly convinced was an addiction as well.

Tabby had cut Steve an awful lot of slack through the years. She saw how he was able to continue writing through the alcohol- and coke-induced fogs, and she'd seen him when he wasn't writing: it wasn't pretty. She too worried that if he stopped drinking and drugging, he would not be able to write a word, and that he would be much more difficult to live with than now.

Like many writers with an inclination toward booze and drugs, Steve believed if he stopped snorting cocaine and drinking, his output would slow to a crawl. He felt the same way about psychotherapy: talking about his deep-seated demons would automatically dilute the ideas and terrors that seemed to fuel his stories and novels.

But even he realized that things were getting out of hand. The blackouts were becoming more frequent. Tabby had long ago gotten used to sleeping alone night after night, padding down the magnificent mahogany staircase in their twenty-four-room restored Victorian mansion each morning only to find her husband passed out in a puddle of vomit in his office. The creature lying in the middle of the floor, her husband, was starting to resemble Jordy Verrill from the movie *Creepshow,* the character Steve had played, where, little by little, a nasty green fungus enveloped his entire body, finally asphyxiating him.

Now, the same thing was happening with Steve's alcoholism—yes, Tabby could finally use the word to describe one of her husband's addictions—he was suffocating.

Aside from hangovers that lingered into the afternoon, while he put on the horrormeister face for his public and his devil-may-care face for his family, he *was* starting to worry that booze and coke were affecting his work. The bashing *The Tommyknockers* received was a tiny wake-up call.

While his addictions were interfering with his output, they were also starting to trump plain old common sense: Steve was beginning to think he was immortal. The volume of his work had actually increased through the years along with his consumption, despite the blackouts.

Tabby had finally had enough. One day she combed through Steve's office gathering up everything that wasn't being used in moderation or for its original purpose. Some of it was in plain sight: empty beer cans, and empty bottles of NyQuil and Listerine. Some of it she had to dig for, because Steve still denied he was using cocaine.

"I didn't just have a problem with beer and cocaine, I was an addictive personality, period," he admitted later. "I was smoking two packs of cigarettes a day, I loved Listerine, I loved NyQuil, you name it. If it would change your consciousness, I was all for it."

Tabby went through the bookcases and found tucked into file folders and underneath unopened office supplies the drug paraphernalia: plastic bags with the residue of white powder inside, coke spoons, everything. She loaded everything into a garbage can and, in a confrontational exercise straight out of the AA playbook, gathered up the kids and a few friends and upended the loaded can onto the floor in front of her husband.

She was no longer in denial. Tabby issued an ultimatum: he could either continue on his current path or get sober. If he chose to do himself in, his family sure as hell wasn't going to stick around to watch.

"The worst side effect of addiction is the inability to see what you're doing to yourself and to others," she said. "I made Stephen acknowledge that. Then he decided to save himself."

Steve sat there stunned as he stared at the evidence. Scattered and hidden around the house, it didn't seem like much. But now, as he stared at the detritus of twenty years' abuse, it took up more space than he thought. A *lot* more. It was time to face the truth. He knew if he didn't do something about his addiction, he'd be dead within five years, ten tops.

When Tabby told him he was basically hungover seven days a week until the middle of the afternoon for years on end, and that he started drinking for the day as soon as the clock chimed five o'clock and didn't typically stop until seven hours later, he didn't believe her. Toward the end, he was drinking and taking drugs around the clock. Over the winter and spring of 1986, he revised and edited *IT* while he was in a nonstop blackout.

So he started to think about cutting back. But that's all he was doing, thinking about it. He did dabble a bit with moderation: maybe only one six-pack a night, or two instead of three, and cutting the coke down by half, snorting up only five lines instead of ten.

"I was looking for a détente, a way I could live with booze and drugs without giving them up altogether," he said. "Needless to say I was not successful in this."

He'd pull off moderation for a few days, then he'd be right back where he'd started. The alternative—no drugs, no booze, stone-cold sober twenty-four hours a day—scared him more. He'd been drinking almost as long as he'd been writing. He didn't always write when he was drunk or stoned, but his primal belief was that alcohol made it possible for him to write, and without it he'd have to sweat out each word. If his brain was forced to stand on its own, without a crutch, he was deathly afraid that his writing ability would shrivel up and blow away.

It took a full two years of hits and misses, false starts, broken promises, and the quiet realization that he couldn't simply do it himself before he got 100 percent sober—and stayed that way. He finally realized he had to go cold turkey in 1989.

It took two weeks of absolute torture. Once he'd checked each item off his list on his journey through withdrawal—the dry heaves, nausea, constant tremors, and insomnia—Steve knew he'd made it. He'd never pick up another beer or snort another line of coke again if it meant he had to repeat the previous two stinking, miserable weeks. He felt strange and unsettled as his body and brain adjusted to his new reality.

"My coke addiction was a blessing in disguise," he said. "Without coke, I'd have gone on drinking until the age of fifty-five and I would have died of a stroke. Once you add the coke, you eventually tip over, that stuff eats you from the inside out."

His body and mind were not accustomed to sobriety.

The calm was so loud it buzzed. For someone who wasn't used to the sensation—after all, Steve had started drinking when he was barely a teenager—it was unnerving. Steve turned to the one thing that had saved him time and time again through the years, had distracted him from illness and poverty, and had ultimately made him wealthy and famous behind his wildest imagination:

He sat down to write.

In a plot twist at once so horrifying and ironic it could have come straight out of one of his own books, his greatest fear of all came true.

He couldn't. The words wouldn't come, his sentences were complete gibberish, and each letter might as well have been a hieroglyph. For years, he had imagined that if he stopped drinking and drugging, his ability to write would simply shrivel up and blow away. And it finally had. Now what?

Steve seriously considered the pros and cons of a relapse, returning to his old ways. He knew he could live without the booze and the coke. What he couldn't live without was his writing. He was prepared to sign a deal with the devil in blood, and he knew it would be worth every drop. So what if he died early? Look at the body of work he already had to leave behind.

He considered it *very* seriously.

During these early, fragile days, Tabby could read her husband's mind, and she wasn't buying any of it. She sat with him, cried with him, and kept him on a short leash until she felt the danger was past. She knew how easy it would be for him to slide back into his old ways.

They both knew if he did, she'd be out of there. That knowledge was enough to carry him through the rough spots. She helped him write one word at a time. He wrote a lot of crap trying to recapture the rhythm of writing without the input from either a high or a low. Little by little, his ability to tell a story came back.

In 1988 he started going to AA and NA meetings and found great irony—and truth—in the organization's slogan. "Nobody lives one day at a time like a drug addict," he said. "You don't think yesterday or tomorrow, you just think *now*."

About a year after Tabby's ultimatum, Steve was driving on I-95 outside Bangor. At the time, he was still playing around with the idea of moderation, whipsawing between swearing off booze and coke forever, then partaking from his hoarded stash in secret, always with an eye on the closed door to make sure Tabby didn't suddenly come barreling through it.

The section of the highway between Augusta and Bangor is a pretty tedious stretch of road, not much more than asphalt and pine trees as far as the eye can see. It was perhaps the perfect place for King to experience the epiphany that he would later credit with saving his life.

He was by himself. The day was cloudy. As was his norm most afternoons, he was thinking about getting high later in the day once he returned home. Then, out of the blue, came a voice that told him to reconsider.

You don't have to do this anymore if you don't want to was the exact phrase he heard. "It's like it wasn't my voice," he said later.

And that, as he's said in his books, was that.

When he decided to give up drugs and alcohol, he thought it would be a good idea to see a therapist, primarily because he felt that he needed to learn how to deal with the substantial void that getting sober would leave in his life. Though it did help him, he decided to tread carefully, however, because he was afraid it would affect his writing. "I'd be afraid that it would put a hole in the bottom of my bucket, and then everything might go out the wrong way," he said. "I don't know if it would exactly destroy me as a writer, but I think it would take away a lot of the good stuff."

Once he got sober, he looked at other parts of his life that needed some cleaning out. One of the victims was Kirby McCauley, King's longtime literary agent. Steve ended his long relationship with McCauley and hired Arthur B. Greene, a personal manager who would handle agenting responsibilities along with financial matters. Greene's first task was to negotiate a new contract with NAL, with Steve responsible for writing only one book a year for the next four years. Though he was writing again, King was still newly sober and didn't know what to expect every day when he woke up in the morning.

Nineteen eighty-eight was a quiet year when it came to Steve's publishing career. The first trade paperback edition of *The Gunslinger* was published in September. Then in November, *Nightmares in the Sky,* a book of gargoyle photographs by F-stop Fitzgerald, an independent photojournalist, was published, and Steve had written the commentary for the book.

His reduced output was a wise move as the hard truths about his addictions started to emerge in small doses. He finally realized what he had turned into, as well as the stress he'd put his friends and family through.

He had been addicted to cocaine for about eight years. "I was high for most of the eighties. It's not a terribly long time to be an addict, but it lasted longer than World War Two," he said. "And that's how it felt a lot of the time. I didn't hide my drinking, but I hid my drugs because right away I knew it was a problem.

"The kids accepted my drinking as a part of life. I didn't beat up on them or anything. Basically I don't think I was so different from a lot of dads who have three or four martinis when they get in from work."

"He covered well," Joe later said about his father's drug and drinking problems.

As another way to do some housecleaning in his new life, King decided to make a change with WZON, the radio station he'd owned for five years. In October, he switched WZON to a noncommercial format, similar to how public radio stations operate. Instead of generating revenue from commercials and live remote broadcasts, the station would make money from listener contributions and corporate grants, and Steve would make up the difference if necessary.

The following year, Stephanie Leonard decided to shut down *Castle Rock*, the newspaper. The quality of the publication had seriously deteriorated over the past year, mostly because Steve had stopped contributing, and all that remained were short stories by his fans and fawning reviews of his latest books. Newly sober and fragile, he needed to spend his energy and time more carefully. But more than that, he decided not to do anything he didn't want to do. His family came first, then his work.

Nineteen eighty-nine brought the publication of several limited editions that had been in the works for a while, including *My Pretty Pony* and *Dolan's Cadillac*. King's only full-length novel published that year was *The Dark Half*, which came out in November.

My Pretty Pony was published in a limited metal-bound edition of 250 copies by the Whitney Museum, which published one limited-edition book each year as a fund-raiser. When the museum contacted him, King sent along "My Pretty Pony," an unpublished, hundred-page short story about an elderly man who teaches his grandson about the quick passage of time. The book's cover was made from stainless steel and had a digital clock embedded on the front. Even at $2,200, the book sold out immediately. King then assigned the mass-market rights to the publisher Alfred A. Knopf for a printing of fifteen thousand copies with a cover price of $50.

The Dark Half was the last novel King would write before becoming totally sober, and perhaps not coincidentally, the plot revolved around the two personalities of one man. "I started to play with the idea of multiple personalities, and then I read that sometimes twins are imperfectly absorbed in the womb," he said. "I thought, 'Wait a minute. What if this guy is the ghost of a twin that never existed?' I wrapped the whole book around that spine."

With every additional day Steve spent without alcohol or cocaine, more scales fell from his eyes. Despite agreeing to license the rights to "My Pretty Pony," Steve was starting to sour on the idea of limited editions. "You just have a book I once had in my hand, and I signed my name to it. So what?" he said. "Just because I touched it with my pen? I don't completely understand it, other than it's not normal."

Though Steve had always participated in benefits and fund-raisers for a variety of causes, he decided to expand his efforts and commitments to others, not only through his foundation but by tying his creative output to local community and economic-development projects. He agreed to sell the movie rights to *Pet Sematary* only to a production company that agreed to film the story in Maine. The movie, released in April 1989, was a commercial success and brought more film crews to the state in coming years.

In the meantime, King's relative calm, and sobriety, continued. He signed up as assistant coach on his son Owen's Little League team and helped the team win the state championship in the summer of 1989. His family had grown closer since Steve had kicked drugs and alcohol, and no one was happier than Tabby and the kids.

In 1990, Steve found himself reunited once again with his original publisher, Doubleday, for the publication of *The Stand: The Complete and Uncut Edition*. He was finally going to have one of his best-loved works published in the version he had originally intended. First, he restored the hundred thousand words that had been cut from the original edition. Then he updated it by adding a new beginning and end, along with a dozen illustrations by Bernie Wrightson, a well-known fantasy artist. Steve had admired his work for years and thought Wrightson's art would enhance the expanded book.

Doubleday, of course, was still Steve's last choice for a publisher, but because they had published the original novel, they still owned the rights. In the intervening years, however, Doubleday had been purchased by Bertelsmann and merged with Bantam and Dell into BDD, so Steve was dealing with an entirely new set of faces. Many people in the company were doubtful that they could be successful with what was essentially a previously published book with some new material. They did not consider the mythology and anticipation that had built up over the years about this uncut book. In its first week of sale in May 1990, at a then hefty cover price of $24.95 and at 1,153 pages, *The Stand: The Complete and Uncut Edition* rocketed to number one on the *New York Times* bestseller list, where it stayed for many weeks.

By the time of its publication, Steve had celebrated a full year without drugs or alcohol. Some things were becoming clearer to him. For one, he felt his writing was more effective now that he was sober:

"I actually feel more creative. I went through a period where I felt a bit flat, like a cup of seltzer water where all the bubbles have departed. But now I feel like myself again, only with wrinkles."

IT was first broadcast as a four-hour miniseries on ABC-TV on November 18, 1990, and King was thrilled that what he considered his magnum opus was dramatized the same year that the full-length version of *The Stand* was published. But much as he struggled with reducing the length of his books, he frequently felt constrained by not only network censorship but also by the length of time available for a broadcast. Perhaps that's why, in recent years, he had pulled back from writing the teleplays for miniseries based on his books. "If I'd written the script for *IT,* it would have been a thirty-two-hour miniseries," he joked.

Four Past Midnight, published in September 1990, was a collection of four novellas: "The Langoliers," "Secret Window, Secret Garden," "The Library Policeman," and "The Sun Dog."

As usual, the idea for one of them came out of the blue, when Steve was doing his usual mundane tasks. One morning Steve was having breakfast with Owen, when the twelve-year-old asked to borrow his father's library card to take out a few books for a school project. When King asked why he couldn't use his own card, Owen said he was afraid.

Of course, that got Steve's attention. "What are you afraid of?" he asked. When he was six years old, one of Owen's aunts had told him that he always had to return his library books on time or else the library police would show up at the house and punish him. When Steve heard his son's story, it brought him back to his own childhood.

"When I was young, I'd always check the due date on library books, because I worried about what would happen if I brought the books back a year late," he said, adding that on several occasions he'd lost a book and gone into a total panic.

Many scholars and fans who are intimately familiar with every word that Stephen King has ever written would point at April 16, 1990, as the turning point in his metamorphosis from horror writer to one who could actually tell a pretty good story without once drawing on horror, blood and guts, or the supernatural.

That was the issue date when "Head Down," a story about his son's Little League team and Steve's experience as an assistant coach, appeared with his byline in the *New Yorker,* the elite literary weekly magazine. One can only imagine the outrage when his byline appeared.

"I think a lot of people in the literary community look at horror as a gutter genre," said Chuck Verrill, King's longtime editor. "You don't think of Philip Roth and Stephen King in the same sentence, but I think the door has been finally opened for him."

King donated the payment from the *New Yorker* to the Bangor Little League. "It was the hardest work I'd done in ten years," he said. "My method of working when I am out of my depth is brutally simple: I lower my own head and run as fast as I can, as long as I can. That is what I did here, gathering documentation like a mad pack rat and simply trying to keep up with the team. Hard or not, 'Head Down' was the opportunity of a lifetime, and before I was done, Chip McGrath of the *New Yorker* had coaxed the best nonfiction writing of my life out of me."

Jonathan Jenkins grew up in Bangor and graduated from Bangor High School in 1990. The first couple of summers after graduation, he worked for the Growing Concern, an Orono-based landscaping company contracted to mow the lawn and maintain the gardens at Stephen King's Bangor house. Jenkins compared the job to painting the Golden Gate Bridge in San Francisco. Despite that he rode a self-propelled commercial mower that cuts a swath about five feet wide, the Kings' lawn was "so big that as soon as we finished, we went back and started again," said Jenkins.

Though Jenkins had grown up in Bangor and knew what the Kings' house looked like, he wasn't initially familiar with the elaborate gardens that Tabby had designed and planted because they were mostly in the back of the house. When Jenkins heard he'd be working at the house, at first he expected to be maintaining grounds that looked as if they were straight out of *The Shining.* "I kept picturing the kid running through the maze at the end of the movie," he said.

But the grounds were more humble, with no topiary and no six-foot-high hedges. Instead, a good chunk of the area behind the house consisted of elaborate flower beds. Tabby was beginning to lose her sense of smell, so perhaps she kept adding more annuals and perennials to compensate.

Jenkins's most vivid memory of mowing Stephen King's lawn was the tourists, an endless stream of people. Some would camp out in front of the house, tightly gripping the bars of the wrought-iron fence, straining for a glimpse of Steve in one of the mansion windows. Others would drive by the house slowly, leaning out a car window with a video camera trained on the towers. "They'd head down the street, turn around, and drive by the house again," said Jenkins. "It was a constant procession all day long. Every so often a guy would stick his head out the window and yell, 'Hey, Lawnmower Man!'" Other times, people would come up to the gate with Polaroid pictures of the house and ask Jenkins if he could get Steve to sign them.

Steve occasionally wandered out into the yard with the dogs when the landscapers were working and would exchange a few words with Jenkins and the other workers, but Tabby was clearly in charge of the gardening effort. She set most of the flower beds in back of the house so she wouldn't be on display to the gawkers. "I don't ever recall her going out front," said Jenkins. "Usually if she had an issue or wanted to talk to us, it would be out back or on the side of the house."

One day Jenkins was out front mowing while a car full of teenagers was parked in the street. They kept asking him if Mr. King was home, then all of a sudden Steve pulled up in front of the automatic gate in his Suburban. Jonathan threw a glance toward him as a warning, but they followed his gaze and saw Steve just as he was driving through the gate. "They ran towards the Suburban and had just about reached it when he floored it and closed the gate behind him as fast as he could," said Jenkins.

In addition to remembering the persistent tourists camped out in front of the house, Jenkins was impressed by Steve and Tabby's generosity. One of his high school friends from Bangor was an aspiring actor who desperately wanted to go to college and earn a degree in theater, but his parents wanted him to go to medical school. "He got into a huge fight with his parents, and when word got out, Tabby told his parents she and Steve would pick up the tab for him to go to college," said Jenkins.

It was too early in the season for Jenkins to be mowing the lawn when a man named Erik Keene broke into the Kings' house on April 20, 1991, at six in the morning. Tabby was the only one home at the time, and after hearing the sound of glass breaking, she encountered Keene in the kitchen. He waved a box wrapped in brown paper at her and told her he had a bomb and was going to blow up the house because he claimed that King stole the plot for *Misery* from Keene's aunt. Tabby ran out of the house in her nightgown and headed for a neighbor's house to call the police.

With a bomb-sniffing dog in tow, the police searched the house and found Keene holed away in the attic. When they opened the box he had threatened Tabby with, they found about two dozen pencils with paper clips wound around them. Keene was arrested and prosecuted and served just over eighteen months in jail before he was extradited to Texas for a parole violation.

After the break-in, the Kings increased security at the house by extending the wrought-iron fence all the way around the yard, adding gates with access codes, and installing closed-circuit surveillance cameras. Spooked by the incident, the family lay low for most of the year.

In August 1991, *The Wastelands,* the third book of the *Dark Tower* series, was published. Eager fans got their hopes up that Steve would get back up to speed and bring the projected next four books of the series out in quick succession. Unfortunately, after *The Wastelands* appeared, readers who wanted to find out about the exploits of Roland Deschain would have to wait more than six long years until the next installment.

Steve's next novel, *Needful Things,* the first book he wrote while completely sober, was published in October 1991. "I was in a sensitive place, because it was the first thing that I'd written since I was sixteen without drinking or drugging," he said.

He intended the book to be a comedy about the Reagan years, but neither readers nor the critics seemed to get the joke. "I thought I'd written a satire of Reaganomics in America in the eighties," he said. "The idea being that this man came to a small town, opened it like a junk shop and you could buy anything that you wanted, but you ended up paying with your soul."

With its huge cast of characters, King viewed *Needful Things* in the same vein as *Salem's Lot* and *The Stand,* but in retrospect, his opinion of the book has changed: "Over the years I've come to think that maybe it just wasn't a very good book."

Stephen Edwin King was born at the appropriately gothic-looking Maine General Hospital in Portland on September 21, 1947. (George Beahm)

King inciting his fellow students as student council president to protest the Vietnam War in 1969. (*UMO Yearbook*/George Beahm)

King posed for the cover of the January 17, 1970, issue of *The Maine Campus*, which earned him a comparison by more than a few student to Charles Mason. (*The Maine Campus*/George Beahm)

After graduating from college in 1971, King worked at the New Franklin Laundry in Bangor for $1.60 an hour. The facility handled laundry from commercial establishments and businesses. (George Beahm)

Even with a full teaching load at Hampden Academy, King was found with his nose in a book – or *Mad* magazine – more often than not. (*Hampden Academy Yearbook*/George Beahm)

Though he'd be spending his writing time teaching freshman English at Hampden Academy, Steve could still ham it up with students. (*Hampden Academy Yearbooks*/George Beahm)

Note the change in expression from one year to the next. The caption says it all: King was about to become a published author. (*Hampden Academy Yearbooks*/George Beahm)

In 1978, King returned to teach at the University of Maine at Orono for a year in order to give back to the school. (*UMO Yearbooks*/George Beahm)

"I wish someone had told me how little I knew and how gruelling it was going to be," King said of his first directing experience on the 1985 film *Maximum Overdrive*. "I didn't know how little I knew about the mechanics and the politics of filmmaking." (*LTI Stock*/Corbis)

King and cat on the set of *Sleepwalkers* in 1992. King admitted his creative vision would sometimes clash with that of the director's. A plaque on his garage wall reads: "If you're not the lead dog, the view never changes." (*SNAP*/Rex Features)

Tom Hanks and Rita Wilson hold King up at the premier of *The Green Mile* in 1999. King was bound to his crutches for many months after being hit by a van in a near fatal accident. (*Gregory Pace*/Corbis)

From writer to rock star. King hits the stage in literary musical group The Rock Bottom Remainder. The band of best-selling authors that includes Amy Tan and Frank McCourt performs once a year to raise money for charity. (*Lynn Goldsmith*/Corbis)

King and son Joe Hill take in a Boston Red Sox baseball game. Although clean-shaven here, King often sports a beard between the end of the baseball World Series and the opening of spring training. (*Elise Amendola*/Press Association Images)

Needful Things was billed as the last novel King would set in Castle Rock. He knew he would still write stories about Maine, but in the wake of his drawing attention to the Pine Tree State, a new group of writers had recently written novels about Maine. Except for a few—such as *The Beans of Egypt, Maine,* written by fellow native Mainer Carolyn Chute—Steve didn't hesitate to lash out at those writers who wrote about his beloved Maine and got it all wrong. He was provincial and protective about his native state, and he believed that the Johnny-come-latelies shouldn't even be writing about Maine.

"You can write about Maine if you are from away, as long as you write a story about somebody who's from away who comes to Maine," said Steve. "But if you want to write a story about Maine and Maine people, I think you have to grow up here."

As 1991 ended, Tabby finally felt she could breathe easier. Steve was faithfully attending AA and NA meetings, the house was as secure as they could make it, even though King had made it clear he didn't "want to live like Michael Jackson or Elvis at Graceland," and he would continue to attend his beloved Red Sox games and appear at book signings.

Gerald's Game came out in May of 1992, and to call the novel a departure for Steve was the understatement of the year. Faithful readers who had no qualms about devouring King's usual stories of murder, mayhem, supernatural creatures, and occasionally blood and gore threw down the book with horror when they learned it was about a couple who played sexual-bondage games in bed.

The idea for *Gerald's Game* began when Steve thought he'd like to revisit the primary theme of *Cujo,* where one or two characters are essentially trapped within a small space. What would happen if a woman was trapped in a room by herself and couldn't get out? And why was she there?

"She's handcuffed to a bed," participating in a bondage game, was the first thought that popped into his brain. "I started to consider what causes people to do this sort of thing, so I read a little bit about it and the whole thing struck me as a bit Victorian. There was something very Snidely Whiplash about the whole thing."

Reading about sex games wasn't the only research King had to do, unusual in itself for a man who professed to hate doing research. "I remember thinking that Jessie would have been a gymnast at school and she could simply put her feet back over her head, over the headboard, and stand up." But he had his doubts. So after writing about forty pages of the book, he wanted to test the theory and he asked his son Joe to play guinea pig.

"I took him into our bedroom and tied him with scarves to the bedposts. At one point, Tabby came in and asked what I was doing, and I told her I was doing an experiment," Steve said. After trying a few different positions, Joe couldn't do it. Though he considered making Jessie double-jointed, King thought that was the easy way out, so it was back to the drawing board.

All the loyal fans who refused to buy the book because of the perceived subject matter would be surprised to hear King's take on it: "*Gerald's Game* is a book about child abuse. It's an ordinary, grim story about a little girl who is abused by her father and grows up to be a certain kind of woman. She is chained to the bed because she has been chained in a certain kind of life." Reviews were mixed: *Entertainment Weekly* called the main character Jessie Burlingame's struggle 150 of the most excruciating, exhilarating pages in recent thriller fiction, yet a few sentences later lambasted King for his "stick-on feminism." As predicted, many readers were offended by the sexual overtones of the book, pretty much a first in King's oeuvre.

Like the publication of "Head Down" in the *New Yorker* two years earlier, *Gerald's Game* was another departure for Steve. But the story made sense to him as a metaphor for his own struggles of the last few years. Not only was the novel set inside one room, but also within one woman's brain. While a day didn't go by when he didn't want to drink a case of beer or snort up countless lines of coke, Jessie taught him the grace in the "one day at a time" motto of AA. He used the experience of his own sometimes overly long days to drag out Jessie's minutes and make her story as horrific as possible to the reader.

In addition to his broadening horizons in his writing career, another surprising thing happened: once he had more than a tenuous hold on his sobriety, his marriage changed for the better. Steve and Tabby almost felt they were on a second honeymoon.

"People think that the kid stuff of love—you know, the romance, moon-June-spoon, and all the rest of it—ends with marriage, or shortly after," he said. "When romance comes again, it comes as a complete surprise. And it's much more uplifting 'cause you feel so grateful to have it return."

Tabby agreed: "Sometimes creative people get creative about their marriage and find ways to revitalize it. Change happens, and you have to let it. Ultimately, it's about contentment, partnership, and friendship. The other thing about marriage, if you get out early, you'll miss the surprises, and some of them are wonderful."

They also continued their charitable giving, primarily to Maine organizations. In 1992, they donated $750,000 for a new pediatric unit at Eastern Maine Medical Center.

Steve was still intimately involved with baseball, following the Red Sox and coaching Owen's Little League team. When Owen turned thirteen and moved on to Senior League, the difference in the quality of the fields was night and day: the field was pockmarked and uneven, and the equipment looked as if it came from a yard sale.

"I thought it was shame that kids have to adjust to substandard fields with shoddy equipment," King said. "It's not on a par with world peace or ending hunger here in Bangor, but I was taught that charity begins at home."

So with a $1.5 million contribution from the Stephen and Tabitha King

Foundation, he decided to build a regulation AA baseball field for teenagers in and around Bangor. The Shawn T. Mansfield Stadium is named in memory of fellow coach Dave Mansfield's son, who died of cerebral palsy.

The stadium, which Mansfield has dubbed "Stephen King's Field of Screams," can seat fifteen hundred, is fully lit for night games, and has a state-of-the-art public address system. The infield is made of Georgia clay, and sod was painstakingly placed by hand in the outfield and around the pitcher's mound. A full-size electronic scoreboard complete with a six-foot-high, six-hundred-pound, lit analog clock sits beyond the right-field fence.

In addition to his philanthropic efforts, Steve continued to be generous to small presses and publishers. Occasionally, he'd send a story over the transom to an editor who had no clue it was coming. In the spring of 1992, King sent the story "Chattery Teeth" to Richard Chizmar, founder of the magazine *Cemetery Dance*. Founded in 1988, *Cemetery Dance* is a horror magazine that pays homage to the old *Twilight Zone* TV show and publishes short stories, book reviews, and author interviews. King was a regular reader of the magazine, and when the story was published in the fall issue, his byline helped raise the profile of the magazine.

Not two years after Tabby's encounter with Erik Keene, another fan began haranguing King. In the summer of 1992, Stephen Lightfoot showed up in Bangor, camping out in a van covered with messages that blamed King for John Lennon's murder.

The police generally left him alone, but told him he'd be arrested if he strayed anywhere near Steve or his family. Not long after receiving the warning, Lightfoot showed up at a political rally in Portland for Representative Tom Andrews, and Steve and Tabby were in the audience.

A few of the volunteers on Andrews's campaign saw Lightfoot's van and watched as he approached some of the people in the audience. The volunteers called police, who said their hands were tied because Lightfoot hadn't broken any laws. However, Steve was not the first famous person to appear in Lightfoot's crosshairs; he was also warned to stay away from the Bush family compound in Kennebunkport, Maine, earlier that summer.

Sandy Phippen has firsthand experience with the sheer determination of King's fans. When Phippen lived in Orono, one Sunday morning he went to pick up a newspaper at a local store and ran into a couple who'd driven all the way from Oklahoma just to take a photo of Steve's house. "This happens all the time to anyone who lives near Bangor," Phippen said. Usually he just gives directions, but this time he actually drove them to Steve's house.

Based on his expertise as a book reviewer for *Down East* magazine, Phippen started to lead literary tours of Bangor for tourists. "Of course, all anyone wanted to see was Stephen King's house," he sighed. Once he had a busload of tourists from Youngstown, Ohio, who were librarians. "There have been lots of other writers from the Bangor area through the years, and poor ones too," he said. "But everyone just wanted to go to Stephen King's house, and to see the Paul Bunyan statue. Finally, because it was getting dark and they wouldn't be able to take pictures outside Steve's house, I gave in."

Shortly after *Gerald's Game* was published, Steve appeared at the annual convention of the American Booksellers Association (ABA) in Anaheim, California, the largest publishing trade show in the United States. This year, however, in addition to talking with booksellers and reporters, he'd be doing something a bit different: he'd be playing his old electric guitar in a band made up solely of other bestselling authors at a charity gig.

He took the stage as rhythm guitarist in a band called the Rock Bottom Remainders, where his bandmates included Amy Tan, Dave Barry, and Barbara Kingsolver, among others. They planned two performances during the convention—one on the convention floor, another in a local club. Their motto didn't mince any words: "They play music as well as Metallica writes novels."

The band was the brainchild of Kathi Kamen Goldmark, a San Francisco–based media escort who ferried authors from one interview to another when they came to town to plug their books. The conversations during the long days would often wander, and Goldmark would mention that she also sang in several small country bands.

She said the reaction from authors was universal: they all wished they could play in a band; perhaps they'd played in high school but had let their musical aspirations lapse over the years.

"I just kept hearing the same story, and we were all around the age of forty and thinking about the things we didn't get to do," she said, before the epiphany hit. Why not? Somehow she talked about a dozen authors into starting a band. In addition to Tan, Barry, and Kingsolver, other members included Ridley Pearson and Robert Fulghum. A friend who knew that King played guitar told Goldmark and suggested she invite him to be in the band. He accepted immediately.

She asked the members to fax lists of songs they'd like to play, keeping in mind that none of the authors knew anyone else, and what they all had in common was that they were amateurs. "Easy three-chord rock and roll was the only thing I had in mind," she said.

Once word got out that Steve was playing in the band, everything changed. Tickets to the two scheduled concerts began to sell briskly, and booksellers called to see if Goldmark could arrange a private dinner with King, among other requests.

The first order of business was to find out just how bad they were. Goldmark and musical director Al Kooper, a songwriter and producer who helped to form the band Blood, Sweat, and Tears and also played the organ on Bob Dylan's classic "Like a Rolling Stone," booked a few days in a practice studio near the convention hall.

"I walked into a band rehearsal room in Anaheim, California, in 1992 and there were a bunch of people playing instruments loudly and badly," said Dave Barry, prize-winning humorist and columnist at the *Miami Herald*. "In the middle, thrashing away on his guitar, was Stephen King. I picked up my guitar and started thrashing away, adding to the bad music set."

During the phase when Goldmark had the musicians faxing song lists back and forth, Barry thought that maybe he was getting in over his head: "Some of these people sounded like they actually knew what they were doing, with chord charts and the like flying through the air." Though he'd played in a band during college, he knew he wasn't that good. Once the rehearsal began, however, Barry relaxed: "I was relieved when I got there and saw how bad we all were."

Ridley Pearson, whose books included *Blood of the Albatross* and *Undercurrents,* also showed up that first day feeling a bit intimidated, not as much for his musical skills, but because Steve was in the band. "I was a big fan of his," he said. "I read his books early on."

When they finally met, Pearson was disarmed by King's demeanor. "He turned out to be this teenagery, goofy tall guy who is not entirely comfortable with himself, but incredibly smart and very funny," said Pearson. "Somehow I expected this guy dressed all in black. But he's this blue jeans and T-shirt dude who has never grown past the age of fifteen, which is true of all the Remainders, which is why we all get along."

Once they got past the first couple of awkward rehearsals and started to hang out, Goldmark noticed the breadth of Steve's knowledge of popular culture. "He knows about everything," she said. "You can't mention a song or artist or a book that he's not familiar with. Name a song and he'll quote the lyrics. It doesn't matter if it was a recent hit or something from thirty years ago, he'll know it."

Tabby also came on board for the rehearsals and performances. To Goldmark's relief, she fit right in. "She's very unpretentious and no-nonsense and very funny," said Goldmark, who booked a tour bus to take the band the ten blocks from the hotel to the gig and back. "She went out and bought a bunch of extralarge boxer shorts and got a bunch of people to throw them at the stage during the performance. As fun as the gig was, I think the bus was more fun."

During the performances, Goldmark thought that Steve looked like a little kid at Christmas, and he acted like one too. Though King focused mostly on playing along on rhythm guitar, he did sing a few songs, including "Last Kiss" and "Teen Angel."

"Steve would get going and kind of spontaneously mutate the lyrics," said Dave Barry. "One night, on 'Last Kiss,' he sang, 'When I awoke, she was lying there and I brushed her liver from my hair.'" The other band members cracked up and had to stop playing for several minutes.

No one—Kathi Goldmark or the authors in the band—expected the reaction to the Remainders to be so big, or to continue beyond the two shows. But it turned into a huge story not only with the national media, with the morning television stations frantically jockeying to get first dibs on the story, but also with the publishing industry all abuzz. After the final encore for the second performance, the band filed offstage, their heads still ringing with the thrill of playing for hundreds of screaming fans.

As Ridley walked behind Steve, suddenly Steve looked at him over his shoulder and said, "Ridley, we're not done here."

Within days, plans were being solidified for future performances as well as a road tour in 1993, which needed to be financed, so Steve proposed the idea of a book to his publisher, Viking, which they instantly agreed to. The working title was *Mid-Life Confidential: The Rock Bottom Remainders Tour America with Three Chords and an Attitude.* Everyone in the band would contribute, Tabby would take photos, and Dave Marsh, a music critic who had written biographies of Bruce Springsteen, Elvis Presley, and the Who, would edit the book.

The Rock Bottom Remainders would play again.

After *Gerald's Game* caught many Stephen King fans off guard, he continued to surprise them when *Dolores Claiborne* was published, the story of a woman who has led a long, hardscrabble life. When the story opens, she has been accused of murder, and not for the first time. Steve said he patterned Dolores's life after his own mother's, and that many of the stories in the book were those he had heard from Ruth when he was growing up.

To longtime fans who asked what happened to the horror, he assured them it would return, and soon. "Don't say that I'm stretching my range or that I've left horror behind," he said. "I'm just trying to find things I haven't done to stay alive creatively."

For a while, he actually considered combining *Dolores Claiborne* and *Gerald's Game* into one novel, since both involved the abuse of a woman. But after working on a few different angles, he decided to keep them separate. Since he was already working on *Gerald's Game* when the idea for *Dolores Claiborne* came along, he opted to finish *Gerald's Game* first.

In addition to branching out with the kinds of stories he told, he was also changing in at least one other way with his writing.

"The worst advice I've ever received is 'Don't listen to the critics.' I think that you should, because sometimes they're telling you something is broken that you can fix," he said. "If you stick your head in the sand, you won't have to hear any bad news and you won't have to change what you're doing. But if you listen, sometimes you can get rid of a bad habit. Hey, none of us like critics, but if they're all saying something's a piece of shit, they're right."

For most of his novels, and quite a few of his short stories, movie studios and production companies snapped up the film rights even before the books saw print. *Dolores Claiborne* was no exception, but he was starting to lose patience with film projects that were not true to the original story.

The simple reason why films such as *Children of the Corn II* got made in the first place was because of a contract loophole where, in addition to buying the rights to the story, the producers also obtained the rights to the title. So while the first movie out of the gate was typically faithful to King's stories and novels, subsequent movies weren't. But Steve had no way of stopping them.

"They suck!" he said. "*Carrie 2*? What's the point? There are thousands of good scripts and screenwriters out there, but their work is going begging because these people are so intellectually bankrupt that they have to do *Carrie 2* or *Children of the Corn VI*."

Sometimes They Come Back spawned *Sometimes They Come Back . . . Again,* followed by *Sometimes They Come Back . . . for More.* Steve predicted that the fourth and fifth in the series could be called *Sometimes They Come Back . . . for Dinner* and *Sometimes They Come Back . . . for Low, Low Prices.*

"They're like walking around with a piece of toilet paper on your shoe," he said. "People tell me they thought it was really a kind of a piece of junk. And I didn't even know it got made."

In most cases there wasn't anything he could do about it. He did prevail in one instance, when New Line Cinema released *Stephen King's Lawnmower Man,* which starred Pierce Brosnan. The producers also had a script titled *Cyber God,* and they killed two birds with one stone by incorporating a few elements from King's story into *Cyber God,* but ran it under the title *Stephen King's Lawnmower Man.*

Steve was so incensed at how they'd abused his name and his story that he sued New Line to have his name and the title of the story removed from the film and promotional materials. Two separate courts found in his favor, but New Line refused to change the film's title, and the first editions of the video still had Stephen King's name in the title. Only after the company was ordered to pay him $10,000 a day and full profits did they remove his name from the movie.

While *Lawnmower Man* was an extreme example, he was sanguine about why so many of the movies based on his books or short stories turned out to be bombs: he referred to it as the Hotel Towel Problem. "You steal all the towels in the hotel room and try to get them into a single suitcase," he said. "You sit on it and move the towels around, and it still won't shut because there's too much material." A parallel issue involved film producers. "They're like the sharks you see in horror movies. They're nothing but eating machines that buy and option books, and then the projects just sit on their desks while they wonder what the fuck to do with them."

While some might suggest that he could perhaps help reduce the number of bad movies produced by not selling any more film rights, he refused: "I can't get frozen on either side by saying that I can't take on one more project, or what if I say these people can't do this and they would have made a fantastic film?" For example, several people told him he was making a huge mistake to give Frank Darabont the option for his novella *Rita Hayworth and Shawshank Redemption,* let alone sell it for only a thousand bucks. Darabont had previously written several episodes for the TV series *Tales from the Crypt* and *The Young Indiana Jones Chronicles,* and his directorial debut was *The Woman in the Room,* a Dollar Baby short film that he'd made from one of King's short stories. "I think that you have to take some risks, and you can't do everything yourself because there's just not enough life or enough time."

One reason Steve decided he could throw the dice was because he had worked out a sweet deal with the production company Castle Rock Entertainment, a company that actor Rob Reiner and several Hollywood executives had founded in 1987 that dates back to *Stand by Me.* "They can have my work for a buck, and what I want in exchange is script approval, director approval, cast approval, and I want to have the authority to push the stop button at any point regardless of how much money has been invested," Steve said.

"What I get on the back end is five percent from dollar one, every dollar spent at the box office, I get five cents. *Needful Things* grossed twenty million domestically and I made half a million. With *The Green Mile,* I made twenty-five million."

Steve had also learned to put his foot down when it came to another visual medium as well: photographs of him. "If I see the red gels and the underlighting come out when someone is photographing me, I walk out," he said. "All that shit to make me look spooky. I ask them when they're photographing a black writer if they bring a watermelon and a barrel for him to sit on."

He wasn't soured on all moviemakers; there was still one director he wanted to work with, though it looked as if the planets would have to align first.

"Steven Spielberg and I have tried to work together three times, first on *The Talisman,* then on *Poltergeist,* and then on an original idea," King said, but things never worked out. "It's a case of two strong creative personalities, and Spielberg is fiercely creative, and unless you're very, very quick, he's always two steps ahead of you." Steve admitted that in terms of his own creativity, he's become accustomed to getting his own way. He cited a plaque that hangs in his garage that reads, *If you're not the lead dog, the view never changes.* "That was basically the problem with us, who was going to be the lead dog."

For Steve and Tabby, exactly twenty years after they'd first received word that their lives had changed with the sale of *Carrie,* life was running smoothly and the family was calm.

Tabby's fifth novel, *One on One,* was published in the spring of 1993. The book was the fourth in her Nodd's Ridge series and was billed as a modern-day *Catcher in the Rye.* As she saw her husband switch gears and begin to experiment with different genres, Tabby became inspired in her own work.

"The biggest influence he's had on my writing is that he taught me not to set limits on myself, that I was the only one who could decide what the limits were," she said. "He's also taught me the legitimacy of ordinary things in fiction."

She had returned to a regular schedule of writing, though it in no way resembled her husband's output: "I live with somebody who writes a lot faster than me, so I tend to think I'm a very slow writer." Steve carried on as usual: *Nightmares and Dreamscapes,* a collection of mostly previously published short stories, including "Head Down" and "Dolan's Cadillac," was published in October 1993. The story "The Fifth Quarter" also appears in the book, which is the only published story King wrote under the pseudonym John Swithen, when the piece originally appeared in the April 1972 issue of *Cavalier.*

In the spring of 1993, Steve and the other members of the Rock Bottom Remainders went on a ten-day tour of eight East Coast cities from Providence to Miami. Tabby came along as photographer for the book that they'd collaboratively write about the experience: *Mid-Life Confidential.* After a few days of rehearsal in Boston, the band set out on the road in Aretha Franklin's old tour bus with a playlist that included Dave Barry singing "Gloria," Amy Tan doing lead vocals on "Leader of the Pack" and "These Boots Are Made for Walkin'," and Steve singing "Teen Angel" and "Stand by Me."

Though they had gotten a taste of it the previous year during the two-night Remainders stand in Anaheim, one of the first things the other author/musicians noticed was how much different Steve's life was from their own.

"No matter where you are, no matter what time of day, we were stopped, mauled, and interfered with because Stephen King just happened to be traveling with us," said Pearson. "The guy does not have a private moment in his existence, but he does a beautiful job of dealing with it."

Barry concurred: "He's amazingly polite considering that there are times when people can be very intrusive. I've heard him explain to people that he can't give them an autograph because he wasn't working that day, and if he signs one, he'll end up signing four hundred. Some people get it and some people don't. Sometimes you see them get mad like he owes them."

Sometimes the fans employed the other Remainders to get King's autograph. After performing at a Philadelphia club called Katmandu, everyone hustled onto the bus for the long ride to Atlanta for the next concert. Barry was the last one on the bus, getting there just in time to see a huge crowd of people hanging around the bus all clutching Stephen King books. Steve was already on the bus, and people immediately corralled Barry and begged him to bring Steve out to sign their books.

"So I gave a little speech, telling them that they just got to see him play for two hours, he's exhausted, we're all exhausted, and we had a long bus ride ahead, so thanks for coming, but just let him be now," Barry said. "They were all watching me and nodding at everything I was saying, and as soon as I finished, they started up again, asking me to drag him out of the bus. They didn't hear a single word I said. And nobody asked for my autograph, either. Al Kooper said if the bus crashed, the headlines would read, 'Stephen King and 23 Others Dead.'"

Later that night, a few hours out of Philadelphia, the bus stopped at a rest area. "We all pile out to go take a pee at this truck stop at four in the morning, and when we came out maybe fifteen minutes later, there were four people standing out in front of our bus holding copies of *The Stand*," said Pearson. "Which meant that the gas jockeys had called their friends, woke them up, they got dressed, grabbed their copies of *The Stand*, drove to the truck stop, and were standing there in ten minutes to get Stephen's autograph at four in the morning."

The behavior of some fans inside the clubs and concert venues was no less bizarre. At one performance, a man who thought he was going to hear an actual band lit a cigarette just before he stomped out in disgust. "Somebody next to him was just drunk enough to think, 'Oh, yeah,' and lit his lighter next, and pretty soon we had that old Bob Dylan moment going," said Pearson. "A thousand people swung back and forth with their lighters for our ridiculous band."

Five minutes later, Pearson glanced into the audience. "There in front of Steve is this perfectly attractive forty-five-year-old woman, her mouth open in total adoration, holding both hands up just like as if welcoming him to hug her," said Pearson. "And all ten of her obviously plastic fingernails were on fire.

"I shouted over to Dave, 'I never want to be that famous.'"

Goldmark would be the first to admit that the band would not have been the same without King, and not just because of the crazed pyromaniacs. "He made it bigger," she said. "He made it different, and he gained the band a lot of notoriety and interested a lot of people."

But despite his obvious visibility onstage, Steve saw the band as a kind of refuge. "His life is just really different from anybody else's, but he makes a real effort to be a regular guy, to roll with it, to take the regular seat on the airplane instead of getting the upgrade," said Goldmark. "I felt that was really important to him. He hung with the group and I was really impressed by that."

The few times that Steve and Tabby had to leave the tour on other business, even for a few hours, they regretted it. Once they reached Miami for the ABA Convention, she and Steve stayed at a different hotel from where the band was based. "In retrospect, it was a mistake," she said. "Once we were at the American Booksellers Convention, Steve wasn't part of the band anymore, instead he was Stephen King Public Figure, bug in amber. From the silly bitch who threw herself into the limo to announce that she was in love with his mind to eating in a restaurant so full of publishers it might as well have been in New York, the tour felt like it never happened."

As band photographer, Tabby found the tour to be a welcome respite from their public lives as well. "After the first day, we all forgot that she was taking pictures," said Goldmark. "We already knew her from the first year, and it made much more sense to have her as the photographer than having some strange person with a camera come on board. The whole thing was just so much fun, like a weird, wonderful little summer camp."

When the tour ended in Miami, everyone agreed that they would perform at least once a year at ABA.

Insomnia came out in April 1994. The story is about a widower who starts suffering from a severe lack of sleep. Soon, his sleep deprivation becomes so bad that he believes he's hallucinating—at first, that is. The truth slowly sinks in, and soon the main character, Ralph Roberts, is in battle with a slew of supernatural demons intent on taking the town of Derry and its inhabitants by force. At 832 pages, compared with the comparatively anemic length of *Gerald's Game* at 331 pages and *Dolores Claiborne* at 305, it appeared that King was back in his old stomping grounds.

Though *Insomnia* fell within the same category as Steve's usual horror books, he was still reaching out into new areas. With the publication of *Insomnia,* some critics automatically categorized *Gerald's Game* and *Dolores Claiborne* as experimental works in King's lifelong opus, and his latest book only proved that he was still entrenched in the horror niche and would remain there until his last book was published. King dismissed this theory out of hand: "I'm sure that I could make a very nice living just being Stephen King for the rest of my life. But if it came down to just doing that, I'd rather not write at all."

King has suffered bouts of insomnia on and off through the years. His "What if?" moment for the book came during a particularly bad stretch of sleepless nights, and writing the book only exacerbated his condition: "While I was writing it, I hardly slept at all."

But the book almost didn't see the light of day. After he'd spent four months writing and had about 550 pages of the manuscript, he suddenly decided it wasn't publishable.

Steve had long held the theory that in writing, all he's doing is unearthing stories that already exist, extracting them from the earth as intact as possible. "I really think that the stories are found articles and the story basically tells itself," he said. "When I'm working on something, I see a completed book. In some fashion, that thing is already there. I'm not really making it so much as I am digging it up, the way that you would an artifact, out of the sand. The trick is to get the whole thing out so it's usable, without breaking it. You always break it somewhat—I mean, you never get a complete thing—but if you're really careful and lucky, you can get most of it."

He believes this so deeply that he bristles whenever someone suggests that he has created his stories and characters out of thin air. "Actually, when I feel that I'm creating, I feel that I'm doing bad work," he said. "I don't feel like a novelist or a creative writer as much as I feel like an archaeologist who is digging things up and being very careful and brushing them off and looking at the carvings on them."

In that way, *Insomnia* felt as if he had created it. And he was not happy. "Taken piece by piece and chapter by chapter, it's good," he said. "But I didn't get this one out of the ground. It broke. And I sometimes go back and think I can fix it, but then I remember that I can't, because of something in the story."

He put the manuscript away for a while, and one day about a year later he picked it up and finished it in a white-hot heat. When the book was published, he did a cross-country promotional book tour on his Harley-Davidson Heritage Softail, stopping only in independent bookstores to do signings along the way. *Insomnia* spent fourteen weeks on *Publishers Weekly*'s bestseller list and *Booklist* deemed it marvelous.

Despite his success of almost twenty years and publishing dozens of books, Steve still faced blocks of his own making: "For me, a lot of times the real barrier to get to work—to get to the typewriter or the word processor—comes before I get there." He often has days when he is unsure whether he can write that day, this coming from a man who is obsessive about his writing and who has spoken of retiring countless times. "I have a lot of days like that. I think it's kind of funny really, that people think that just because I'm Stephen King, it doesn't happen to me." Usually his hesitation comes when he knows he has to write a difficult scene, but like many other writers, once he sits down at the desk and puts his fingers on the keyboard, he falls right back into the story.

On May 8, 1994, *The Stand* debuted as a four-part miniseries on ABC.

"*The Stand* is the most important project, in terms of film, that I've ever done," he said. "It was a huge effort and more work than any two or three novels I've ever done in my life."

When Steve set out to write the screenplay for the book, he had originally intended it to be a movie for theatrical release. Try as he might, he couldn't condense the story enough, and he and director George Romero thought about turning it into two separate films before farming it out to another writer, but then ABC approached Steve about turning it into a miniseries.

Once the script was finalized—the length of the miniseries was pegged at over six hours—Steve broke with his usual hands-off approach when selling movie rights to his books and was on the set of *The Stand* for most of the 125 days of shooting, serving as coexecutive producer. There was no way he'd miss it; after all, it was his baby.

"I was mostly making sure that they were doing what they were supposed to do," he said, but he occasionally caught a mistake that few other people would have picked up on. When Ray Walston, Gary Sinise, and Corin Nemec were on Walston's porch, Nemec, who played Harold, wanted to go to Stovington, but Sinise, in the role of Stu Redman, said there was no need, since the people there were all dead.

Nemec's line in the script was "Let's just say I'm Missouri." After three takes, King interrupted the actors to ask Nemec to repeat the line. Nemec pointed to the script where it read, "I'm Missouri," which turned out to be a printing error.

"You're supposed to say, 'Let's just say I'm *from* Missouri,' meaning 'Show me,'" King said. "This was not a case of an actor being stupid, this was the case of an actor with so much reverence for the script, apparently, he didn't want to change a word."

Little noticed on the set was Steve's son Joe, who joined the crew as a production assistant during a semester off from college. And Steve decided to take a cameo role in the miniseries to play the part of Teddy Weizak, who gives Nadine a ride and also serves as a border guard.

"I actually have a part this time that isn't a total country asshole," he said. "Starting with *Creepshow,* I got sort of typecast. I've played a lot of hick morons in my career."

The Shawshank Redemption followed in theaters that fall, and the movie received raves from critics, even those who had previously automatically panned a movie or book simply because King's name was attached.

In fact, *Shawshank* stood out simply because many moviegoers had no clue that Steve wrote the story that the film was based on. It was no secret that many of his previous movies had turned out to be clunkers. But people who couldn't be bribed to walk into a movie theater to watch a Stephen King movie—or to read one of his books—loved the film and dragged their friends along to see it.

Case in point: One day Steve was in a grocery store in Sarasota when a woman approached him to tell him she was happy to meet him, but that she didn't read his books or watch his movies because she didn't like horror. He asked her what she did like, and she rattled off a list of movies including *Shawshank Redemption.*

"I wrote that," he said.

"No, you didn't," she said.

"Yes, I did."

"No, you didn't."

Steve excused himself to pay for his groceries.

Somewhat less publicized in the mass media, but much discussed among New York literary insiders, was the appearance of a short story with a Stephen King byline in the *New Yorker.* "The Man in the Black Suit," published in the October 31, 1994, issue, was King's second appearance in the magazine. Was a new, more literary game afoot for King? Or were the definitions of high and low literature being blurred?

Steve had shown Chuck Verrill, his longtime editor, his stories from time to time for consideration for future short-story collections. Verrill thought that a couple of his nonsupernatural stories might be a good fit for the *New Yorker.* Verrill sent them along to Chip McGrath, then the fiction editor at the magazine, who said he'd rather have one of King's typical stories. Verrill sent along "The Man in the Black Suit," and the magazine published it in the Halloween issue. Steve's reaction was mixed: "I don't want to bite the hand that feeds me, and I'm grateful for the exposure, but it's still a little bit like being a prostitute and being put at the head of a float on National Whore's Day."

Yet, the stories he wrote that strayed outside his well-worn horror path were much harder for him to write. "It's like having to learn to think all over again," he said. "At this point, writing on a nonsupernatural level is like learning to talk after you've had a stroke."

THE GOLDEN YEARS

Nineteen ninety-five was characterized by the fast and furious release of movies based on King's novels and stories. Both *The Mangler* and *Dolores Claiborne* came out on the big screen in March, while *The Langoliers* appeared as a made-for-TV movie two months later. *Rose Madder*, Steve's only novel to be published that year, followed in July. It's the story of an abused woman who escapes her violent husband to look for a new life and, through a mysterious painting she got by pawning her engagement ring, discovers her power. Obviously, a critic at *Entertainment Weekly* did not go along with King's new direction and panned the book, grading it C-minus, asking, "When did Stephen King stop being scary?"

The year unfolded with reprints of previously published novels, audiobooks, and short fiction and nonfiction appearing in a variety of magazines and journals. Perhaps the biggest surprise was when Steve's *New Yorker* story "The Man in the Black Suit" won first prize in the O. Henry Awards. It would be published in the accompanying anthology, *Prize Stories 1996: The O. Henry Awards*. Yes, it was *that* Stephen King. He hypothesized that the only reason he won was because the stories were submitted without the authors' names. "There's an immediate attitude that anyone who's reaching a large, popular audience, what they're doing is crap," he said. "You've got these two places: high literature and popular fiction. In between is this great big river of misunderstanding. There are a lot of people who are dedicated to keeping the clubhouse white."

While he was pleasantly surprised and gracious at his win, even he doubted the award. "It made me feel like an impostor, like someone made a mistake."

In the meantime, Steve and Tabby's kids were beginning to make inroads into their own writing lives. In the academic year 1994–95, Joe was a senior at Vassar College when Owen entered as a freshman. Joe spent most of his free time writing short stories and novels and had already started to submit work to literary magazines and fellowships. His first published story, "The Lady Rests," would appear in an obscure publication called *Palace Corbie 7* two years after he graduated under the byline of Joe Hill, and he would go on to win awards and accolades including a Bradbury Fellowship and the World Fantasy Award for Best Novella.

For Joe, the influence from his early days growing up as the son of an internationally famous novelist ran deep. "When we were growing up, what we talked about around the dinner table was books and writers," he said. "It seemed perfectly natural to me to spend your days going into an office and making stuff up. It was as normal as if I came from a family that had a pizza shack and mom and dad went in to throw the pizza dough every day."

His brother, Owen, was also developing his writing chops. Though he dreamed of a career playing pro baseball, his real talents lay elsewhere, and he first set his sights on a writing career while in high school. "I never had much ability besides manual labor and writing, so I figured I'd give writing a shot first," he said. "This is the family business, what I grew up around, so I don't think they were all that surprised."

While Owen readily admits that he comes from a privileged background, he said that his upbringing has kept him grounded: "I love Bangor, it will always be my home. Growing up there and going to public school is something I treasure. I was not sheltered from real people. I grew up with parents that are celebrities and very wealthy, and yet they were treated as part of the community."

As for Naomi, after attending a few colleges, from the University of Southern Maine in Portland, Maine, to Reed College in Portland, Oregon, she opened a restaurant in July 1994 at 94 Free Street in Portland, Maine. Her partner in the twenty-two-table bistro was Patty Wood, and they christened the restaurant Tabitha Jean's, a combination of their mothers' first names. Wood, an experienced chef, was in charge of the kitchen while Naomi ran the dining room. They described the menu as eclectic American cuisine, specializing in grilled entrées, seafood, and vegetarian dishes with an extensive wine list of 150 different vintages. Their primary market was the gay and lesbian community, though Naomi was quick to say the restaurant also attracted a significant number of straight patrons as well.

Naomi's upbringing was evident in that she guaranteed that celebrities could dine in total anonymity at her establishment. In this, she shared her mother's disdain for the unwanted attention their father attracted wherever he went. The official policy was that staff would plead total ignorance when queried by the media about the famous people who frequented the restaurant.

"The different celebrities I've known want to go to places where they can be anonymous, and where the waitstaff will shield them from autograph seekers," she asserted, citing her own experience in instituting the guidelines, though Portland has never been known as a hotbed of celebrity activity. "I have no ability to be a private citizen just like everybody else," she said, adding if she'd had her choice, she would have opted for a nonfamous father. "I think that if anybody went through it, they'd prefer to have their privacy."

Like her daughter, Tabby felt the need to expand her horizons beyond Bangor. She was working on *Survivor,* her seventh novel, and for the first time in sixteen years that she had written about a place other than Nodd's Ridge, a Maine college town by the name of Peltry. "I've thought that I needed to take a vacation from Nodd's Ridge for a long time," she said. "There are some unsettled matters that need to be dealt with there, but for the moment, Peltry is where I have to get some urgent work done."

The idea for the novel came when she was visiting Owen and Joe at Vassar College. She was driving on campus, and out of the blue a student walked in front of her car. She stopped in time, but after the shock wore off, her mind hung on to the image, and before she knew it she was hard at work on a new book. Her views about marriage emerge loud and clear in the story, about a woman named Kissy Mellors who avoids hitting two female college students with her car only to witness a drunk driver behind her plow over them instead, killing one. The novel explores the aftermath in Kissy's life and in those of others who knew the girls.

Like her husband, she tends to overwrite first drafts. "I rarely write a manuscript under a thousand pages, and then we cut and cut and cut. I like big fat novels. I think readers do too. It's only publishers who sort of groan and start worrying about production costs. I think it's too bad that there's such an emphasis on stripped-down stories, because people's lives aren't."

Also like Steve, she writes for three or four hours a day, though her work style is different. "Steve will rewrite the entire book, but I do it a page at a time as I go along, and subsequently my rewrites after the completion of my first draft are usually pretty minor tweaks."

When her editor asked her to change the ending of *Survivor,* she disagreed, saying that her ending was more in keeping with what would happen in real life. Stephen got involved and sided with the editor—of course he would, he prefers happy endings—and Tabby changed the ending.

Survivor would be published in March of 1997.

In 1996, Steve began work on his first nonfiction book in eighteen years, since *Danse Macabre*. He thought that the proposed book, *On Writing*, would mean he would no longer have to answer the same old questions his fans still asked more than twenty years after *Carrie* was published. The number one offender, "Where do you get your ideas?" still elicited a groan. Partway into the project, however, he became distracted by an idea for a novel and put *On Writing* aside. When he returned to it a few years later, it would turn out to be a very different book from the one he had originally envisioned.

The midnineties were a golden time for King and his family. His kids were forging lives of their own, Steve had been sober for almost a decade, and his writing was hitting the sweet spot, pleasing his fans and surprisingly winning over critics who had previously regarded his work with undisguised contempt. He decided now to experiment with the literary roots of his youth: serial fiction. Between March and August of 1996, his six-part series, *The Green Mile*, was published, one installment each month, all in paperback by Signet. Predictably, each book hit the bestseller charts.

In a way, it was a deliberate response to fans who flipped ahead in his books to see how they ended, as well as an homage to his mother. As a boy, Steve had watched as Ruth would occasionally turn to the last page of a book to discover how the story ended. With a serialized novel, the ending wouldn't be published for another six months. At the same time, the project was also a direct challenge to himself.

"I wrote like a madman, trying to keep up with the crazy publishing schedule and at the same time trying to craft the book so that each part would have its own mini-climax, hoping that everything would fit, and knowing I would be hung if it didn't," he said. "There was less margin for screwing up, it had to be right the first time. I want to stay dangerous, and that means taking risks."

What made the situation even more tenuous was that he had no idea how the story would end, as he was still writing the last volume even when the first two books in the series had been published. He added another aspect to his high-wire act when the 1997 publication of the fourth *Dark Tower* book was announced in the back of the third book of *The Green Mile*. His fans were on alert.

When the final *Green Mile* book was published in August of 1996, all six of the books in the series appeared on the *New York Times* bestseller list at the same time, creating an outcry at the newspaper. From then on a book would only appear in one slot on the list regardless of how many different volumes were in the series.

King continued his interest in serialized fiction the month after the last *Green Mile* book came out, albeit with a twist. Two more novels would follow in the fall: *The Regulators,* a Richard Bachman book, came in at just under 500 pages, while the 704-page *Desperation* was published under his own name. He billed the two as companion novels and insisted they both come out on the same day: October 1, 1996. With *The Green Mile* books still selling well, King had an astonishing eight different books on some bestseller lists at the same time, which would be a difficult record for him, or anyone else, to beat. On a few bestseller lists where the mass-market edition of *Rose Madder* hit the paperback list, he held nine separate slots.

King described his two new novels as the equivalent of fun-house reflections of the other: "The same characters populate each book, but they have been shaken up, turned inside out, and stood on their heads. Think of the same troupe of actors performing *King Lear* one night and *Bus Stop* the next."

The idea for *Desperation* came on a cross-country trip when Steve was driving Naomi's car from Oregon to Maine. In Ruth, Nevada, a small town that looked totally uninhabited, the only sign of life was a burly policeman walking toward his car parked on the street. Suddenly, a thought popped into King's head: "Oh, I know where everybody is, that cop killed them all." He then wrote a story set in a town named Desolation in the Nevada desert with a population of one: Sheriff Collie Entragian, who has a special purpose in rounding up motorists unlucky enough to pass through the town.

The Regulators had a longer gestation time. In the early eighties, Steve had been working on a screenplay called *The Shotgunners*. In 1984, Kirby McCauley set up a meeting between Steve and Sam Peckinpah, a movie director whose films included *The Wild Bunch, The Getaway,* and *Convoy*. Peckinpah was sniffing around for an idea for a new picture to direct, and Steve had *The Shotgunners*.

Peckinpah liked what he saw and gave Steve some ideas for revamping it, since it was still essentially a first-draft screenplay, but Sam died of a stroke in December 1984 before anything was hammered out. Steve put the screenplay away until he started work on *Desperation*, when he thought some of the ideas from both stories could work well in tandem in a companion book.

Some readers were offended by the outright mention of God in *Desperation,* particularly through the character of David Carver, a young boy whose fervent belief and faith helped him to lead the others.

"The idea of using God as a character in *Desperation* was the engine that made the book go," Steve said. "While I don't see myself as God's stenographer, He's always been in my books. It depends on the people I'm writing about." In a way, Steve just decided to take a break from the evil that's inherent in most of his books. "So I thought, what if I treat God and the accoutrements of God with as much belief, awe, and detail as I have treated evil. Some people say the God stuff really turns them off, but these guys have had no problems with vampires, demons, golems, and werewolves in the past."

He still retained his basic religious beliefs from childhood: "I've always believed in God. I also think that the capacity to believe is the sort of thing that either comes as part of your equipment, or at some point in your life when you're in a position where you actually need help from a power greater than yourself, you simply make an agreement to believe in God because it will make your life easier and richer to believe than not to believe. So I choose to believe."

Due to the demands and challenges of publishing two books on the same day with a combined print run of over 3 million copies, Viking begged King to publish the two books separately, but Steve insisted they appear simultaneously. In the end, Viking published *Desperation,* while Dutton, another imprint under the Penguin umbrella, published *The Regulators.* To further complicate matters, Dutton was in charge of bringing out the limited edition of *The Regulators* while publisher Donald M. Grant would publish the limited edition of *Desperation.* Neither publisher felt it could handle bringing out two limited editions at the same time.

A problem arose in the middle of producing the limited edition for *The Regulators.* When the time came for Steve to sign the pages for the book, he balked, as production manager Peter Schneider recalled. "How can I sign these books?" Steve asked. "*The Regulators* was written by Richard Bachman, and as you know, Bachman's dead. I said you could do a limited edition—I never said anything about signing them."

Schneider contacted Joe Stefko, the freelance designer in charge of the limited edition, who recalled that another small press had run into the same problem with a limited edition by Philip K. Dick, who had died a few years earlier. "They purchased canceled checks from Dick's widow, cut out the signature, and used them as the signature," said Schneider. In the continuing story line of the fictional Richard Bachman, his widow had discovered a few unpublished manuscripts after her husband's death. "What if she also found a number of canceled checks?" Schneider mused.

In the end, each of the numbered-and-lettered limited-edition copies of *The Regulators* had a canceled check signed by Richard Bachman—in Stephen King's hand—included on the first page. The fun part was that each check not only had a different number, from 1 to 1,000, but that each was made out to a character or business mentioned in a past King novel, or a prominent establishment from King's own past, with a pertinent note in the memo line. For instance, check number 306 was made out to Annie Wilkes for $12; the memo read "axe and blowtorch." Number 377 was made out to *Cavalier* for eight bucks for a back issue of the magazine containing "The Cat from Hell."

After having eight new books come out in one year, Steve understandably needed to take a bit of a breather. Indeed, 1997 and 1998 would be relatively quiet by comparison, with only one book to appear each year: the fourth *Dark Tower* book, *Wizard and Glass,* would be published in November of 1997, and *Bag of Bones* in September 1998. Also in November 1997, he'd win the Horror Writers' Association Bram Stoker Award for Best Novel for *The Green Mile* series.

In perhaps the biggest upheaval of that period, with his last contract to Viking fulfilled, King decided to shop around for a new publisher. Viking had earlier come under the publishing umbrella of Penguin when they'd bought NAL, which meant that he and Tom Clancy now shared a publisher. Clancy had been with Putnam since 1986 when they'd published his second novel, *The Hunt for Red October,* and Steve felt that the marketing the company had done on his previous titles was less aggressive than Putnam's campaign for Clancy. In addition, they categorized Clancy as mainstream while King was still classified in the horror genre, despite his recent efforts to branch out.

But probably the more compelling reason for Steve to look elsewhere was that after a relationship of almost two decades, he and his publisher had grown complacent with each other. He felt stale. He didn't even offer Viking a chance to propose a new strategy; he just wanted out.

But he made a serious gaffe in the search for a new publisher, mostly because the drama was played out in public. For years, Steve had maintained that the money didn't matter, all he wanted to do was write his books, but given that, his next move didn't look so good. He could have been bluffing, or maybe he just wanted to leave Viking so badly that he made such an outrageous demand for the advance on his next book that he knew Viking would never agree to it. He asked for a whopping $18 million for *Bag of Bones,* which actually wasn't that outrageous when his previous price per book was $15 million. A commonly bandied-about figure in the publishing industry is that 90 percent of the books published with a traditional advance and royalty agreement never sell enough books or subsidiary rights to earn their advance back, and King was no exception. However, when the publisher turned thumbs-down, he took the opposite tack in the search for his next publisher.

After almost twenty-five wildly successful years in the bestseller realm, he didn't need the money. So he tossed out another insane idea to the next round of publishers and suggested an up-front payment of a mere $2 million for each of three books. King would pay for half of the production costs, and the profits would be split the down the middle. Publisher Susan Moldow at Scribner, part of Simon & Schuster, agreed to his unorthodox proposal, and they got busy. Steve's longtime editor, Chuck Verrill, followed him to his new publisher.

The financial arrangements weren't the only unusual thing about his new deal. The first book, *Bag of Bones,* was a big departure as well, the story of a widower who was a bestselling author who'd suffered from writer's block in the three years since his wife's death. It was billed by King's new publisher as alternately a love story and a literary read, a departure for him, even though he seemed to be in his typical form when he exclaimed with glee, "I just loved that, killing off a major character right at the start!"

When he began writing the book, he had in mind a gothic novel, both within the scope of his storytelling and how he traditionally defined the term: "It's a novel about secrets, about things that have been buried and stay quiet for a while and then, like a buried body, they start to smell bad."

He cited a traditional gothic classic as his inspiration for the book: *Rebecca,* by Daphne du Maurier, the story of a woman who marries a man who is tormented by the memory of his previous wife, now deceased. One aspect of the novel represented a real departure for him, but he found it was the only way the story could work: "There's a narrator, a first-person voice, which I haven't used very much in my longer fiction."

As usual when the main character was a writer, Steve gave a disclaimer in case some readers would think he was writing autobiographically: "Mike is probably as close as you could get to me, even though I've been careful to distance myself from him. He's not as successful, he has no children, his wife is dead, and he has writer's block. But our take on what the writing is about and how the writing works is very similar."

The jacket copy played it to the hilt, highlighting his recent O. Henry Award. CNN called the book a "classic ghost story," and like clockwork it hit the *New York Times* bestseller list the first week it was published and stayed there for a month.

As he made the promotional rounds for *Bag of Bones,* Steve was still talking about retiring, or at least taking a little bit of time off. But even as the words left his mouth, he realized the odds were not good: "You know how when you're on the turnpike on a hot day, and you always seem to see water at the horizon? *That's* my year off, right there! Whenever I get there, it's always a little further along."

Steve and Tabby's kids were grown, out of the house, and forging paths of their own. Though Joe and Owen were pursuing writing careers full speed ahead, Naomi needed to have a serious operation in 1997. She was still running the restaurant, but business wasn't as good as she and her partner had projected, and she was mulling over her path in life when she was hit by a drunk driver and forced off the road.

The other driver was never found. According to an eyewitness, the car bore no tags or registration. Naomi was seriously injured, her back refracturing along an old spinal injury. The accident shook her world.

"My first reaction was to pray really hard for survival," she said. "My later reactions were anger, fear, and grief because there were significant losses and no way to recoup them." She said for years afterward she was incredibly nervous whenever faced with a situation where she found herself in traffic merging to her right. "I had a choice to make: to reopen my heart that was scarred with anger, fear, and grief, or to live confined in an emotional spiritual cage."

She was an active member of the First Universalist Church of Yarmouth, near Portland, and before she entered the hospital, over one hundred parishioners gathered to pray for her. She later said that her most memorable spiritual experience was that healing service. "Words fail to describe it," she said. "Your pulse merges with a sense of unity. You can feel the heartbeat of the world."

A few days after her operation, those same church members said that they had visions of her going to seminary to become a minister. She dreamed about it too.

"I kept having a dream about a closet full of robes and vestments and clerical garb," she said, "but everyone knew that no gay girl kid was going to be able to do that."

In the aftermath of what turned into a lengthy recovery, Naomi decided to close Tabitha Jean's, her Portland restaurant. Her priorities were changing. She was beginning to heed the call she'd heard to attend seminary and become a Unitarian/Universalist minister, though the fact the business was struggling helped strengthen her resolve. While the restaurant did well at lunch, a dinner crowd never materialized the way she had envisioned.

Following in her father's philanthropic footsteps, Naomi donated all equipment from the restaurant to several local charities, including the Preble Street Mission, a Portland homeless shelter and soup kitchen; the East End Family Workshop, a local child-care center and resource service; and the First Universalist Church of Yarmouth, her home church.

Health problems were starting to weigh Steve down as well. Though he had always worn Coke-bottle glasses for his severe myopia, his eyesight was getting worse. In 1997, he was diagnosed with macular degeneration, with total blindness the eventual outcome. The following year, he suffered a detached retina. His vision primarily deteriorated in his straight-ahead perspective, but not in the peripheral vision. He didn't seem too disturbed by it.

"That's the part I want to keep, as a man and as a writer, is what I see out of the corners," he said.

Tabby had also experienced her fair share of health issues. Not only had she lost most of her sense of smell, but she was diabetic as well. And a few years earlier, she'd had an operation where, according to Rick Hautala, "the doctors came out with some or all of one kidney in a bucket."

It was a poorly kept secret that Steve never liked Stanley Kubrick's version of *The Shining,* and he'd always wondered what a remake would look like. He finally got his chance in April 1997 when Mick Garris directed a three-part miniseries that aired on ABC-TV.

Through the years, Kubrick was unhappy with Steve's continued criticism of his 1980 film. ABC was happy with *The Stand,* so they invited Steve to work on another miniseries for the network. He replied that he'd like to rework *The Shining* into a miniseries, and this time he'd like to write the screenplay. To remake the movie, a deal unusual for Hollywood was struck between three parties, Steve, Kubrick, and Warner Brothers, who had produced the original film: the miniseries would only get made if Steve kept his mouth shut about Kubrick's version. He agreed, the standards and practices department gave his script a green light, and production began.

This time, he wanted to see how much he could get away with, since the network was obviously pleased with his treatment of *The Stand,* despite a number of questionable scenes. "I wanted to push the envelope, and I'd worked enough with them that I felt confident enough that they would let me do just that," he said. He sensed that the censors knew they were working within a pretty broad gray area, so Steve tried to stay away from scenes that he knew they'd want to cut.

"We had a number of problems with the network in terms of the violence between a man and his wife," said King. "The last hour of the show is very harrowing. He's chasing her, she's trying to protect the kid, and he's got a mallet which he's hitting her with, and hitting her and hitting her. In the movie he was hit once but she wasn't."

Ironically, the horror sailed through with flying colors, but a stumbling block was Wendy Torrance's telling her husband to stick his job up his ass. The censors refused to budge, so Steve changed the line to "Take this job and stick it!" Yet the issue of Danny's life being endangered was overlooked by the censor's red pencil. When the miniseries aired, ABC received a number of complaints about the harrowing scenes when Jack pursued his son, practically nonstop. After *The Shining* aired, censors at all three networks agreed that from now on, in programs airing before 9 p.m., they'd excise any scenes or situations where children would be placed in physical and emotional jeopardy.

On December 1, 1997, Michael Carneal, a fourteen-year-old freshman at Heath High School, in West Paducah, Kentucky, shot and killed three students at a school prayer meeting and wounded five others. Carneal had a copy of *Rage,* the first novel by Richard Bachman, in his locker.

Barry Loukaitis, just shy of his fifteenth birthday, killed two fellow students and his algebra teacher on February 2, 1996, at Frontier Junior High in Moses Lake, Washington. After he shot his teacher, fifty-one-year-old Leona Caires, Loukaitis was overheard quoting from *Rage,* "This sure beats algebra, doesn't it?"

In the wake of the shootings, and after the Columbine High School massacre in April 1999, where thirteen people were killed and twenty-three wounded, King made an important decision. "I sympathize with the losers of the world and to some degree understand the blind hormonal rage and ratlike panic which sets in as one senses the corridor of choice growing ever narrower, until violence seems like the only possible response to the pain," he said. "And although I pity the Columbine shooters, had I been in a position to do so, I like to think I would have killed them myself, the way one puts down any savage animal that cannot stop biting."

The FBI asked King to help set up a computer profile to identify teenagers who have similar tendencies. He declined, but realized he'd had enough.

"I've written a lot of books about teenagers who are pushed to violent acts," he said. "But with *Rage*, it's almost a blueprint in terms of saying, 'This is how it could be done.' And when it started to happen, I said, 'That's it for me, that book's off the market.'"

He told New American Library, the publisher of the early Bachman novels, to declare the book out of print.

During the New England ice storm of 1998, which toppled trees and knocked out power across the region for up to two weeks or more, Steve and Tabby's opinion toward Maine winters began to change. He was walking one of their dogs in the driveway, taking baby steps down the icy surface to get the mail, when a chunk of ice fell off the mailbox, barely missing the dog. "That's when we asked ourselves, 'Why are we still here in the winter?'" The only answer they could find: "Because we always have." So they decided to start spending the winter months near Sarasota, Florida. "The first thing I always do in the morning is turn on the TV and see what they're getting hit with up North," he said.

He and Tabby typically made their annual pilgrimage back and forth by car. Steve's fear of flying was still as strong as ever, though he tended to joke about it. "There's no breakdown lane up there. If it stops, it's over, forget it," he said, adding that he prefers to fly first-class not only for the advantages and service, but also, "If there's going to be an accident, I want to be the first to the crash site. On the other hand, if you're in the last row, at least you don't have to linger in a burn ward."

Once when he was flying on a small jet, he commented that he wouldn't mind flying if he could just get knocked out for the entire flight, but without resorting to the drugs and booze that he had kicked in a hard-won fight a decade earlier. One of the pilots said they could do it by lowering the oxygen back in the passenger section. Steve brightened and told them to do it, but they refused.

Once he had a real scare when he was flying on a Learjet and the plane hit clear-air turbulence. "It was like hitting a rock wall in the sky," he said. "The oxygen mask came out and I thought that we were dead. You *never* want to see an oxygen mask, except in the film at the beginning." The turbulence was so bad that his seat was ripped from the floor and he landed lying on his side still strapped into the seat.

It took a while for him to get on a plane again.

Older and wiser, Steve was starting to become more sanguine about not only his place in the canon of popular fiction, but also about the reality of the publishing marketplace. He recognized that his decision to not focus strictly on writing horror had driven away some readers. "Over the years, I've lost readers," he said. "After all, I'm not exactly providing the same level of escape that *Salem's Lot* or *The Shining* did. People tell me I never wrote a book as good as *The Stand,* and I tell them how depressing it is to hear that something you wrote twenty-eight years ago was your best book."

Regardless of the topic or approach he took in a new novel, the process was always the same. "Once the actual act of creation starts, writing is like this high-speed version of the *You Can Make Thousands of Faces!* flip books I had when I was a kid, where you mix and match," he said. "You can put maybe six or seven different eyes with different noses, except in writing a novel there aren't just thousands of faces, there are literally billions of different events, personalities, and things that you can flip together."

Even though some of the readers who had been with him from the beginning were falling away with his new brand of books, he was about to embark on a project that would bring millions of new fans into the fold, all saying—just as had happened when *Stand by Me* and *The Shawshank Redemption* were released—"I didn't know Stephen King wrote that!"

Production began for *The Green Mile,* with Frank Darabont directing and serving as screenwriter. Steve visited the set a few times and said that Tom Hanks stayed in character the whole time Steve was there. "He strapped me into the chair, tightened the straps, and put the hood on my head and screwed it down. I said, 'Okay, I've got the idea, now let me out of here,'" Steve said.

Then he asked Hanks to trade places. Hanks refused, telling King that since he was in charge of the block, he could *never* sit in the chair.

Steve continued to branch out even on TV. Instead of adapting his novels and stories for miniseries, he was invited to write an episode for the fifth season of *The X-Files,* which aired on February 8, 1998. He had appeared on *Celebrity Jeopardy!* with David Duchovny and Lynn Redgrave in November 1995, and Steve won, donating his proceeds of $11,400 to the Bangor Public Library. After the show Duchovny, who played the role of Fox Mulder on *The X-Files,* suggested that Steve write an episode for the series. He returned to Bangor, watched a few shows, and started talking with Chris Carter, who created the series.

The episode, named "Bunghoney," was classic Stephen King. Gillian Anderson, in the role of Dana Scully, takes a rare weekend break to a town in Maine, where she meets a number of residents who have clawed out their eyes. She volunteers her services to the police in town and discovers the cause to be a single mother with a supposedly autistic daughter whose favorite doll, named Chinga, appears to be possessed and the cause of the discontent in town. According to King, Carter radically edited his original script, which revolved around the theme of the government pursuing the little girl.

But Carter wanted King to focus on Chinga, so Steve rewrote the script. Carter still wasn't happy with the revisions, so instead of giving it back to Steve for another try, he instead rewrote it himself. The episode that finally aired bore little resemblance to Steve's initial idea.

Though Steve had dreamed for years about finding his father—or at least, what happened to him—he'd never actively pursued it, perhaps afraid of what he'd discover.

One day in the late nineties, someone did the digging for him.

A crew at the CBS television network was working on a documentary on Steve, and they interviewed David King, his brother. The issue of their father came up, and though both brothers typically dismissed the question, this time David gave the producers Donald King's Social Security number. After a bit of research, the crew found a trail that had long gone cold. Steve's premonitions from the eighties were right on track. In November 1980, Donald King had died in the small town of Wind Gap, Pennsylvania, known as the Gateway to the Poconos, and ironically five miles west of Bangor, Pennsylvania.

Though Steve and David had mixed feelings about the news, the producers presented them with photos of the new family their father had started, which included three boys and a girl, their half brothers and half sister.

King believes that his father's widow, Brazilian by birth, had no clue of her late husband's past. "Bigamy is a very severe offense, which would have serious consequences for those children," Steve said. "I couldn't do that to them, bring that knowledge. Let sleeping dogs lie, I say."

MISERY

The last year of the millennium began beautifully for Steve. He had four solid projects scheduled: *The Storm of the Century,* the story of a stranger who shows up in a small town in Maine just before a massive blizzard and who knows all the residents' secrets, would debut as a miniseries in February. The novel *The Girl Who Loved Tom Gordon* was slated for publication in April, and *Hearts in Atlantis,* a collection of stories that link a group of friends from childhood through adulthood who are influenced by the Vietnam War, was scheduled for September. The eagerly anticipated *Green Mile* movie would reach theaters in December, just in time to attract the Christmas crowds.

Stephen King had been scaring the bejesus out of readers and movie lovers all over the world for a quarter of a century. He decided to throw himself a party on the anniversary of the first publication of *Carrie.* After an exquisite dinner and lots of champagne—except, of course, for the host—the highlight of the night finally arrived: the lights were dimmed, a projection screen was lowered, and the invited dignitaries were treated to a best-hits version of the bloodiest, scariest snippets from films based on King's novels.

He could have chosen any venue in the entire world and flown two hundred of his closest friends and colleagues in via first class and it wouldn't have made a dent in his bank account. But staying true to form, he wanted his celebration to be held at nothing less than Manhattan's Tavern on the Green, which fit his persona as the hick from Bangor perfectly, as the landmark restaurant is a place most New Yorkers would disdain as suitable only for tourists who don't know any better.

Though he still sold movie rights and usually eschewed getting involved in the script or the production, he would occasionally go to the other extreme and write the screenplay, serve as executive producer, and spend as much time on the set as possible. *Storm of the Century* was one of those projects.

"I think that the best rule is to either be all the way in or be all the way out," he said. "With *Storm of the Century* I was all the way in, and I really enjoyed the process."

In developing the story for the four-part miniseries, King returned to a theme he had explored countless times before: the secrets that people in a small town know about each other but rarely give voice to. Not until a stranger enters the community do the secrets and long-held resentments finally get aired, which leads to a total meltdown for the town and the people.

As he had done previously with *The Stand* and *IT,* King had to shape the screenplay to get by the ABC censors. By this time, he'd had a lot of practice in what they'd accept and what they'd give a thumbs-down. He'd figured out a sneaky trick: "I build in three or four paper tigers that I can let go in trade for the stuff I feel is really important, and generally that works pretty well."

The one tug-of-war with *Storm of the Century* occurred when a deputy says, "You know, this is gonna be one bad mother of a storm." The censors told Steve to take out the phrase. Steve's reply: "Every sitcom on American TV is salacious in tone. We argued back and forth, but finally, I got my own way. Usually, with TV, if you whine enough, you do."

Traditionally, his least favorite part of a new book or movie project was the dog and pony show that any publisher, magazine, movie director, or TV network wanted him to do to promote it. With *Storm of the Century,* the big surprise was that he didn't balk at going on talk shows and meeting with reporters. In fact, he enjoyed it so much that he wanted to do another project for ABC and pondered the possibility of adapting *Bag of Bones* for a TV miniseries. "What I'd like to do is to have the *Storm of the Century* experience again, which is one of the reasons that I've done most of the promotion that they've asked me to do," he said.

Critic Tim Goodman said the miniseries suffered from the same affliction as King's books: "It's edge-of-the-couch good in some spots. The trouble is that it has too many spots. So many that the title should have been changed to *Story That Lasts a Century.*"

Steve still spoke of retiring, but he was becoming more realistic about the remoteness of the chances: "I can't retire until I finish the *Dark Tower* books, because there are people out there who would slaughter me if I didn't finish. I feel like Conan Doyle after he tried to kill Sherlock Holmes by sending him over Reichenbach Falls. A lot of people will not let me rest until I finish with Roland."

In March, one of Steve's professor friends, Anthony Magistrale, associate chair of the English Department at the University of Vermont, invited Steve to spend three days in Burlington to give a lecture, read from his work, and meet with students who were studying his work. To Magistrale's great delight, Steve accepted.

They were walking to the chapel before his lecture when King asked Magistrale a curious question.

"Why are thirty-five hundred people coming here?"

"I said, 'Oh, come on, do I have to answer that?' But Steve just shook his head and said, 'I will never understand this.' And you know, he wasn't just being false humble," Magistrate said. "He really doesn't get why people have this attachment to him or how he went from the guy who went to the University of Maine at Orono on an academic scholarship with one pair of blue jeans and ended up Horatio Alger."

A similar thing happened when they had a few hours to kill and played a few rounds of tennis. Tony asked Steve if he wanted to take a sauna. "He looked at me and asked, 'A sauna?' like I was asking him to copulate with an animal. I saw it as a testament to his working-class background, and no one he knew would ever take a sauna, that was for people with money," Magistrale explained.

At the end of the three days, Tony handed Steve a check for $15,000 for three days' work. "I apologized that it was so small, but then he turned it over and gave it back to me."

"Use it for something else," he said.

The Girl Who Loved Tom Gordon was published on April 6 to coincide with Opening Day for the Red Sox, since the Tom Gordon in the title is a relief pitcher for Boston. King described the 224-page book in this way: "If there was such a thing as a Stephen King young-adult novel, it would be *The Girl Who Loved Tom Gordon*." It was the second book of his three-book deal with Scribner, and it immediately hit the top of the bestseller charts.

Also in the spring of 1999, Steve and Tabby became grandparents for the first time. Joe and his wife, Leanora, had a son, whom they named Ethan. Grandpa started early on his grandson's indoctrination, bringing the infant to his first Red Sox game at Fenway Park at the ripe old age of ten days.

Steve was reenergized and began to talk with Peter Straub about collaborating on another novel, *Black House*, and *Hearts in Atlantis* was scheduled for September publication.

He was hitting the sweet spot. Life was good.

In June of 1999, King was in the middle of writing a new novel, *From a Buick 8*, and had also decided he was ready to return to his nonfiction work-in-progress *On Writing,* when fate horribly intervened.

At 4:30 p.m. on Saturday, June 19, 1999, Steve was doing what many in the area consider his daily ritual: he was walking against traffic on the shoulder of Route 5 in North Lovell. As usual, he was reading a book on his walk. That day he was reading *The House* by Bentley Little, the story of five strangers who begin to experience hallucinations and nightmares, and the only thing they share in common is that they all lived in identical houses during their childhoods.

When Steve hit a stretch of the road with no sight line at the crest of a hill, he stopped reading but continued to walk. A light blue Dodge van careened toward him, and King thought that the driver would realize his mistake and veer away. Instead, another split second later, Steve realized it wasn't going to happen, and so instead he turned away from the vehicle that had not slowed down and, if anything, was picking up speed.

"Steve turned a little," said Matt Baker, a deputy with the Oxford County sheriff's office, and the first officer to show up on the scene. "If he hadn't turned, it would have hit him square on and he probably wouldn't have made it." He landed in a patch of grass instead of an outcropping of rocks. "If he hit those rocks, he would have died."

The deputy estimated that the van was going forty miles an hour when it hit King. "I went out like a light," Steve said, "and when I came to, my lap was kind of on sideways and I thought, 'Oh, boy, I'm in trouble here.'"

Bryan Smith, the forty-two-year-old man who was driving the van, left the scene to call the police, then returned. He sat on a rock watching Steve as he lay there unconscious, and he was the first person King saw when he came to. Smith told him an ambulance was on the way.

As Steve recalled, Smith told him he'd never even gotten a parking ticket in his life. "Here it is my bad luck to hit the bestselling writer in the world," he said, before adding, "I loved all your movies."

As Tabby was summoned along with an ambulance, she had no idea of the extent of Steve's injuries or the painful path that lay ahead.

"I got a phone call to meet the policeman," she said. "I didn't understand the extent of his injuries for some time. He was conscious, his head was very bloody, but he was still talking and coherent.

"Time stopped," Tabby said later. "And then it started up again, all different."

The details slowly emerged in the aftermath of the accident.

Smith had been veering from one side of the road to the other for at least a half mile before he hit King because one of his rottweilers, named Bullet—he had another rotty at home, named Pistol—was in the back of the van trying to get into a cooler full of meat. From the driver's seat, Smith was trying to swat the dog away from the cooler.

When he first felt the impact, Smith thought he'd hit a small deer. He pulled over to the side of the road and discovered he'd hit a grown man when he saw a pair of blood-covered eyeglasses sitting on the front passenger seat and saw a bloodied, twisted body lying in a patch of grass just off the road. He headed off on foot to find a pay phone to call for help.

King was transported to Northern Cumberland Memorial Hospital in nearby Bridgton, where he was stabilized. The doctors there quickly arranged to fly him to Central Maine Medical Center (CMMC) in Lewiston via helicopter once they realized the extent of his injuries.

En route to Lewiston, King's lung collapsed. He said, "I remember one of the guys saying, 'Oh, shit,' and then I heard the crackle of something being unwrapped. Somebody said he was going to stick me, and then I could breathe again after they had intubated me and pumped up my lung."

Then his hands started to swell. The EMTs cut off his clothing, took off his shoes, then told him they had to remove his wedding rings. He wore one on each hand: the original he'd bought with Tabby's ring at $15.95 for the pair, and the other one she gave him years later. The ring on his left hand they were able to pull off, but they had to cut off the one on his right.

At one point, an EMT asked him to wiggle his toes, and Steve complied, but then asked, "Were they moving?"

The EMT nodded. "Good wiggle."

Even through his haze of pain and shock, Steve didn't believe him. "Do you swear to God, are my toes really moving?'

"Yes, they are."

"Am I going to die?"

"Not today."

Once the helicopter arrived at CMMC, the paramedics rushed him into the operating room, and surgery began around eight thirty, about four hours after he was struck by Smith's van.

King was in surgery for hours, then was moved into the critical care unit at 3:30 a.m., where he remained until Sunday afternoon.

"If there was a bone on the right side of my body, it was broken, with the exception of my head, which was only concussed," he said.

A preliminary list of his injuries included his right knee, split down the middle; his right hip, fractured; four broken ribs; a deep gash to his head that required twenty stitches to close; and his spine, which was chipped in eight places. His doctors had to decide whether to amputate his right leg below the knee, since it was broken in at least nine places. Steve later joked that the bones were like marbles in a sock.

The doctors decided to first try to stabilize the leg by attaching an external fixator, a device resembling a wire cage that goes over the leg to immobilize the bones and the joints.

Steve went back into the OR on Monday for another round of surgeries that lasted almost ten hours.

When he woke up in a hospital bed after the first couple of surgeries, he had a phenyltol patch on his arm and was hooked up to a morphine drip and a slew of different painkillers. He took one look and thought, "My God, I'm a junkie again. I was as grossed out by that as I was by the injuries. If I thought anything was unfair about what had happened to me, it was that after struggling and winning a battle to get off all sorts of drugs and alcohol, it was that I had to take them again."

He decided that the only way to deal with the number of highly addictive painkillers being infused into his body—such as Percocet and Vicodin, which he would happily have knocked back a little over a decade ago—was to be conscious of how many painkillers he was taking and try to stay below the recommended dose. "On the other hand, I didn't get sober to suffer, so if I'm in a situation where I'm miserable and medication will help that suffering, I'm going to take it," he said.

On Tuesday, June 22, the day after his second round of surgeries, his doctors told him they would like him to start walking by the end of the week, then asked him if he had any short-term goals he wanted to shoot for.

Steve replied that the All-Star Game was at Fenway Park on July 13. "Do you think I could get down there in a wheelchair?" he asked.

"Two nurses in the room threw each other these pitying looks, and it put chills in my heart."

He went back in for surgery on Wednesday, June 23—his third round of procedures in five days. He was on the operating table that night when a fierce thunderstorm hit eastern Maine, which caused power outages throughout the state. The electricity at the hospital flickered on and off and the lights dimmed a few times throughout the night, but at no point did they lose power thanks to battery backup and the hospital's two generators.

He was scheduled for another marathon in the operating room on Friday, but the medical team canceled it, concerned about the amount of anesthesia King had received for three major bouts of surgeries in just five days. By the end of the first week, Steve was able to take a few steps with the help of therapists and a walker.

Steve would spend the next three weeks in the hospital and undergo two more extensive surgeries.

An investigation later showed that when Bryan Smith hit Steve, he was driving from a campground where he was staying to a local store to pick up a few Mars's bars. One of the sheriffs met with King in the hospital and commented that the can of Pepsi Steve was drinking had a higher IQ than Smith. King would later say, "It occurs to me that I have nearly been killed by a character right out of one of my own novels. It's almost funny."

Though Smith had told King at the accident scene that he'd never even gotten a parking ticket, it was far from the truth. In reality, the list of Smith's driving offenses was lengthy, with some charges going back to when he was a juvenile and had only his driver's permit. Some of the more recent convictions included several DUIs as well as failure to stop for a police officer. His license had been suspended three times in 1998 alone.

Surprisingly, on June 19, Smith had not been tested for drugs or alcohol at the accident scene.

When Steve returned home to West Broadway, his life looked radically different. He had lost over forty pounds, had round-the-clock nurses, was swallowing at least a hundred pills a day, and began daily sessions of excruciating physical therapy.

The first goal of his PT was to flex his knee to allow the leg to bend ninety degrees. "The pain was just excruciating, and I filled the house with my howls," he said. "I can't imagine how my poor wife ever stood it, but the physical therapist would just laugh and tell me to do a little bit more. I'd tell her I couldn't and to let me stop, and she wouldn't."

After he'd been home for a few weeks, one of the nurses confided in him that before they were assigned to his care, a supervisor had told each one that under no circumstances were they to make any *Misery* jokes. Steve appreciated her candor and said that none of them had even broached the topic, though given his penchant for black humor, it might have taken his mind off his pain for a short while.

In addition to dealing with the physical agony, Steve was plagued by weakness and wasn't sure if he'd be able to write again, given the myriad effects of so many different medications. But five weeks to the day after the accident, he started to write. Though it wasn't the longest hiatus he'd ever had from writing, he had been forced into it against his will and it was the most painful one to endure.

But writing was much harder than he'd anticipated: "At first, it was as if I'd never done this in my life. It was like starting over again from square one. There was one awful minute when I didn't know if I knew how to do this anymore." He wasn't sure if it was from a lack of confidence, a side effect of all the medication, or a memory lapse from spending so much time away from it. He wrote for ten or fifteen minutes before stopping. A few days passed before he worked up the nerve to read what he had written. The sentences were a bit clunky, but his biggest concern was if they still made sense, and they did.

He slowly built up his tolerance, writing a little more every day until he could write for an hour and a half. His fractured hip made it painful to sit at his desk. He could write at the kitchen table as long as he was sitting on a large pile of pillows. He resumed *On Writing,* the nonfiction book he was working on at the time of the accident.

Sometimes he wrote on a laptop, other times he wrote by hand with a Waterman fountain pen because it was more comfortable for him and he could write for longer stretches of time. Instead of having his fingers fly over a computer keyboard, he was forced to slow down, which changed his writing. If he wrote at night, instead of working by the overhead light he lit a candle and worked in the light of a flickering flame.

The writing helped his life to become as normal as possible under the circumstances, while also distracting him from the constant pain. He began writing *Dreamcatcher* in mid-November.

Though he had long been accustomed to calling the shots in his life, he realized that given his current physical state, it was pretty much impossible, and he had to cede total control to others. "I've become a totally passive person," he said. "You recognize immediately that you've been seriously hurt and you can't deal with your own life and that you're going to have to depend on other people to pull you through, so you just kind of let go."

However, despite his vigilance, Steve was soon taking more medication than was necessary, specifically OxyContin, which one of his doctors had prescribed after he came in to check on him after his first surgery and noticed King was hitting the morphine pump a little too often. King realized that he had fallen back into the abyss of addiction, as the pain from the fractures and breaks and subsequent surgeries was too much for him to bear without massive amounts of painkillers. The difference between his addiction now and the one he had kicked more than ten years earlier was that this time he was fully aware of what was happening, and he vowed as soon as the pain let up, he'd kick drugs for the second time in his life.

But he wasn't quite ready for that to happen yet: "I took the pills until I didn't need them anymore, but then I continued to take them because pain is subjective. The addict part of my brain began inventing pain just to get these painkillers."

Not long after the accident, due to an overload of morphine and a bevy of other painkillers to get him through the pain of three marathon surgeries in the first week, he began to hallucinate. In one, Steve believed that Tom Gordon from his most recent book had murdered his family, and the only reason King was in the hospital was because he knew about the crime and he thought the Red Sox player was hunting for him and would kill him next.

He also imagined that one man who visited him in the hospital looked like a gym teacher dressed all in white, and that he was a character in one of his books. Instead, the man was Steve's primary orthopedic surgeon. Steve added that several times during his hospital stay "I seemed to be a character in one of my own books, and that was a very frightening place to be."

On September 30, 1999, the Oxford County grand jury indicted Bryan Smith on two charges: aggravated assault and driving to endanger. Smith objected to the indictment, saying he hadn't committed a crime and referring to the June 19 tragedy as "an accident without a cause."

Steve and Tabby were pleased with the indictment. "I believe that by indicting Bryan Smith, the grand jury did the right thing, and I am very grateful to them for doing it—not only as the injured party, but as a citizen of the State of Maine," said their statement. "The indictments send a powerful message: when we slide behind the wheel of our vehicles, we are responsible for the lives of others and must be held accountable when we fail in that responsibility."

In case Smith or a relative got the idea to cash in on the gruesome history of the van, King's friend and lawyer Warren Silver offered Smith $1,500 for the vehicle, which he accepted. For a while, Steve played with the idea of using the van for a fund-raiser for a Bangor charity—five bucks buys you three swings with a sledgehammer—but Tabby discouraged him. In the end, the van was crushed and cubed.

The pair of Steve's glasses found on the front seat of Bryan Smith's van made out better than Steve's body did. The wire frames were bent, but even after the impact of the van at forty miles an hour, the lenses were fine. He chose to reuse the lenses and put them in new frames.

That fall, as he recovered and began to give interviews, his typical humor returned. King vowed that if the external rotator was still on his leg in late October, he would hang a string of Halloween lights on the clamps of the device.

He also realized it was time to quit his painkillers. While he was aware the pain was fading away, from several previous decades' worth of heavy addiction to alcohol and drugs, his body was beginning to invent new pain in order to justify the drugs. "I was manufacturing the pain to get the medication. There was a point there where either I stopped using or I would have to get my Vicodin prescription filled in a wheelbarrow," he joked. The only choice was to go cold turkey. "Kicking a prescription like that is physical. It took about two weeks. You kick it and you sweat, you're awake nights, you twitch, and then it's gone."

By the time *The Green Mile* movie came out on December 10, Steve was well enough to attend the premiere. Roger Ebert of the *Chicago Sun-Times* wrote, "By taking the extra time to allow the movie to run for three hours, Darabont has made *The Green Mile* into a story which develops and unfolds, and has detail and space. The movie would have been much diminished at two hours." Janet Maslin of the *New York Times* said that "unassumingly strong, moving performances and Mr. Darabont's durable storytelling make it a trip worth taking just the same."

Undoubtedly, that woman in the grocery store would have denied that it was a Stephen King movie too.

SOMETIMES THEY COME BACK

The new century brought King many new challenges and events, some of them strange, some of them expected. Recovery continued slowly, but he persevered. Though he could only write up to an hour and a half at a time, his productivity obviously did not suffer. He completed the draft of *On Writing*, wrote the e-novella *Riding the Bullet*, penned the screenplay for *Kingdom Hospital*, a thirteen-episode TV series, and cranked out *Dreamcatcher*, which weighed in at a mere 624 pages. He also resumed his collaboration with Peter Straub on *Black House*.

He had finished writing *From a Buick 8* a couple of months before his accident, and it was scheduled for publication in 2000, but his publisher, Susan Moldow, thought it would be in bad taste to publish the book so shortly afterward since a horrific car accident is prominently featured in the novel.

After the accident, Steve and Tabby decided to stick to the routine they'd started a couple of years earlier and spend the winter in Florida. They would be away from the doctors who had been treating and closely monitoring him, but they were fearful of what a harsh Maine winter could do to Steve's legs and hips, which were still held together by a convoluted network of pins and rods. Not only would the cold aggravate his pain and stiffen his joints, but if Steve slipped on the ice, he'd be almost back to square one.

A few benefits came from smashing up his body. When he visited the Red Sox camp during spring training in Fort Myers in the spring of 2000, the moment he showed up, he was mobbed by the players. "Nomar [Garciaparra] comes over, Bret Saberhagen comes over, Tim Wakefield comes over, and Tim goes, 'Come on, get it up, get it up!' They all wanted to see my leg," Steve said.

Peter Straub visited Steve and Tabby for a week in February so they could resume working on *Black House*, the sequel to *The Talisman*. They collaborated on a forty-page bible that spelled out the bones of the story along with an outline and other details. Their working method was different this time around: When they worked on *The Talisman*, they spent a lot of time together at Steve's home in Maine and Peter's in Connecticut and taking long drives to nowhere to hash out the details. For *Black House,* they corresponded via e-mail and gabbed on the phone, then began to write. Steve would crank out the novel in a chunk of approximately fifty pages before forwarding it to Peter, who'd read it over and write his own fifty-page segment before sending it back.

Straub said they had more fun writing *Black House* than *The Talisman* and the work proceeded more quickly as well, though their writing styles and methods of working are quite different. "Steve is more straightforward than I am, far less given to complexity of both plot and characterization," said Straub. "We both love the sweep of narrative and are both attracted to grandeur, and we are intensely interested in the various manifestations of evil. And our senses of humor coincide at many points, because we can reduce each other to helpless laughter."

Steve thought of Peter like a big brother. As they worked on the second novel, they wrote with an eye toward a third. "There was never any question that there would be another book," said King. "It's just a question of trying to find the time."

Stanley Wiater characterized their relationship as yin and yang: "Peter is a man who gets up in the morning, puts on a suit, and walks around looking like a million bucks. Stephen King gets up, puts on blue jeans and his shit-kicker boots, and he looks like he's going to go out and drive a garbage truck. Peter Straub is very refined. He'll look at the wine list and immediately know the best one. In his drinking days, Steve would always pick the Miller or Budweiser."

In the first few months of 2000, electronic books were starting to gain some traction in the world of publishing, though there were no hard figures yet and many people both in and outside of the industry viewed reading a book on a computer screen as a novelty. Ralph Vincinanza, Steve's foreign-rights agent, suggested that he think about trying out this new medium. "It would be nice to get an idea of what this market is like now," said Vincinanza.

Steve pondered it and told his agent he had a novella that would work as an e-book. When Vincinanza read *Riding the Bullet,* he thought it would work well in the new format. "I thought it was a really good story in terms of subject matter, but also in terms of length," he said.

"It was a way of saying to the publishers that I don't necessarily need to go through them," said King. "I wanted to break some trail for some other people, and it was a way of keeping things fresh." He was also curious to see what the response would be.

Within twenty-four hours after it first appeared as a downloadable PDF file in e-book and Windows formats on several Web sites—Amazon and Barnes & Noble initially offered the book at no charge, while netLibrary and a few other sites charged $2.50 per download—*Riding the Bullet* had been downloaded four hundred thousand times.

The success of *Bullet* got Steve thinking of other stories to experiment with in electronic format. He and Tabby frequently joked that after his brush with death, they were living in the Bonus Round, and so he felt freer to experiment on his own. The Internet was still the equivalent of the Wild West, and he loved gunslinger stories.

In 1982, Steve and Tabby had grown weary of sending out the same old Christmas cards every year, so he decided to start a serial novel that he would bind and send to friends. *The Plant* was the story of a houseplant named Zenith the Common Ivy that is anything but common; in fact the story bore an eerie resemblance to *Little Shop of Horrors*, an off-Broadway musical from 1982 about a giant man-eater of a plant as well as a classic 1960 horror movie by Roger Corman and starring Jack Nicholson. *The Plant* was King's first self-publishing effort through his Philtrum Press. He printed 226 copies of the handsome green chapbook.

In 1983, he sent out the second chapter of *The Plant*. In 1984 he gave *The Plant* a year off, publishing in its stead the limited edition of *The Eyes of the Dragon*, the book he wrote for Naomi. In 1985 he published and sent out a third installment of *The Plant*.

Little Shop of Horrors was made into a movie for the second time in 1986 and was the major reason why there would be no fourth installment. He felt that the stories were just too similar and didn't want to be accused of copying someone else's idea.

After the success of *Riding the Bullet*, he thought about experimenting further with electronic publishing by offering *The Plant* for download. But first he wanted some feedback from readers. He posted a query on his Web site asking (a) if he should publish *The Plant* in serial format, and (b) if people thought readers would pay for it on the honor system, like an unattended roadside farmstand where people take what they want and leave the money in a coffee can.

His fans, as expected, eagerly responded and encouraged him to proceed with his experiment.

The first serial appeared on the Web site in July, with a new edition appearing each month until December. After the sixth installment had appeared, Steve announced that he was stopping his experiment, at least temporarily. About

75 percent of the people had paid up, though he admitted that while some were freeloaders, others had failed to fork over the dollar for each installment because they were stymied by the technology.

But also, Steve had lost interest in the story. He'd decided to publish the story for public consumption because he wanted to motivate himself to work on it again, but that didn't work. Essentially, the six parts of the electronic version of *The Plant* were the three versions published back in the eighties, and he wrote little new material for the e-book.

But he couldn't entirely be faulted; understandably, he still wasn't back to full steam ahead since his accident. And three other projects were consuming his attention: *Black House*, *Dreamcatcher*, and the fifth *Dark Tower* book. He departed from his usual strategy—write first, research later—on *Dreamcatcher*, the story of four childhood friends who reunite in adulthood to fight both psychological and supernatural demons. He compared his new novel to a Tom Clancy book, where the story line required more details about the military—particularly helicopters and Humvees—than he knew, so he approached the National Guard base in Bangor for help.

He asked for a ride in a Humvee, and a couple of soldiers took him, with a brace still on his leg, out into a marshy area near the barracks. Steve was thrilled. As a result of his research, he offered to appear in a thirty-second public service announcement to promote the Maine National Guard's college tuition-assistance program.

In a scene reminiscent of his old American Express commercials from the early eighties—"Do you know me?"—King started his spiel in the TV spots by saying, "You know, one of the few things scarier than my books and movies is trying to pay for college."

The PSAs were so successful that the "commercial" was pulled from the airwaves two months early, with fifty-five new recruits enlisting in the Army Guard and twenty more signing up with the Air Guard. The original $300,000 in the program earmarked for troops pursuing undergraduate and graduate degrees was boosted to $500,000 with the help of additional federal funds.

In June 2000, Steve and Tabby flew to Nashville to witness a "ceremony of union" between Naomi, thirty, and her fifty-four-year-old professor at Meadville Lombard Theological School, who goes by the name of Thandeka. Naomi had enrolled at the seminary in 2000.

Thandeka is an ordained Unitarian Universalist minister and received her doctorate in the philosophy of religion and theology from Claremont Graduate School. She and Naomi met at Meadville, and like Naomi she had undergone a change of heart in midlife and decided to go to seminary after spending sixteen years as a TV producer.

In 1984, the Bishop Desmond Tutu blessed her with her Xhosa name, which means "one who is loved by God."

Steve was still on crutches when he and Tabby flew to Nashville, but by the time his birthday rolled around in September, he was walking unassisted. He still had some pain in his hip and needed to work on his range of motion, but his leg was as good as it was going to get, with no pain. "My body is fifty-two years old except for my hip, where it's about eighty-five now," he said. "I never think anymore, 'I'm going to New York.' It's more like 'I'm taking my leg to New York.'"

On September 21, Steve and Tabby were celebrating his birthday when word arrived that Bryan Smith, the man who had caused him so much pain and agony and lost work time over the past fifteen months, was dead of a drug overdose. King offered a brief statement:

"I was very sorry to hear of the passing of Bryan Smith. The death of a forty-three-year-old man can only be termed untimely."

On Writing, King's first nonfiction book in two decades, was published in October with a first printing of five hundred thousand copies. Though he had always shied away from writing his autobiography, this was as close as he would ever get, albeit in a selective way, by focusing on a few choice events from his childhood in a section he entitled "C.V." In a separate section, he also described the details of his accident and subsequent recovery, assembling it as best he could from the bits and pieces he recalled, and from what others had told him.

Steve, who once said, "Facts don't bother a novelist," confided that writing the book, especially the second half when he was still recovering from the accident, was more difficult than he had expected. "It's like sex in a way," he said. "You'd rather do it than write about it."

At 288 pages, the book was one-fourth the length of *The Stand.* He worried that after more than twenty-five years of publishing novels, it was only a paltry book and asked himself, "Is this all you really have to say about the art and craft of writing?" He was satisfied that it was, yet he realized that some folks would be put off by the idea of Stephen King writing a book on how to write: "It's like the town whore trying to teach women how to behave."

Just as happened when he turned in his scripts for miniseries to the networks, his editor came back with some objections to his manuscript for *On*

Writing, particularly because one of the markets for the book would be high school students. When told to tone down the language a bit, Steve knew that he had accomplished what he'd set out to do as he viewed the book as a renegade primer, "an outlaw text." He said, "If you give a book to a kid and tell him to take it home, put a book jacket on it, and give it back at the end of the year, they think it's a dumb book. But if it's something that they have to go and buy themselves, they take it more seriously."

He also resumed working on the fifth *Dark Tower* book, though at the time he started it, he intended the last three books to be published as one. Though his fans breathed a great sigh of relief, his reasons for returning to Roland Deschain were selfish: "I decided that I wanted be true to the twenty-two-year-old who wanted to write the longest popular novel of all time. I knew it was going to be like crossing the Atlantic in a bathtub, and I thought I'm just going to keep on working, because if I stop, I'll never start again."

January 2, 2001, marked a milestone in Steve and Tabby's lives: their thirtieth wedding anniversary. Their friends and colleagues were not surprised that they'd lasted this long.

"They have one of the best and healthiest marriages you can possibly imagine," said Otto Penzler. "She knows him so well and he's dependent on her. She's his crutch. Tabby has gotten him through a lot of stuff."

George MacLeod, Steve's college buddy, agrees, adding that Steve would never think of straying: "Steve is very conservative in that regard. He's a one-woman man, that is his nature." In at least one regard, according to MacLeod, Tabby and Steve are complete opposites. "There's a side of him that is still some nervous kid, while I've never seen that in Tabby at all. She's very, very comfortable with herself and very up-front when she needs to be. My guess is that he probably still depends on that in her, and she runs interference for him."

"Tabby keeps the monsters away," said Steve.

"You never know what you're going to get with Tabby, she's very mercurial," said Rick Hautala. "Sometimes when I see her, she'll give me a big hug and a kiss and tell me that she's happy to see me, and the next time she'll hold back and just say hi."

While Steve has been known to rattle off a list of his most common fears, adding more as the years go by, Tabby has struck many of their friends as completely fearless. "Tabby's not afraid of him, or anything," said Dave Barry.

"I think that people fear things they shouldn't and don't fear things they should," she says. "Like anybody else, if the plane drops, I'm going to scream. But fear stops you from moving forward and keeps us from knowing things."

Steve admits that without Tabby he wouldn't have generated the sheer number of pages that he has. "When people ask me how I've managed to remain so prolific, I tell them that I haven't died and I haven't gotten divorced. I've had a fairly settled life, and that's made it possible for me to contemplate some god-awful things in my fiction."

Despite his output, however, King doesn't think he writes a lot. "I just write every day and keep it rolling along. I think a lot of writers have a tendency to stand back awhile and sort of sniff around a project if it's not going well. That never works for me; I find that once I get out of the driver's seat, I don't want to go back in. The story gets old for me very quickly, and I begin to lose whatever feelings I had for the characters. So when I run into tough sledding, my impulse is to push straight ahead and the material piles up. If it's bad, I can always rip it out later."

Have any famous actresses caught his eye? "There are always temptations when you're off on tour and doing the conventions, and plenty of groupies," he said. "But no wife wants to be traded in for a trophy wife. What helped was that my father deserted my mother and I saw what my mother's life was like after that, what the consequences were when the man leaves."

Both maintain that they've been faithful through their decades of marriage. Says Tabby on the prospect that Steve would fool around, "I would cut something off and then I would shoot him."

"They really love each other, number one," said Sandy Phippen. "They're wonderful together, and I love the way she takes over. And they also play off each other all the time. They make fun of each other, and I think he lets her handle everything."

But all that togetherness only goes so far. Neither Steve nor Tabby think they could write a book together. "Sounds like a quick ticket to divorce court," he joked. "I don't think we could do it, though the thought has crossed my mind."

"I've never sought out collaboration," said Tabby. "I've seen other people do it, and I think it takes a lot of generosity and a willingness to let go of control to some degree. I've seen my husband do it, but I don't think he lets go of control. I think he just bullies his way into what he wants like a freight train."

But another problem was at hand. "We did once talk about doing a project together, but the minute the businesspeople got involved, it turned into Steve's project," she said. "It was like I wasn't even in the room. I ended my involvement immediately."

She has also ruled out writing a book with either of her sons. "We read each other's shit and offer suggestions that may or may not be taken, and that's the end of it," she noted.

In February 2001, King filed a lawsuit against his insurance company, Commercial Union York Insurance, stemming from his accident two years earlier. The insurance company had paid him $450,000—Commercial Union stated that amount was the limit of his policy—while Steve sued for the full value of his $10 million umbrella policy to cover his medical bills and lost income. The lawsuit estimated his total losses to be $75 million.

The media had a field day and his loyal fans questioned why, when Steve had more money than God and had always claimed that money mattered little to him, he'd suddenly got greedy.

To those who knew him, however, it wasn't a surprise. "The money was irrelevant, it was the principle of the thing," said Stephen Spignesi. "If he had not gotten what he believed the policy entitled him to, he would have felt that he was wasting the money, and growing up dirt-poor in rural Maine, it was a sin to waste money. And if he has a contract in place with an insurance company and they're screwing him so that the money would come out of his pocket, it would be a waste. *That's* why he sued."

In the end, the two sides settled the lawsuit when Steve suggested that the insurance company donate $750,000 to Central Maine Medical Center in Lewiston, where he'd spent three weeks recovering after the accident, and the company agreed.

Dreamcatcher, the novel he began writing a few months after the accident, was published in March 2001.

"It's a book about guys," he said. "I wanted a truer version of *Iron John.* I wanted to write a book about how guys act with other guys and what it means to be a man among other men."

The book seemed a way to overcompensate for the spate of novels he'd written over the years featuring strong female characters, though other messages clearly wormed their way into the story line. "There is a terrifying fear of the government that runs throughout the book, that they would rather kill all of us than tell us the truth," he said.

He couldn't help but use his recent pain and recovery in the novel. "The character in the tree stand had been hit by a car and was recuperating, and I obviously knew how that felt. When I wrote about it, I didn't think about the pain as much. It was like being hypnotized. But there are things in the book that are extremely gruesome, and I found myself pulling back a bit."

His original title for the book was *Cancer,* but Tabby talked him out of it, since she thought it would be bad karma.

The month after *Dreamcatcher* was published, one of Steve's stories appeared in *The Best American Mystery Stories of the Century.* Editor Otto Penzler selected "Quitters, Inc.," a story about a man who wants to quit smoking and hires an agency that promises to help him no matter what, for the anthology, which put Steve in the esteemed company of some of his childhood heroes, including John D. MacDonald and Shirley Jackson.

He'd written "Quitters, Inc." back in the seventies, when he habitually listened to blasting rock and roll while he wrote. Now, however, he started to gravitate toward a subgenre of country music called cross-country, a cross between rock and country. While he still listened to rock and roll, he no longer listened to it blaring through the speakers while working on a first draft of a short story or novel. Now when he was working on a first draft, he worked in complete silence, a first for him.

One thing hadn't changed, however: the more rabid fans still camped out in front of the bat-garnished wrought-iron fence for hours in hopes of a glimpse of Steve. They'd occasionally throw packages over the fence, books and presents, and sometimes harangue people driving through the gate. After September 11, however, the entire country was skittish, including Steve and Tabby, who had dealt with crazed fans for years. One day not long after the terrorist attacks, a fan left a package on the walkway leading up to the house and the police were called. But the parcel was not an explosive device: instead, a copy of *IT* got blown to bits, tiny shards of paper littering the entire neighborhood after the bomb squad was called in.

September 11 also had an adverse effect on *Black House,* since it was to be published on September 13. Steve and Peter were scheduled for a heavy-duty publicity tour that included national TV talk shows and interviews and book signings, but in the end everything was canceled. "It was almost like the book never happened," said King. "I called Peter on the phone and told him I didn't think anyone would want to read about a supernatural cannibal after what just happened. The book eventually did pretty well, but not at the time. Nothing did really."

Stephen King's Rose Red, a three-part miniseries with an original script by King, debuted on ABC on January 27, 2002. Scribner wanted to publish a book to tie in with the movie but preferred a prequel to the story, not just a novelization of the miniseries, and they came up with the title: *The Diary of Ellen Rimbauer: My Life at Rose Red.* Stephen was busy writing the script for the miniseries, so they asked him for some suggestions for writers who could handle the job. Ridley Pearson's name came up from his association with Steve playing in the Remainders. Since Pearson had first joined the band, he'd written several well-received novels, including *Chain of Evidence* and *Beyond Recognition.*

Steve immediately agreed, though it was the first time he allowed a book to be written as a prequel to his work, as well as not by his own hand. Ridley flew out to Seattle, where he and Steve spent several days on the movie set, hashing out the story line and interviewing the actors. "He's an amazingly generous guy," said Pearson. "We split royalties on the book and he helped me immensely whenever I had questions about the story."

Though they had spent time together with the band, this was the first time they were able to sit down and talk one-on-one, not only about the book and the show, but also about life itself.

"He's a sixty-year-old man who acts like a goofy teenage boy who also happens to be the smartest man in the room," Ridley said, adding that he never got the sense that Steve was comfortable with his physical self. "He's a big man, and you know how some big guys carry themselves like if the door's in his way he's going to knock it down? Stephen isn't that way. He's more gawky and geeky. He carries himself as if he doesn't want to be as tall as he is."

One time Ridley visited Steve and Tabby in Bangor, and she took him on a tour of the underground part of the house. She led him to the library, where Steve had an old-fashioned paperback rack from a drugstore, with "lots of fifties paperbacks because I love the covers, and a certain amount of pornography from the sixties, paperback pornography that was done by people like Donald Westlake and Lawrence Block, just because it amuses me," said King. "You see little flashes of their style."

Tabby nonchalantly mentioned to Ridley that the library held around seventeen thousand books. "We got to the end and there was one little cabinet that had a label that said *TBR* on it, with about thirty books in it," he said.

TBR stood for "To Be Read." Pearson pointed at the label and she nodded, which meant that Steve had read every book in that library except for the thirty books in the cabinet. "I said, 'That's not possible,' and she said, 'I assure you he has read them all.'"

When *Rose Red* was published, it hit the top of the bestseller lists the first week it appeared and stayed there for almost three months. It was Pearson's first number one bestselling book. Though Steve was pleased that Pearson had written the prequel to *Rose Red,* he warned his friend about the fallout that would come after the book was published.

"He called me up and said, 'Ridley, watch out because from here on out, mark my words, the reviewers are going to savage you.' And he was absolutely right," said Pearson. "That was the beginning of the end. Before that everybody loved me. After that everybody hates you." Steve knew from firsthand experience that once an author becomes popular and hits the bestseller lists, many critics no longer believe his work is any good, and their disdain will show up in their reviews.

Steve and Tabby had fallen into a comfortable rhythm of spending half the year in Maine and the other half in Florida.

After spending several winters in Florida, the Kings decided to spring for a house in Osprey, about ten miles south of Sarasota. They paid $8.9 million for a waterfront, seventy-five-hundred square-foot, contemporary home on Casey Key, which set a record for the highest-priced house in Sarasota County; it took another five years for a pricier house to sell.

Steve spent every day he could at Red Sox spring training, just down the road in Fort Myers, and admitted that the location of their house had more than a little to do with his favorite pastime. "I'm not going to say that we moved down here the way that alcoholics move into barrooms, but there might have been an element of that involved," he admitted.

Tabby usually stayed home. "I stopped being interested in professional sports a long time ago," she said. "I'll watch a little hockey and a little ball, but it's a boys' club with no girls allowed. So to hell with it."

But her then eighty-two-year-old mother, Sarah Spruce, loved to talk baseball with her son-in-law, often tying up the phone line for the entire game to offer comments and opinions and commiserate when necessary.

"She's Steve's baseball buddy," said Tabby. "She's one of those Maine women who's been following the Red Sox forever."

Steve had become so well-known as a long-suffering Red Sox fan that baseball fans flocked to the games as much to see him as to see the game. "I've become sort of a Red Sox mascot," he said. People approach him to gab but also to give him gifts, such as CDs, baseball caps, and even fake bloody socks, after the stitches in pitcher Curt Schilling's ankle let go during Game 6 of the AL play-offs against the Yankees in 2004 and again in Game 2 of the World Series against the St. Louis Cardinals; Steve's collection of bloody socks stood at seven.

For the most part, however, fans just wanted to talk baseball with him. They'd ask his opinion on the prospects for the coming year and the merits and weaknesses of the players on the roster. They'd spend an afternoon happily watching the game and offering commentary.

By the time *Everything's Eventual,* a collection of short stories, was published in March of 2002, Steve was hard at work writing the final three books of the *Dark Tower* series. Though he was always a fast writer, he worked even more feverishly with these books than any others he'd written since he had quit cocaine, which had admittedly been a big part of the reason for his marathon writing sessions in the early eighties.

So why rush now? "Because it seemed to me that once I got started with the actual writing, this time it felt like one of those WWF wrestling matches where it's for all the beans," he said. "And I felt like if I didn't finish this time, I never would, so I just hammered away until they were done. And once they were done, there was no reason not to publish them as soon as possible." Though he wanted all three books to be published at the same time, the publisher didn't concur.

Due to the long gaps between the first four books, Steve also knew that many readers didn't want to start reading the first book knowing that the last one wasn't even written yet. NAL decided to reissue the backlist in June 2003, then Scribner scheduled the publication of *Wolves of the Calla,* the first of the new *Dark Tower* books, five months later, in November. *Song of Susannah*—number six—followed in June 2004, and the final book, *The Dark Tower,* was published on Steve's fifty-seventh birthday, September 21, 2004. "I think it made up for all the waiting people had to do, to be able to say to them that these books are going to come in fairly rapid succession," he said.

Like clockwork and despite his feverish workload, Steve announced—for maybe the fourth or fifth time in his career—that he would be done writing books after the few more required by his contract. He made the announcement in anticipation of his next novel, *From a Buick 8,* which would be published in

September 2002. He was worried that he was starting to repeat himself and that people would regard his new novel as a reworking of material he used in *Christine,* since both stories featured a supernatural car from the 1950s.

His editors, fans, and family had all heard it before, and so their first inclination was to say, "Yeah, right," and nod right along to humor the boy who cried wolf. "Of course, for Steve that means that instead of three books a year, he'll only write one," said Stanley Wiater.

Some believed that his public announcements of never publishing another book had ramped up in the years since he had quit drinking and drugging as a way to replace the countless times through the seventies and eighties he had promised Tabby he would quit the booze and cocaine, or at least cut back. Saying he was going to retire and not following through had just replaced his pronouncements of earlier years.

"Work is his only drug," said Wiater.

"I have nightmares when I'm not working," Steve admitted. "I think that basically what doesn't come out on the page just has to come out some other way."

"Steve used to say he'd commit suicide if he couldn't write, which has always pissed me off," said Tabby. "I tell him if he pulled an Ernest Hemingway on me, I'd kick his body into the street and dance on it!"

But people had a real concern that maybe this time he was serious. After all, the accident had created lots of changes in his life, and also in his demeanor. He seemed calmer, more resigned to the onslaught of time and to the decrease in his fan base somewhat due to the well-trumpeted charges that he had turned literary. His books stayed on the top of the bestseller lists for only a few weeks now; previously, they would perch at number one for months.

"I've killed enough of the world's trees," he said, quickly tacking on that it didn't necessarily mean he would stop writing. "I've always rejected the idea that every book had to be available to every consumer, but I'd never stop writing because I don't know what I'd do between nine and one every day, but I'd stop publishing. I don't need the money."

He simply explained that after the last of the *Dark Tower* books was published in 2004, he felt that he had said everything he had ever wanted to say in his life, and then some.

Despite that he insisted that *this time* he was really going to retire, no one around him believed him, least of all those people in the business who had heard it all before. Susan Moldow, the publisher of Scribner, didn't believe a word he said. In the five years since King had signed with Scribner, she estimated that he'd threatened to retire at least six different times.

Even Peter Straub concurred. "I have a great deal of difficulty believing it," he said, joking that *From a Buick 8* "might be his last novel for the year."

Two months later, Steve reiterated his desire, though he tempered his words a bit: "I can't imagine retiring from writing. What I can imagine doing is retiring from publishing. If I wrote something that I thought was worth publishing, I would publish it."

But this was just another of those times he was toying with his fans, and his constant threats to retire were in reality a long-running tongue-in-cheek joke that most people were in on. "A year from now, people will say the idea that this guy was going to retire is a laugh," he said.

Even he knew he was a hopeless case: "I'm like a drug addict, I'm always saying I'm going to stop, and then I don't. When I'm not working, my mind doesn't take kindly to being unhooked from its dope. I get migraines and very vivid nightmares. It's almost like the d.t.'s, like my mind and body are trying to scare me back to work."

As 2003 began, it looked as if King were doing the impossible and sticking to his guns about kicking back and retiring. He wrote numerous articles for magazines and newspapers and contributed new introductions to revised editions of his work. His only book published that year was *The Dark Tower V: Wolves of the Calla*. According to his prediction, after the last two books in the series were published, the world would have seen the last new Stephen King book.

In June, the first four books of *The Dark Tower* were reissued, and the first book bore significant changes from their original versions. "I rewrote the whole thing," he said. "After all, they were written when I was young. It always seemed to me like I was trying too hard to make it be something really, really important, so I tried to simplify it a little bit."

In August, he started writing a regular column for *Entertainment Weekly*, reviewing new books, movies, and music. It was a culmination of everything he'd loved about pop culture through the years and bore great similarities to "The Garbage Truck" column he wrote in college.

"It's exactly the same," said Tabby. "He's engaged with pop culture in a way that I'm not. Most of the new-music suggestions come from our children. He goes to movies, and I don't. I'm old enough to have seen every damn movie, and all they're doing is remaking them at this point."

His taste in music would surprise those who knew him as an aficionado of loud rock, the harder the better. In particular, he confessed his admiration and appreciation for the rapper Eminem.

"I understand Eminem," said Steve. "He's funny and clever and really angry. And he's a kindred spirit."

He was also beginning to realize that he was on the downhill side of life and started to cooperate with old friends and colleagues who were in a position to help shape and interpret his legacy. He granted Tony Magistrale, his old buddy from the University of Vermont, an interview for his new book, *Hollywood's Stephen King*.

Though Steve maintained that he was fully recovered from the accident, Tony was taken aback when he first saw his friend; after all, the last time he'd seen him was a couple of months before the accident.

"He had changed physically, he looked fragile and he was still walking with a cane," Tony said. "He showed me his leg, and it was a mess. He was still working with the doctors to come up with a cocktail of medications that would be effective, allow him to sleep and allow him to experience life without too much pain. So he was still struggling."

Magistrale added that he saw an emotional change in his friend as well. "There was a period there for about five or seven years where he was obsessed with the accident, which manifested itself in *Kingdom Hospital*," a TV series that King wrote and produced and debuted in March 2004 and ran for one season on ABC.

But happily, Tony saw that some things about Steve hadn't changed. Tony asked him to recommend a few places to eat in Bangor, and the only places he named were diners.

One day Tony asked him outright, " 'Steve, you made fifty-five million dollars last year. What are you doing in Bangor, Maine?' He looked at me like I was some sort of bug."

Steve answered, "Where would you like me to live, Tony? Monaco?"

"We both had a good laugh at that," said Magistrale.

The literary establishment was up in arms again when it was announced that the National Book Foundation's Medal for Distinguished Contribution to American Letters would be given to Stephen King at the annual awards ceremony in November. He was tickled at the idea; finally, after decades of selling millions upon millions of books all around the world but having the literary world thumb their noses at him, here he was, getting the recognition he'd always craved and felt he deserved.

The backlash began almost immediately. Self-professed keeper-of-the-literary-keys critic and Yale professor Harold Bloom thundered, "Another low in the shocking process of dumbing down our cultural life." However, this exact prize had four years ago been given to Oprah Winfrey, without this sort of controversy. Previous recipients included Ray Bradbury, Studs Terkel, and Toni Morrison.

"I thought it was absurd for them to say, 'Don't give this award to Stephen King.' It wasn't as though they were giving me a National Book Award for a novel I wrote," he said, joking, "They were giving me it the way they give the Miss Congeniality Award to a girl who's not going to be Miss America."

Steve admitted the award was more important than that, but he was extremely bothered by the continued prejudices of people who consider any novel that hasn't been christened as literary to be beneath them and not worth the paper it's printed on. "There's an unstated prejudice that if it's popular, it can't be good because the reading taste of the American public is idiotic," he said. "That kind of elitism drove me totally insane as a younger man. I'm better now, but there's still a fair amount of resentment toward that."

Steve made the rounds of TV and radio talk shows and interviews with newspaper reporters. He wasn't feeling great, and his doctor had diagnosed him as having pneumonia and warned him against traveling and speaking. But the recognition was too great for King to pass up, so he continued a jam-packed promotional schedule in the days leading up to the awards dinner on November 19, which undoubtedly weakened him further.

"That award nearly killed me," he said later. "I was determined I was going to accept it and make my speech." He returned home after the ceremony and was hospitalized four days later with double pneumonia, the result of a long-festering problem dating back to the collapsed lung he suffered in the wake of the car accident. "My lung had collapsed and the bottom part of it had not reinflated, but no one knew that," he said. "It stayed collapsed and got rotten and infected the rest." He remained in the hospital for almost a full month; surgeons performed a thoracotomy, a major surgical procedure that allowed doctors to remove fluids and infected tissue from the lung.

While he was in the hospital, he contracted a bacterial infection that lasted for three months. By the time it had cleared up, he weighed only 160 pounds, "a skeleton on feet," as he described it. In fact, he came closer to death during this hospital stay than as a result of his car accident.

Despite vomiting every few hours, he continued to write. "Even when I felt dizzy and weak, the words were always there for me," he said. "The writing was the best part of the day."

When the doctors told Tabby they were sure he was out of the woods, she asked him a question: "Can I redo your office?"

"I said yes because with a tube in my chest and another one down my throat, that was all I could say," he said. "She knew I couldn't argue."

When he returned home a week before Christmas, he asked about her renovation of his office, but Tabby told him not to go in there because she thought he'd be upset. So, just as he had told generations of schoolkids to run out and read his books the second a grown-up told them they shouldn't, one night when he had insomnia, he made a beeline to his office. The room was devoid of furniture, the rugs were rolled up, and the books were all in boxes. "It was like the ghost of Christmas yet to come, a vision of the future," he said. "This is what it will be like in twenty or twenty-five years when I'll be in a coffin and Tabitha will have rolled up the rugs and will be going through all my effects, all the papers and unfinished stories. It's the clearing up after a life. My brother and me did it when my mother died of cancer."

He thought back to the story he'd written a couple of years earlier, "Lisey and the Madman," which was slated to be published in a forthcoming anthology, *McSweeney's Enchanted Chamber of Astonishing Stories,* with Michael Chabon editing, in November 2004. As he had done countless times before, he took two apparently disparate ideas and, just like a kid playing with a chemistry set, combined them to see what happened.

"Ideas come along and I have to follow them," he had previously said whenever he announced his pending retirement and then didn't. He started working on what would turn out to be the novel, *Lisey's Story.*

He was off and running, writing about the wife of a famous novelist who is still muddling through daily life two years after his sudden, unexpected death. He later explained *Lisey's Story* as transmogrifying from a novel about a still-grieving woman to a story about repression and how people tend to conceal not only things but feelings. Steve maintained he was writing a love story.

The novel had faint echoes of his 1998 book, *Bag of Bones,* which was also billed as a love story. The theme of that book was also about a dead spouse and a prolific novelist, except the roles were reversed, with a widower who wrote bestselling books but suffered from writer's block for three years after his wife's death.

THE END OF THE WHOLE MESS

As 2005 began, Steve and Tabby had fallen into a comfortable rhythm of spending half the year in Maine and the other half in Florida. As his schedule continued to slow down—maybe there was something to this "retirement" thing after all—his kids started to ramp up their careers.

Joe's first collection of stories, *20th Century Ghosts,* was published in 2005 in a limited edition of two thousand copies by PS Publishing, a small specialty publisher, after every American publisher who had taken a look rejected it. The book won two Bram Stoker Awards and a World Fantasy Award—other winners that year included Haruki Murakami and George Saunders—and the British Fantasy Award for Best Fiction Collection.

Joe wanted to distance himself from his father as much as possible, choosing to make it on his work alone. When he first began to write seriously and submit his work shortly after graduating from college, he chose his namesake, Joe Hill, for his pen name. "I figured if I wrote genre fiction as Joseph King, it would look like a grab at my dad's coattails," he explained. "Whereas I could write whatever the hell I wanted as Joe Hill. I had ten years to write and not have the pressure of being a famous guy's kid."

His work style is very different from his dad's. "I'm not the kind of guy who can or wants to write thirty stories a year," he said. "It takes me a month or more to write a good story, not a week. I try like hell not to be boring and make an effort to avoid adverbs, which is how I describe my fiction: horror stories with few adverbs."

Joe met the woman who would become his wife, Leanora LaGrande, in the MFA program at Columbia University. "A lot of people marry their moms," Joe said. "I kind of married my dad. I'll go from the manuscript I gave her and the manuscript I gave him and go back and forth, and it's the same comments." Joe adds that Leanora reads Steve's manuscripts too.

Like his father, Joe started to work in other venues. He got in touch with an editor at Marvel Comics and wrote "Fanboyz," an eleven-page tale for *Spider-*

Man Unlimited. "Working on that story was the fulfillment of a very intense childhood fantasy," he said.

Like his older brother, after Owen attended Vassar College, he got an MFA from Columbia, though he had reservations about entering grad school. "Writing programs aren't for everyone, and if you want to write straight genre stories, you'll have a real battle on your hands," he said. But he benefited greatly from the time he spent at Columbia. "I had wonderful teachers who focused very hard on the details, on the precision of good writing, and helped coax work out of me that I'm very proud of."

Unlike his brother, however, he decided to keep his name intact. "Obviously I have an advantage as a writer in terms of name recognition, but it's also a disadvantage because people expect it just to be a nepotistic exercise and for you to suck," he said, which is the major reason why his stories are different from his father's. "I write more contemporary straight fiction with no supernatural elements. I wanted to find my own place in the world, not make any bread off his name."

Owen's first book, *We're All in This Together,* a collection of one novella and four short stories, was published by Bloomsbury in June 2005. As with his father, the inspiration for the title novella came from two disparate places: "I was morbidly depressed after Bush won the election in 2000, and I had this crazy idea that he'd step down because he didn't get the popular vote. I thought about what kind of person would actually do something about it and how he'd get his point across." He thought back to a family from Bangor that would write slogans and draw pictures on a billboard outside their house according to the season. He combined the two concepts into the novella.

Also like his brother, Owen met his future wife, Kelly Braffet, when he was in graduate school at Columbia. When reporters interviewed him for his book, they never failed to mention that the couple lived in a deconsecrated Catholic church in Brooklyn. Braffet, author of the novels *Josie and Jack,* the story of a brother and a sister who are psychologically dependent on each other, and *Last Seen Leaving,* about a mother and a daughter who are estranged from each other, said that Owen takes after his father as far as his work habits. "Owen works a hell of a lot more than I do, which makes me feel guilty, which makes me work more," she said.

Owen's thought trajectories also follow his father's. Braffet says that he'll come home from a simple trip to the corner store for a sandwich with an idea for his next novel. "I've got a great idea for a story," he'll say. "See, there's this birthday-party clown with Tourette's and he's got a brother who's a financial adviser, and they go deep-sea fishing in the Mediterranean surrounded by all of these urns of ancient olive oil."

For his part, Steve enjoys both his sons' works, though he does see clear differences: Joe clearly gravitated toward writing genre fiction, while Owen studiously avoided it. "I read Joe's stuff, and I relate to it because it's plot-driven and high conflict," Steve said. "Owen writes more like Bret Easton Ellis, flavor-of-the-month New York relationships.

"There are two great things about this. The first is that what Owen is doing doesn't bear any resemblance to my writing. And the second thing is, thank God he's good."

Naomi was also finding a firm foothold in her chosen field of the ministry. She graduated with a master's in divinity from Meadville Lombard Theological School in June 2005, where she won the Robert Charles Billings prize for excellence in scholarship, awarded to the student with the highest academic standing. After graduation, she was ordained by her home church, the First Universalist Church in Yarmouth and was assigned to her first parish later that summer: the Unitarian Universalist Church of Utica, New York.

As in her days as a restaurateur, she bristled whenever anyone asked about her parents. When asked what drew her to the Unitarian faith, she replied, "We begin and end with primary experience: awe, wonder, fear, trembling, amazement. Everything else is commentary."

After she got settled in upstate New York, Steve had to change the automatic response he'd given over the years whenever someone asked where he got his ideas from. "I used to say that I got my ideas from a small used-idea shop in Utica. I'd bring them down, dust them off, and they worked just fine. When Naomi became a pastor in Utica, I had to stop making jokes about it."

But that didn't mean he had to stop joking with her. "I tell her that Unitarianism is God for people who don't believe in God, and she just laughs."

In the summer of 2007, she left her position as pastor at the First Unitarian Church in Utica, New York, to become the minister at the River of Grass Unitarian Universalist Congregation in Plantation, Florida.

The Unitarian/Universalist faith is known for its acceptance of gay and lesbians, and even though she was warmly acknowledged by her own church, Naomi became easily enraged at those who weren't able to see past her sexuality and felt like shaking her fist at the world even though she was an ordained minister.

"I struggle with tolerating the theology that doesn't allow me to exist," she said. "Hellfire and damnation for gay and lesbian people, for women in ministry, for Unitarian Universalists. My paradox is learning to love more fully people who don't see those of us who are also people, created and beloved of God."

She maintains that she hasn't entirely abandoned the family business: "Everyone in my family tells stories. They use the written word and I tell stories through sermons."

The way she talks about giving a sermon sounds a lot like how her father has described writing. "To me, giving a sermon is thrilling. It's like dancing for a long time. Your sense of beginning and ending disappears, and you never know what will happen."

She has also followed her father's habit of incorporating popular-culture icons into her sermons. In the fall of 2007, she mentioned the Island of Misfit Toys, Winnie-the-Pooh, and *Harold and the Purple Crayon* in her sermons, among others.

Steve and Tabby are understandably proud of their grown-up brood. "It's such a surprise when kids are suddenly strong adults," said Tabitha. "For a long time, my basic standard of parenthood was nobody's in jail."

When editor Charles Ardai first got in touch with Steve about the Hard Case Crime series, a new line of original and reprinted detective paperback novels, the most he hoped for was a cover blurb for one of the books. A big fan of the genre, King decided he'd rather write a book than a blurb, with the result being *The Colorado Kid,* which was published in October 2005 to lead off a season including books by Lawrence Block, Ed McBain, and Donald E. Westlake. The novel was extremely short by King's usual standards, only 184 pages, but it was just a warm-up for King's next project. And it looked as if he had returned to his old ways, starting to crank them out again.

Steve finished writing *Cell* in July 2005 after he spent four months on the first draft. The next book scheduled to be published was *Lisey's Story,* in the fall of 2006, but Scribner switched gears and wanted *Cell* to come out first, almost instantly, as it turned out. Their target date was January 2006, because John Grisham didn't have a novel coming out that month, as he usually did, which meant there was a slot to fill. Publisher Susan Moldow also wanted to publish *Cell* first because she believed it would boost *Lisey's* numbers when it came out.

Steve turned around the final two drafts by October, and *Cell* was published in January.

Chuck Verrill edited *Cell,* as he had done with most of Steve's other books. But Steve wanted Nan Graham, who edited Frank McCourt's bestseller *Angela's Ashes* and has worked with Salman Rushdie and Toni Morrison, at Scribner to edit *Lisey's Story,* because he thought it needed a woman's touch. "I thought Chuck got a little out of joint about it because he had done all the other ones, but he did a great job on *Cell,* and Nan did a great job on *Lisey's Story,*" Steve said. "The books were like apples and oranges, so editing *Lisey's* had to be different from *Cell,* which really was an instant book."

For his part, he even handled his second and third drafts on each book differently. With *Cell,* Steve edited the book on a computer to respond to Chuck's comments and questions. When Steve edited *Lisey,* he followed his usual path of editing on paper, incorporating Nan's suggestions into an entirely new draft that he wrote again from the beginning. He viewed the books as falling into entirely distinct categories, along the line of how Graham Greene saw his books: some were novels and some were sheer entertainment. In King's eyes, *Lisey's Story* was a novel, while *Cell* was entertainment.

He was starting to exercise the same managerial style—deciding which editor was best to handle a particular book—when it came to movies based on his stories and novels, even if he had made up his mind that it was a hands-off film project. He wanted to have final casting approval over the actors who would appear in the films, even though he didn't usually object. In one case, however, he put his foot down. A producer was preparing to launch *Misery* on Broadway and sent Steve a list of candidates for the major characters. One of their choices for Annie Wilkes was Julia Roberts, but Steve immediately nixed the idea. "Roberts is a fine actor, but Annie is a big, brawny woman who's capable of slinging a guy around," he said. "Don't give me a pixie!"

After he put the finishing touches on *Cell,* Steve turned his attention to *Lisey's Story.* He'd wanted to write about a long-term marriage similar to his own for a long time.

"You fall in love with someone that every once in a while you'd like to strangle, but it's the relationship that I have enjoyed for the longest time," he said. He specifically wanted to explore how couples develop a secret language all their own. "In a long-term marriage, you might have words that you might not want to trot out in public. They aren't necessarily dirty, but they may be so babyish so as not to sound good inside that environment."

He also wanted to write about how over time a married couple essentially creates two worlds: their own inner world and the outer world. "The whole idea of the book was that it would be centered on their interior existence," he said. In doing so, he knew he would have to dig deeper emotionally. "I wanted to write something like a Hank Williams song that would convey something about the essential loneliness in people, and how you can love, but sooner or later it ends."

But he was also wanted to test out one of his ideas about retirement: that he could continue to write but not necessarily publish, a concept that was solidified when he recalled a story that Bill Thompson, his editor at Doubleday, had told him years before:

J. D. Salinger went into his bank to put a package in his safe-deposit box. A woman at the bank asked if the parcel was a new book. He nodded, and she asked if he planned to publish it. His reply: "What for?"

"What if there was a writer like that and somebody held up the bank, not for money but for the unpublished manuscripts?" Steve theorized, going one step further. "What if a famous writer died and there was a crazy person who wanted the unpublished manuscripts? That turned out to be Dooley in *Lisey's Story*."

Steve poured his very essence into the book, more than he had ever done with any other book, and yet he knew when he finished, he might decide not to publish it.

That decision would be up to Tabby. She read the book in two sittings before she offered her opinion.

"It's about another writer," she said.

"Yeah."

"People will think that Scott and Lisey are you and me."

"I'll tell them it's not," he said.

"This book is important to you, isn't it?"

"Yes."

"What would you say if I say it worries me?"

"Then I'll put it away."

"It does worry me, but it's too good not to publish."

When the book came out, critics said it was the most intimate book he'd ever written, as well as one of his best-crafted novels. "King is as cagey as a veteran pitcher, employing a career's worth of tricks to good effect," wrote Jim Windolf in the *New York Times*.

"It's a very special book," Steve said. "This is the only book I've ever written where I don't want to read the reviews, because there will be some people who are going to be ugly to this book. I couldn't stand that, the way you would hate people to be ugly to someone you love, because I love this book."

In June 2006, Tabby also had a book published, *Candles Burning*. She had agreed to complete an unfinished manuscript left behind by the writer Michael McDowell, a friend who died in 1999.

She referred to McDowell, a supernatural horror writer who had also written the screenplay for *Beetlejuice*, as her soul mate.

They met at a mystery convention, though she was already familiar with his *Cold Moon over Babylon* as well as the *Blackwater Chronicles*, a serial novel published in six monthly installments in 1983.

McDowell had left behind several hundred pages of *Candles Burning*, and Tabby was unaware that her friend had even been working on it. A few years after his death from AIDS, McDowell's editor, Susan Allison, contacted Tabby to see if she wanted to try finishing it. She was eager to take a look, primarily because she knew that he was a great writer to work with. "He collaborated with so many people, on all kinds of things," she said. "That takes a generosity that isn't common."

Once the estate and the publisher agreed that Tabby was the best writer to finish the book, they left her alone with the unfinished manuscript and pages of notes with the instructions to do what she thought was best with this supernatural Southern gothic novel with plenty of ghosts to go around.

To prepare to finish the book, she read the unfinished manuscript and reread a few of McDowell's books, then researched the cities where parts of the story took place, New Orleans and Pensacola, Florida, among them. Though McDowell had not written an outline or provided a firm ending to the story, once Tabby had grounded herself in the work-in-progress, she listened to the characters and started to write according to where they took her.

When *Candles Burning* was published, she already knew what kind of reception to expect: her familial connections would attract a good deal of attention to the book, but in the end the quality of the story and the writing would pull her through. "People tell me, 'I've never read one of your books,' and I say, 'Millions haven't!'" she joked. "Steve set a standard for millions and millions of books sold that no sane person expects to reach."

Though she planned to travel to promote the book, her plans were limited. "I've got a big streak of that Yankee live-in-the-woods mentality," she said.

"Too many people stimulate me too much. I can only take three days in New York and twenty-four hours in L.A. It's unnerving for me to spend that much time with people not looking at you."

As usual, Steve was taking the opposite tack. He decided to challenge himself by setting a novel in a place other than Maine, and since he was spending so much time in Florida, he set it there.

Along with his outlook on life, which has mellowed, his writing habits have changed. "My brains used to work better than they do now," he said. "I wrote something last week and I looked at it the other day and thought it looked familiar, so I went back a hundred pages and found that I had duplicated something that I had written before. Paging Dr. Alzheimer."

He was no longer writing two thousand to three thousand words a day. Now he was happy if he cranked out a thousand words during a writing session.

Life was changing, but life was good.

In February 2007, the first issue of *The Dark Tower: The Gunslinger Born* was published by Marvel Comics in comic-book format. Seven issues were planned to cover the first book in the series and would appear each month through August. The entire seven-issue run of *The Gunslinger Born* was collected into a hardcover edition, released on November 7, 2007.

Though King had always intended *The Dark Tower* to exist only in book form, he jumped at the chance to see how it would look as a comic book. "It's a blast to see them adapted in an illustrated form, and that's all that I wanted out of it," he said.

He was also starting to come around to the idea of having someone rework his epic for the silver screen. Frank Darabont had suggested doing it, but even he realized it was a pie-in-the-sky dream. "The thought of adapting that saga makes me break out in a cold sweat, curl into a ball, and weep," said Darabont. "It's just so metaphysical and trippy. So much of it is almost impossible to visualize on-screen."

In February, Steve announced that he'd sold an option for *The Dark Tower* to J. J. Abrams and Damon Lindelof, creators of the TV show *Lost*. Steve loves the show, and he figured he'd give Abrams and Lindelof a chance to see what they could do. For the privilege, he charged them $19.

That same month, Joe Hill's real identity came out when his first novel,

Heart-Shaped Box, was published. "My real secret to keeping a low profile was failure," he said. "Nothing helps a writer stay under the radar like not getting published. I didn't want someone to publish my book because of who my dad was or what my last name was. And in that sense, I feel like getting turned down was actually a case of my pen name doing its job."

Even before the book was published, however, the online rumor mill had already started to buzz about the resemblance between Joe Hill and Stephen King, not only physically but in writing style and subject matter. "I had pretty much run to the end of my rope around that time," said Hill, describing a book signing he'd done in the UK where readers had commented on the similarities in appearance. "It would have been nice if the book could have come out and been out for a while, but it just didn't work out that way."

While Tabby totally got why Joe chose a pen name, Steve didn't understand why his son needed to hide who he was. Indeed, Hill said it was hard for his father to say nothing: "My dad likes to boast on his kids and isn't used to keeping quiet about anything. Secrecy is not his strong suit. But he did it."

"I didn't offer any advice, just encouragement," said Steve. "Everyone does it their own way. I just told them to read everything within reach and treasure the bad, because that shows there's hope for you."

Just as Steve told readers not to think that the married couple of *Lisey's Story* was a mirror image of himself and Tabby, Joe also warned his fans to avoid a knee-jerk reaction that he's referring to his own father when he writes about bad fathers. "I can write a bad father, and he'll just laugh," Joe said. "He won't see it as a stand-in for himself."

While Joe's book is a bestseller and editors are clamoring for more of his work, he still sounds a bit wistful about the days when he could write under the radar: "If one of my stories appeared in a magazine, people just read it as a story. They didn't have any preconceptions. Now I feel like there's a bit more pressure because there'll be some comparison."

On April 14, 2007, Sarah Jane White Spruce died at age eighty-three. Tabby's mother was gone, and Steve had lost a devoted mother-in-law.

There wasn't much time to mourn, however, because the accolades for Steve's accomplishments in fields other than horror continued. Two weeks after his mother-in-law's death, he attended the annual Edgar Banquet by the Mystery Writers of America and was given the Grand Master Award for 2007. The prize is akin to a lifetime achievement award in the field, and Steve was heartened by the reception of his peers, unlike what had happened at the National Book Foundation award back in 2003.

Then in June, King received a lifetime achievement award from the Canadian Booksellers Association. He was the first non-Canadian to win the award since its inception in 2000.

He also frequently attended awards ceremonies to honor other celebrities. Steve and Tabby planned to attend a dinner in Los Angeles held by a Jewish philanthropic organization to honor the actor Billy Crystal, but Tabby didn't go because she wasn't feeling well. Steve called Kathi Kamen Goldmark, who played with him in the Remainders, and invited her to go with him instead. She said she'd love to. Because she has an informal northern-California style and it was a formal dinner, "I got three calls from his office making sure I knew I was supposed to wear a dress," she said, laughing.

"When we walked through the doors of the hotel to go to the banquet, the explosion of lightbulbs and people jumping out at Steve was terrifying," she said. "I have never seen paparazzi before in my life and I'm sure I never will again, but then I realized that this is something that happens to him all the time."

Goldmark was impressed by how he handled it. "We couldn't have a conversation or even finish a sentence because people were constantly coming over to talk to him. I had a different look at what his life was like in that world and why the band is such a nice, comfortable place for him because people aren't treating him like some weird famous guy."

After a hiatus of several years, Steve played once again with the Remainders at Webster Hall in New York on June 1 in connection with BookExpo America (BEA).

"It's like camp for grown-ups," said Amy Tan. "I'd kill the whales to do this."

King said that he never took the band seriously, and that he just did it for fun. "Somebody once said that the Remainders without Stephen King is like the Grateful Dead without Jerry Garcia, which I thought was really sweet," he said. "It's a lot of fun to go out and do something that is more of a hobby than work."

He was well aware that his bandmates had different ideas. "Dave and Ridley and Greg [Iles] take this very seriously," he said. "It's like watching three type A people prepare for the GREs. I'm just a hood ornament on this band."

Though the band members loved to play music, Ridley Pearson said the primary reason they schedule three-city tours is to hang out with each other. "With a one-night gig, there's not enough time to spend quality time with everybody in the band," he explained. "When we do a tour, we're all trapped in airplanes or buses and that's what we love because we all get to hang out and talk and have fun together. Of course, the band should be a lot better since we've played together for fifteen years, and we aren't. But the friendships are way better."

Though Steve loved going on tour, Tabby had become more cautious. "She's more down-to-earth than Steve and she really looks out for him," said Pearson. "I remember she told me once that she didn't want the band to be Steve's John Lennon moment."

Pearson remembered a gig in Rhode Island where they needed twenty state police to form a human barricade to get Steve through the crowds: "It was just insane, just like the Beatles. People were throwing stuff at us and trying to touch him."

In June 2007, *Blaze* was published. A Bachman book he wrote before *Carrie*, Steve had referred to it as one of his "trunk novels," one written for practice that he had forgotten about long ago.

Frank Muller, a professional audiobook reader who'd narrated several of King's books onto CD, had become permanently disabled from a motorcycle accident in the fall of 2001 and would never be able to work again. Not only did he have no money, but he had no insurance and owed back taxes to the IRS. He had one child and a few days before the accident he found out that another was on the way.

Steve regularly listened to audiobooks, and he's served as a reader on some recording sessions, so he had a great respect for what Muller did. "It's exhausting work because there are a lot of takes and it is very difficult work," Steve said. "I think no book really exists until it has been done in audio. Good work gets better when it is read aloud, and bad work is mercilessly exposed. It's like taking a strong light and shining it on facial structure. When you do that, even good makeup won't hide bad writing."

Steve was tormented about his friend and certainly knew what it took to recover from a life-threatening accident. Steve set up the Wavedancer Foundation in 2002 to help Frank. But that got Steve to thinking about other freelance performing artists who suffer disabling accidents or illness, so he started another nonprofit called the Haven Foundation to provide grants to freelance writers, artists, and performers who are not able to support themselves because of a sudden disability or illness.

Steve invited authors John Irving and J. K. Rowling to perform in a two-night benefit at Radio City Music Hall called "Harry, Carrie, and Garp" so the Haven Foundation could raise enough money to begin offering grants.

Steve had long thought about giving the copyright to one of his books to the foundation, which would then receive 100 percent of the revenue from advances, royalties, and foreign rights sales, and he thought of *Blaze*.

He dug it out, reread it, and thought it really wasn't that bad, just needing some revision and a polish. Scribner published it in June. *Booklist* gave it a starred review, calling the novel a tribute to John Steinbeck's *Of Mice and Men*, and it hit number two on the *New York Times* bestseller list the first week it was out.

In 2007 Steve and Tabby expanded their real estate holdings yet again. In May they bought another house on Casey Key in Osprey, about two miles away from the one they'd bought five years earlier. At $2.2 million, the new one was a bargain compared to their main house, which was now assessed by the county at more than $12 million.

Then in October, Steve and Tabby bought the mansion next door to their home in Bangor. The white Victorian house with a mansard roof, known as the Charles P. Brown House, was built in 1872 and valued then at $10,000. The Kings paid $750,000, according to city records. Steve mentioned that he wanted to turn the house into a library, or perhaps a museum, and he planned to build an underground tunnel connecting the two houses and ride a trolley between them.

"I fantasize about this and Tabby says, 'Why do we need to do that?' And I tell her, 'Because we could!'"

Steve was chosen to serve as guest editor for the *Best American Short Stories 2007*, published in October. In a sense, he'd come full circle. Short stories had given him his start and pulled his hide from the fire numerous times in his early days, a check arriving just as Naomi had come down with an ear infection and Tabby had run out of pink stuff from the toddler's previous bout.

Indeed, Steve was in high demand in the short-story market that year. Otto Penzler planned on asking him to be guest editor of *The Best American Mystery Stories of 2007*, but Heidi Pitlor, the editor of *Best American Short Stories* beat him to it. "I'll just have to ask him again in the future," said Penzler.

The inevitable, grumbling about the dumbing down of American culture came when it was announced that King would serve as editor for the 2007 edition. But he must have been heartened by the company he kept among previous guest editors of the series: Margaret Atwood and Richard Ford, Michael Chabon and Walter Mosley.

Though his previous collection of short stories, *Everything's Eventual,* had come out five years earlier, he maintained that he still loved the form and wanted it to continue even though the number of short-story markets had precipitously declined through the years.

"I've fallen away from writing short stories and thought maybe if I reacquaint myself with what's going on in the short-story landscape, I'll be reinvigorated and want to write them again," he said. "I've never really lost my taste for them, and it would be sad to feel that a skill I once had had slipped away."

He dove into the project headfirst: "I wanted to expand the playing field and find stories online and in magazines that I hadn't seen represented before, like *Ellery Queen's Mystery Magazine* and the *Magazine of Fantasy and Science Fiction.* I don't think I've ever worked harder on a book in my life than I did on this one." Pitlor said she read more than 4,000 stories and passed 120 along to King that she felt were good enough, but by hunting on his own he estimated that he plowed through more than 400 stories.

His gig as editor accomplished exactly what he wanted it to do: it jump-started his short-story writing skills again. About the same time that the anthology came out, Steve sold a story to the *Magazine of Fantasy and Science Fiction,* which paid $500. While some would call it charity on King's part, he disagreed, and the old frugal native Mainer came out:

"I wouldn't say it's charity because I could buy some hot dinners with that, but I'd love to see the magazine reach a wider reading public," the subtext being that because his name was on the cover, the magazine would likely order a higher print run and sell out.

He wrote another story called "A Very Tight Place." When he and Tabby are in Florida, Steve goes for a daily walk on a relatively isolated stretch of road. One late afternoon he saw a Porta Potti at a construction site. The workers had all gone home for the day, and Steve, still a mile from home, thought he'd take advantage of it.

When he stepped inside, he felt it rock slightly and his mind went into overdrive. "If one of those things fell over on its door with a person inside, he'd be in trouble. Immediately I'm thinking about Poe and his story 'The

Premature Burial' and all the buried-alive stories that I've ever read, but I've never read a story about anyone trapped in a Porta Potti. I'm not a particularly claustrophobic person myself, but I thought, 'Oh, my God, this is wonderful!'"

It was continuing to be a busy fall 1997 with the release of *The Mist* in November. Steve wrote the novella back in 1980.

He was living in Bridgton, Maine, at the time and went to the market to pick up a few things for Tabby. He was headed for the checkout line when he suddenly looked up and noticed that the entire front wall of the market was made of plate glass. The first thought that popped into his mind when he saw the window was "What if giant bugs started to fly into the glass?"

As usual, he was off and running. The story appeared in *Dark Forces*, an anthology edited by Kirby McCauley, his former agent.

When Frank Darabont wrote the screenplay for *The Mist*, he deliberately changed the ending of the novella, which had been unclear at best. Though it usually bugged Steve when his story line was radically changed, this time he didn't mind; in fact, he thought Darabont, who also directed the movie, greatly enhanced the story.

"I thought it was terrific but it jarred me," Steve said. "I knew what was coming the first time that I looked at the movie in a rough cut, and it still jarred me. It took a second viewing to get used to the idea that it was probably the only ending in terms of the world that had been created in that story."

Duma Key was published in January 2008 and represented yet another departure for Steve. For one, the novel was set in Florida and Minnesota, but it was also the story of a divorced man who began to pursue artwork as a hobby, both of which were outside King's realm of personal experience.

"I love art, but I couldn't draw a picture of a cat," he said. "So I took what I feel about writing and put it in a book about an artist. After all, the last thing I need in my books is another author."

The initial spark for the novel came when he was out on his daily afternoon walk. "I was walking on this deserted road—the only kind of road I walk on now—when I saw this sign that said *Caution: Children*. I thought, what kind of children do you have to be cautious about? Then I got this image of two dead girls."

Though *Duma Key* was critically acclaimed and hit the top of the best-seller lists the first week it came out, Steve has pretty much accepted that he is no longer at the top of the heap when it comes to bestsellers. Tom Clancy and John Grisham and King are often mentioned in the same breath, but King has had a good degree of attrition among readers, and his numbers have fallen more rapidly than those of the other guys, a trend that can directly be traced back to when he began to stray from the straightforward horror formula that had made him famous. For instance, the first print run for *Lisey's Story* was 1.1 million copies, while the combined print run for *Desperation* and *The Regulators* was 3 million. Also, the bookselling business, and overall readership numbers, have dramatically changed since he first published *Carrie*.

"The bottom line is always sales," he said. "Grisham outsells me four to one, but it's not a big deal to me anymore. I look at the *New York Times* bestseller list and ask, 'Do I really want to bust my ass to be on this list with Danielle Steel and David Baldacci and the born-again books?'"

Though he has long regretted his 1985 statement "I am the literary equivalent of a Big Mac and fries," he no longer feels he has to defend himself against it. "I'm still paying for that remark," he admitted. "What I meant by it is that I'm tasty and I go down smooth, but I don't think that a steady diet of Stephen King would make anybody a healthy human being."

"He glories in popular culture and popular literature," said George MacLeod. "It's just the basic dynamic of who he is, and I don't think he's ever going to change."

After more than thirty-five years since his first book was published, a wide-ranging oeuvre, and the admission that if he couldn't write, he'd die, it would be reasonable to assume that Stephen King has gotten the writing part of his life down to a science, that it's streamlined. But he says that through the years it hasn't gotten any easier, he just knows how to push the right buttons so the work will flow. While he also adds that it hasn't got any harder, he's discovered that he needs to continue to push off into directions that are unfamiliar to him.

He admits that his *Entertainment Weekly* column has gotten more difficult to write as time passes: "I want it to be good, but at the same time I want it to feel casual and off-the-cuff, and that's not easy to achieve all the time."

Steve said, "It's grow or die. If you're only going to get to go to the dance once, you ought to do more than just the box-step waltz." With that, he and John Mellencamp are putting the finishing touches on their collaborative musical called *The Ghost Brothers of Darkland County* and testing it out through readings and workshops before bringing it on the road and ultimately to Broadway.

Mellencamp initially approached Steve with the idea to collaborate on a musical set in the 1950s based on a true story about two brothers in love with the same girl. One brother accidentally shoots and kills the other, and the girl and the remaining brother bring him to the hospital. They're speeding, and on the way to the hospital they drive into a tree and are both killed. Mellencamp offered to write the music if Steve would write the play. He loved the idea and, true to form, sat down and cranked out a sixty-seven-page treatment.

"In a way, John came to me at the right time," Steve said. "He's been doing what he does for a long time, and I've been doing what I do for a long time. He's tried to keep the music fresh and try different things and formats."

The two clicked immediately when they started working together and got along famously. "I love Steve, he's nothing like everyone thinks he is," said Mellencamp, "and we really have a lot in common. He lives in the middle of nowhere, I live in the middle of nowhere. He's not comfortable being around a lot of people and neither am I. We're kinda antisocial guys, and we're big mouths too."

While Steve continued to expand his horizons, he still feared to tread in a few places. For instance, the idea of directing another movie still occasionally crossed his mind: "I'd never say never, and I think it would be great to direct a movie when I wasn't drunk out of my mind and see what came out. But I'm not crazy enough to do it again."

He's long said he writes about the things that scare him most, such as rats and airplanes, but he hasn't yet managed to work up the courage to cover one subject in particular.

"I want to write about spiders because it's the one theme that cuts right across and scares just about everybody," he said. "To me spiders are just about the most horrible, awful things that I can think about."

Today, work is his sole drug, and in one way it's taken up the slack in the vacuum of his drug-free life: when he's not writing, his brain and body go into withdrawal.

He still smokes cigarettes, though he's down to only three a day. He kicked alcohol, cocaine, powerful prescription painkillers, and almost every mind-altering substance under the sun.

"I'm not as angry as I used to be because I'm not twenty-five anymore," he said. "I'm sixty, and that'll kick your ass every time."

Both his charitable organizations, the Haven Foundation and the Stephen and Tabitha King Foundation, are going strong. "Steve believes religiously in tithing, and I don't," said Tabby. "I just believe you can't take it with you, so we try to unload as much as we can. We're happy to do it and we wish we could do more. There's the feeling that it's the teaspoon against the sea."

"Give away a dime for every dollar you make, because if you don't give it, the government's just going to take it," Steve said. "If you think you can't afford it, just look at the taxes you pay on every gallon of gas you buy."

"Steve is coming to the end of what has been an extraordinary career," said Tony Magistrale. "He's got money, he's got popular acclaim, the only thing he doesn't have is for people to take him seriously and recognize that this is not a hack writer."

But even that has been changing in the years since the *New Yorker* published his first story. One senses that he feels a bit torn about the respect. "People ask me when I am going to write something serious, but questions like that always hurts," he said. "They don't understand it's like walking up to somebody and asking how it feels to be a nigger. My answer is that I'm as serious as I can be every time I sit down at a typewriter. It took me about twenty years to get over that question and not be kind of ashamed about the books I write. There'll always be a market for shit, of course. Just look at Jeffrey Archer! He writes like old people fuck."

But one thing hasn't changed: Steve still doesn't understand why anyone would be interested in his life.

"I think we all feel that way," said Ridley Pearson. "After all, we spend most of our time in a little room typing, and there's nothing interesting about that. But that's who he is, he's not an egocentric kind of guy."

That is not to say he isn't competitive, because he's extremely competitive. "Despite the fact that he's already had it thirty-six times, Steve still wants that number one spot on the list every time he publishes," said Pearson. "But he doesn't think that there's anything remarkable about that, and he just feels that there are a lot more interesting people around than him."

He's a grandfather three times over now; Joe and Leanora have three sons: Ethan, Aiden, and Ryan.

The title for Stephen's new short-story collection is *Just After Sunset,* though his original title for the book was *Unnatural Acts of Intercourse.* The book was published in November 2008.

"The appeal of horror has always been consistent," he said. "People like to slow down and look at the accident. That's the bottom line."

Through the years, he's been tempted to hide out, to deny who he is when he's recognized. "The day that I deny my identity, the day that I say that I am not who I am, is the day I quit this business forever," he said. "Close up shop, turn off the word processor, and never write another word. Because if the price of what you do is a loss of your identity, it's time to stop."

ACKNOWLEDGMENTS

As always, thanks must first go to superagent Scott Mendel for shepherding this book through its various hoops and barrels.

Next at bat is Peter Joseph, who edited the book and offered valuable insight and suggestions as I delved into King's psyche.

Once again, transcriptionist Paula Hancock helped make sense of hours of tapes.

Genealogist Margaret Dube of Common Folk Ancestry in Kittery, Maine, dug up some great details about Steve and Tabby's beloved Maine.

Thanks to King's friends, acquaintances, business associates, and assorted others who offered revealing stories and anecdotes, including Dave Barry, George Beahm, Michael Collings, Kathi Kamen Goldmark, Rick Hautala, Peter Higgins, Jonathan Jenkins, Jack Ketchum, Richard Kobritz, George MacLeod, Anthony Magistrale, Ridley Pearson, Otto Penzler, Sandy Phippen, Lew Purinton, James Renner, Samuel Schuman, Stephen Spignesi, Bev Vincent, Stanley Wiater, and Nye Willden.

Kudos to the Buddies for knowing how to deal with me when I'm in the throes of a deadline: Tim Ashe, Leslie Caputo, Bob DiPrete, Doc and Nancy Gerow, Dean Hollatz, Ed Leavitt, Don McKibbin, Spring Romer, Paul and Cary Rothe, and Andy and Donna Vinopal.

This is a chronological list of Stephen King's books interspersed within the events of his life. For a complete bibliography of his works, including short stories, novels, and screenplays, the best source is his own Web site: stephenking.com.

1947 September 21: Stephen Edwin King is born in Portland, Maine, to Donald and Ruth King, who already had a two-year-old boy, David

1949: Donald walks out one evening for a pack of cigarettes and never comes back

1949–58: Ruth and her two boys move from house to house constantly, including in Chicago; West De Pere, Wisconsin; and Stratford, Connecticut

1958 Summer: The Kings settle in West Durham, Maine, to live with Ruth's elderly parents

1962 June: Steve graduates from grammar school

1962 September: Steve enrolls at Lisbon High School in Lisbon Falls, Maine

1966 June: Steve graduates from Lisbon High School

1966 September: Steve enters the University of Maine at Orono as a freshman

1967 October: Steve sells his first short story, "The Glass Floor," to the magazine *Startling Mystery Stories*

1968: Steve meets Tabitha Spruce, a college student a year younger

1969 February: Steve begins writing a weekly column, "The Garbage Truck," for the *Maine Campus*

1970 June: Steve graduates from UMO with a bachelor of science degree in English

1970 June: Naomi Rachel, Steve and Tabitha's first daughter, is born

1970 October: Short story "Graveyard Shift" is published in *Cavalier*, marking the beginning of a steady stream of sales of Steve's short stories to men's magazines

1971 January 2: Steve and Tabitha marry in Old Town, Maine

1974 April: *Carrie* published

1975 October: *Salem's Lot* published

1976 November: *Carrie* movie released

1977 January: *The Shining* published

1977 September: *Rage* by Richard Bachman published

1978 February: *Night Shift* published

1978 September: *The Stand* published

1979 July: *The Long Walk* by Richard Bachman published

1979 August: *The Dead Zone* published

1980 May: *The Shining* movie released

1980 September: *Firestarter* published

1981 April: *Danse Macabre* published

1981 April: *Roadwork* by Richard Bachman published

1981 October: *Cujo* published

1982 May: *Running Man* by Richard Bachman published

1982 July: *Creepshow* book published

1982 August: *Different Seasons* published

1982 November: *Creepshow* movie released

1983 April: *Christine* published

1983 October: *The Dead Zone* movie released

1983 November: *Pet Sematary* published

1983 December: *Christine* movie released

1984 April: *Cycle of the Werewolf* published

1984 May: *Firestarter* movie released

1984 November: *Thinner* by Richard Bachman published

1984 November: *Talisman* published

1985 February: Richard Bachman revealed

1985 April: *Cat's Eye* movie released

1985 June: *Skeleton Crew* published

1985 July: King directs *Maximum Overdrive* in Wilmington, North Carolina

1986 July: *Maximum Overdrive* released

1986 August: *Stand by Me* released

1986 September: *IT* published

1987 February: *Eyes of the Dragon* published

1987 June: *Misery* published

1987 November: *Tommyknockers* published

1988 September: *The Dark Tower I: The Gunslinger* published

1988 November: *Nightmares in the Sky* published

1989 March: *The Dark Tower II: The Drawing of the Three* published

1989 November: *The Dark Half* published

1990 May: *The Stand Uncut* published

1990 September: *Four Past Midnight* published

1990 October: *Graveyard Shift* movie released

1991 August: *The Dark Tower III: The Wastelands* published

1991 October: *Needful Things* published

1992 May: *Gerald's Game* published

1993 January: *Dolores Claiborne* published

1993 October: *Nightmares and Dreamscapes* published

1994 April: *Insomnia* published

1994 May: *The Stand* TV miniseries debuts on ABC

1994 September: *The Shawshank Redemption* movie released

1994 October: "The Man in the Black Suit" is published in the *New Yorker*

1995 July: *Rose Madder* published

1996: King receives O. Henry Award for "The Man in the Black Suit"

1996: March through August: *The Green Mile* is published monthly in six installments

1996 October 1: *Desperation* and *The Regulators* are published on the same day

1997 November: *The Dark Tower IV: Wizard and Glass* published

1998 September: *Bag of Bones* published

1999 February: *Storm of the Century* TV miniseries debuts on ABC

1999 April: *The Girl Who Loved Tom Gordon* published

1999 June 19: King is seriously injured when he's hit by a van while walking

1999 September: *Hearts in Atlantis* published

1999 December 10: *The Green Mile* movie released; Steve and Tabby show up at the premiere

2000 March: *Riding the Bullet* e-book released

2000 July: *The Plant* e-book released

2000 October: *On Writing* published

2001 March: *Dreamcatcher* published

2001 September: *Black House,* written with Peter Straub, published

2002 March: *Everything's Eventual* published

2002 September: *From a Buick 8* published

2003 June: *The Dark Tower* books I–IV reissued

2003 November: *The Dark Tower V: Wolves of the Calla* published

2003 November 19: King receives National Book Foundation award

2003 November 23: King hospitalized with pneumonia

2004 March: *Kingdom Hospital* miniseries debuts on ABC

2004 April 7: King finishes writing *The Dark Tower* series

2004 June: *The Dark Tower VI: Song of Susannah* published

2004 September 21: *The Dark Tower VII: The Dark Tower* published, King's fifty-seventh birthday

2004 October 27: The Boston Red Sox win the World Series

2004 December: *Faithful: Two Diehard Boston Red Sox Fans Chronicle the Historic 2004 Season* published, written with Stewart O'Nan

2005 October: *The Colorado Kid* published

2006 January: *Cell* published

2006 October: *Lisey's Story* published

2007 February–August: *The Dark Tower: The Gunslinger Born* comic books published

2007 June: *Blaze,* a Richard Bachman book, published

2007 October: *Best American Short Stories 2007* published, King as editor

2007 November: *The Mist* movie released

2008 January: *Duma Key* published

2008 November: *Just After Sunset: Stories* published

INTRODUCTION

1 "I'm afraid of everything": *The Mist* press conference, November 13, 2007.

1 "I'll just keep on typing till I get to a safe number": *Bare Bones,* p. 37.

1 "the sums of these numbers add up to thirteen": *Castle Rock,* September 1987.

2 "I can only get it so small": *Dennis Miller Live,* April 3, 1998.

2 "the fact that I'm not doing it nags at me": *Paris Review,* Fall 2006.

3 "gathered at your fence snapping pictures": *Castle Rock,* February 1989.

3 "who wants to be the best at what he does": *New York Times,* August 13, 2000.

4 "because their fathers are gone": *Dream Makers,* 2: 279.

4 "Writers don't outgrow it": *Weekly Reader Writing* magazine, October 2006.

4 "all of this makes him wonderful company": Tenebres.com, 2000.

5 "get on with the work": *Bare Bones,* p. 70.

CHAPTER ONE: APT PUPIL

10 "trouble came easy to him": *Bare Bones,* p. 35.

12 "some years after the fact": *Danse Macabre,* p. 116.

12 "'My, that's *crisp!*'": *Bare Bones,* p. 41.

13 "Write one of your own": *On Writing,* p. 28.

14 "beyond anything I have ever felt": Ibid., p. 24.

14 "about what my name is!": *Fresh Air,* October 10, 2000.

14 "he was an unperson": *Guardian,* September 14, 2000.

15 "Tell them he's in the navy": *Entertainment Weekly,* September 27, 2002.

15 "her other sisters kept their husbands": Ibid.

15 "bulging out as the bat hits it": *Bare Bones,* p. 210.

16 "I'm going to write this junk": Ibid.

16 "in a frame like a movie screen": *Bare Bones,* p. 128.

16 "you can go insane quite easily": Ibid.

16 "worried about my sanity a lot": *60 Minutes,* February 16, 1997.

16 "you were in pain or frightened or sad": *Fresh Air,* October 10, 2000.

16 "you were supposed to behave": *Faces of Fear,* p. 241.

17 "young and very credulous age": *Fresh Air,* October 10, 2000.

17 "a figure of happiness and fun being evil": *Weekly Reader Writing* magazine, October 2006.

17 "I'd get pneumonia and die": *Bare Bones,* p. 39.

18 "into orbit around Earth called *Sputnik*": Ibid.

18 "and it went away": *Faces of Fear,* p. 243.

18 "I spent a lot of miserable hours": *Boston Globe,* April 15, 1990.

18 "by a terrible old lady in black": *Bare Bones,* p. 40.

18 "the corpse opened its eyes and looked at me": *Complete Stephen King Encyclopedia,* p. 19.

19 "as clearly now as when it happened": *Writers Dreaming,* p. 135.

20 "bends your mind a little": Ibid.

20 "and all juvenile fiction for me": *Paris Review,* Fall 2006.

21 "total senile dementia and was incontinent": *New Yorker,* September 7, 1998.

21 "Good God, you're warped": *Bare Bones,* p. 61.

22 "these people are not": *Hollywood's Stephen King,* p. 6.

22 "and get out of his way": *Feast of Fear,* p. 245.

22 "it was in a lot of people": *60 Minutes,* February 16, 1997.

22 " 'here's the starting line, GO!' ": *Stephen King: Master of the Macabre,* TLC/BBC documentary, 1999.

22 "tough even if you weren't": *Bare Bones,* p. 115.

22 "sort of work it out for myself": Ibid., 33, 34.

23 "streaming with sweat": *Complete Stephen King Encyclopedia,* p. 52.

23 "it affected him deeply": Ibid., p. 58.

24 "he was more isolated than we were": Ibid.

24 "a great big Cadillac!": Ibid.

24 "I'd be in another world": *Bare Bones,* p. 25.

CHAPTER TWO: HEAD DOWN

26 "He hit the sidewalk and splattered": *Nightline,* November 15, 2007.

26 "before she finally drowned": Ibid.

27 "you'd always be pregnant": *I Want to Be Typhoid Stevie.*

27 "got in your clothes, your hair": *New York Times,* October 26, 1988.

28 "disembodied vaginas and things that have teeth": *Salon,* September 24, 1998.

29 "nobody wanted to see her change the mold": *Feast of Fear,* p. 11.

30 "never really did very much": *Weekly Reader Writing* magazine, October 2006.

30 "That's why he left the marriage": Ibid.

31 "one of them was retarded": *Feast of Fear,* p. 254.

31 "something awful will happen": *The Mist* press conference, November 13, 2007.

31 "somebody to haul off on me": *Feast of Fear,* p. 90.

32 "jump out at him or scare him": *Weekend Edition,* May 10, 2003.

32 "were taunters instead of tauntees": Keynote address, annual meeting, Vermont Library Conference, May 26, 1999.

32 "which is fine by me": *Weekend Edition,* May 10, 2003.

33 "robots reading my work": *Castle Rock,* March 1987.

34 "making out like crazy in the backseat": Ben Rawortit interview.

35 "with her on his lap": *Stephen King Country,* p. 40.

36 "pissed off and confused": *Mid-Life Confidential,* p. 30.

36 "possibly smoke?": Ibid., p. 31.

37 "Don't ever forget it": *Writer's Digest,* October 1977.

40 "sit right up and beg for it like dogs": *Stephen King from A to Z,* p. 87.

40 "It was very unsettling": *Bare Bones,* p. 66.

CHAPTER THREE: THE GUNSLINGER

41 "already formed even back then": *UMO Alumni Magazine,* Fall 1989.

41 "He created his own world": Ibid.

43 "a place for us at the table": *Bangor Daily News,* January 23, 2008.

44 "my teachers at college": *Dream Makers,* 2: 27.

45 "can be seriously damaged emotionally": *Bare Bones,* p. 43.

46 "these kids just weren't prepared for it": *Highway Patrolman,* July 1987.

47 "really dangerous in a lot of ways": *A Good Read,* Maine Public Television, August 2004.

47 "for a number of different stories I've written": *Salon,* September 24, 1998.

47 "you're going to find in a garbage truck": *UMO Alumni Magazine,* Fall 1999.

48 "occasionally disappear into our own realm": *Maine Campus,* December 18, 1969.

48 "with a filthy mouth and a vapid mind": *Maine Campus,* November 13, 1969.

48 "a serious decision about birth control": *Maine Campus,* August 1, 1969.

49 "but with no control": Ibid.

49 "would write more than horror stories": *UMO Alumni Magazine,* Fall 1999.

50 "a version of himself that rang true": Ibid.

50 "yet public in a loud way": Ibid.

51 "the part of a very wild man": Ibid.

52 "a lot of bullshit like that": Amazon.com, September 1998.

52 "he got a letter into the paper before I did": *New Hampshire Sunday News,* June 27, 1993.

52 "because he couldn't afford shoes": *Biography: Stephen King, 2000.*

52 "even more incredible that he didn't care": *Guardian,* September 18, 2004.

52 "He also was hot for my boobs": *Boston Globe,* June 4, 2006.

52 "as a tough broad": *Time,* October 6, 1986.

53 "from part of the store": *New Hampshire Sunday News,* June 27, 1993.

53 "they couldn't harm me": *Castle Rock,* December 1987.

54 "that didn't get me anywhere either": *Bangor Daily News,* March 4, 1997.

54 "if she likes something": Powells.com, October 2006.

55 "a couple of hundred willing young virgins": *Castle Rock,* June 1985.

56 "how long it took to tell the tales": Amazon.com, March 2003.

CHAPTER FOUR: DESPERATION

57 "in a display of righteous anger": *New Yorker,* April 22, 2002.

57 "would have been talking grand larceny": Ibid.

58 "the forgetful pump jockey": Ibid.

60 "for an extraordinarily long time": *Feast of Fear,* p. 236.

61 "Who the fuck are you?" Ibid.

61 "It used to make me crazy": Ibid.

61 "a Nazi-salute kind of typeface": BBC, *An Audience with Stephen King*, November 12, 2006.

61 "not being in that Saturday evening": *Stephen King Country*, p. 224.

62 "look a doughnut in the face ever since": *Bare Bones*, p. 30.

62 "not seeing each other, it wasn't good": *Writer's Digest*, June 2007.

62 "this traditional family home life": *Boston Globe*, April 15, 1990.

62 "when I was in the laundry": *New Yorker*, September 7, 1998.

63 "an opinion on Willy Loman's depression": *Castle Rock*, February 1986.

63 "twins having sex in a birdbath": *Feast of Fear*, p. 247.

64 "I better slap one together": *Bare Bones*, p. 46.

64 "I didn't really like it": *Lilja's Library*, January 16, 2007.

65 "don't sell too well to *Cosmopolitan*": *Bare Bones*, p. 85.

65 "the better you can do it": Ibid.

66 "Girls are even more mysterious": *Nightline*, November 15, 2007.

66 "when you're badly hurt": *Bare Bones*, p. 94.

66 "I'll help you": *Nightline*, November 15, 2007.

66 "a few different ways to fix it": NPR *Morning Edition*, November 19, 2003.

67 "electrical equipment from the rock band": *Bare Bones*, p. 86.

67 "from behind the desk": Ibid., p. 16.

67 "I felt depressed and really down": Ibid., p. 73.

68 "he always took the time to write": *Stephen King from A to Z*, p. 93.

68 "a pretty good sense of humor": Ibid.

69 " 'we wrote our way out' ": *A Good Read,* Maine Public Television, August 2004.

69 " 'Why don't you get an actual job?' ": National Book Foundation acceptance speech, November 19, 2003.

69 "you can't take it": Ibid.

69 "pissed away half the food budget for that week": *Bare Bones,* p. 31.

69 "why anyone wants to be a social drinker": *Guardian,* September 14, 2000.

70 "by teaching a creative-writing course": *Bare Bones,* p. 32.

70 "to occasional outright hate": Ibid.

70 "she told me she understood": Ibid.

70 "burning of money that drove me nuts": *Biography: Stephen King,* 2000.

70 "underwear had holes in it in those days": *Bare Bones,* p. 83.

70 "we've got to pay as we go": Bankrate.com, October 31, 2006.

70 "channeled into about a dozen stories": National Book Foundation acceptance speech, November 19, 2003.

71 "it's depressing, and it's fantasy": *Bare Bones,* p. 94.

72 "if Doubleday didn't accept *Carrie*": Ibid., p. 33.

73 "I scuttled across those streets, looking both ways": *Faces of Fear,* p. 246.

74 "someone opened a prison door": *Yale Bulletin & Calendar,* May 2, 2003.

74 "we were out of that trap for good": *Bare Bones,* p. 33.

74 "to live with my brother in Mexico, Maine": *New Yorker,* September 7, 1998.

74 "She got very exasperated with me": *Faces of Fear,* p. 246.

75 "but that's okay, let 'em! I'll be writing": *Dream Makers,* 2: 278.

75 "all sorts of things within that framework": *Paris Review,* Fall 2006.

75 "it's vampires from the first": *Bare Bones,* p. 102.

76 "they don't read *Weird Tales*": Ibid.

76 "that just wasn't the same": *Bare Bones,* p. 51.

76 "by God, he *is* too old": *Feast of Fear,* p. 77.

76 "forced out the obstruction": *Bare Bones,* p. 42.

CHAPTER FIVE: RIDING THE BULLET

78 "That could be a snake": *Yale Bulletin & Calendar,* May 2, 2003.

78 "it was so deep": *Bare Bones,* p. 67.

78 "I had the whole book in my mind": *The Province, Dienstag,* April 1997.

78 "because of my brutal impulses": Ibid.

79 "the realities of fatherhood": Ibid.

79 "about my kids that I never expected": *Nightline,* November 15, 2007.

79 "I could kill him": Ibid.

79 "I'm trying to keep the hex off": *Times of London* podcast, January 28, 2007.

79 "when I finished with the scene, it was gone": *Yankee,* March 1979.

79 "I was writing about myself": *Guardian,* September 18, 2004.

80 "performing a kind of self-psychoanalysis": *Nightline,* November 15, 2007.

80 "was to lie about it": *Feast of Fear*, p. 94.

80 "this guy has just written my book": Ibid., p. 98.

80 "and stanch the flow, I'd just die": Ibid.

80 "You carry your place with you wherever you go": *A Good Read*, Maine Public Television, August 2004.

81 "as many books and stories as he could churn out: *Castle Rock*, May 1986.

81 "You don't have to do things you don't want to do": *Writer's Digest*, 1976.

82 "a Sturm and Drang quality that's absent from the film": *Bare Bones*, p. 28.

82 "and they'd step back": *Fresh Air*, November 21, 2003.

83 " 'Thank you for saying that, for articulating that thought' ": Ibid.

83 "like having a Swiss bank account": *Kingdom of Fear*, p. 127.

84 "what people don't want them to know": *Feast of Fear*, p. 253.

85 "because he wouldn't shut up": Ibid., p. 181.

85 "It pops up again, and again, and again": *Bare Bones*, p. 105.

86 "you're entertaining yourself too, you know": *Publishers Weekly*, January 17, 1977.

87 "we feared for both Owen's death and his life": *Castle Rock*, August 1987.

87 "have to introduce him all over again": *Biography: Stephen King*, 2000.

88 "begin to see the light at the end of the tunnel": *Yankee*, March 1979.

88 "ugly and unpleasant most of the time": *Bare Bones*, p. 16.

88 "That's the mad-bomber side of my character, I suppose": Ibid., p. 30.

88 "as though I'd invented it myself": *Creepshows*, p. 89.

89 "we'll kill the messenger that brought the bad news": *Bare Bones,* p. 129.

90 "put them in school for a year abroad": BBC, *An Audience with Stephen King,*
November 12, 2006.

90 "It was like my umbilical cord had been cut": *Times of London* podcast, January
28, 2007.

90 "I swear to you, they don't like being warm": Letter from Susie Straub.

91 "you feel like a freak": *Castle Rock,* March 1987.

92 "responsible for destroying anybody's ego completely": *Bare Bones,* p. 76.

93 "I don't know why": *Writers Dreaming,* p. 142.

93 "they would bury them in the sandbox in our backyard": *Castle Rock,* August 1987.

93 "Then they'd have a little after-burial party": Ibid.

94 "Mommy and Daddy collapsed on the lawn": Ibid.

94 "And that was the end of it. *Almost*": Ibid.

94 "I found that very, very hard to read and deal with": *Biography: Stephen King,* 2000.

94 "maybe I could sell these to a magazine of short stories": BBC, *An Audience with
Stephen King,* November 12, 2006.

95 "So we do for others": *Good Housekeeping,* September 2001.

95 "and not hurt anyone if you can help it": *New York Times,* August 13, 2000.

95 "Hold on, let me finish this paragraph!": *Stephen King from A to Z,* p. 238.

CHAPTER SIX: THE RUNNING MAN

96 "there had to be a way to improve on nature": *Age,* November 25, 2006.

96 "He is not now and never has been an alcoholic": *Mystery Ink,* 1979.

97 "they have all the good munchie food too": *Bare Bones,* p. 206.

97 "I'd order a beer and Steve would order three": *Master of the Macabre,* TLC/BBC Documentary, 1999.

98 "that's why their faces retain a youthful look": *Bare Bones,* p. 38.

98 "I am a dickey bird on the back of civilization": Ibid.

98 " 'that's not funny, that's horrible!' ": *Castle Rock,* March 1987.

99 "a real big plot and subplots": *Times of London,* October 21, 2006.

99 "all the pillows have been treated with low-grade poison gas": *Bare Bones,* p. 68.

100 "which is typical of writers": Ibid., p. 72.

100 "and you let them do that": *Dream Makers,* 2: 277.

101 "I feel like I've earned it": *Bare Bones,* p. 68.

101 "try to convey some of that in my fiction": *Salon,* September 24, 1998.

102 "once you are north of Freeport": *Hollywood's Stephen King,* p. 3.

102 "there are no distractions whatsoever": *Feast of Fear,* p. 254.

103 "I thought it was destiny": *Stephen King Companion,* p. 77.

104 "I capture the bat and put it out while he just screams": *Stephen King Country,* p. 86.

104 "Tabby wanted spiders and webs": Ibid.

104 "I wanted superhero characters, not demonic characters": Ibid.

105 "The chair was empty": "An Interview with Stephen King," by Janet Beaulieu, November 17, 1988.

105 "a medium said she had a message from her": *Highway Patrolman,* July 1987.

105 "denies that there is a link between smoking and lung cancer": Ibid.

105 "I didn't even take the shaving cream off my face": *Feast of Fear*, p. 109.

106 "This is the book": *Bare Bones*, p. 133.

106 "except admire it as sculpture": *Paris Review*, Fall 2006.

106 "There was no moral struggle at all": *Feast of Fear*, p. 100.

106 "my childhood was quite happy, in a solitary way": *Faces of Fear*, p. 241.

107 "only from a more mature perspective": Ibid., p. 222.

107 "and then went where I wanted": Ibid.

107 "it will crystallize a scene for me": *Paris Review*, Fall 2006.

108 "A part of me dies when the World Series is over": *Faces of Fear*, p. 227.

108 "maybe white guys can do something in sports": Ibid.

108 "not only is this house vacant but it's haunted": *Castle Rock*, August 1987.

108 "part of them wants to see you fall as far as you can": Ibid.

108 "The fan had obviously done this often": *Castle Rock*, December 1986.

108 "like the ones Lennon used to wear": *London Observer*, August 9, 1998.

109 "there are real crazy people out there": *Castle Rock*, August 1987.

CHAPTER SEVEN: DIFFERENT SEASONS

110 "some publisher thought they would make sales on the novelty": *Castle Rock*, December 1987.

110 "she had turned out a damned fine piece of work": *Bare Bones*, p. 46.

110 "as he did with mine": *Faces of Fear,* p. 222.

111 "boredom often leads to actual thought, exploration, and discovery": *Onyx Reviews,* May 2006.

111 "But once I start, I'm hard to turn off": *Castle Rock,* December 1987.

111 "and then entering the story": *Writer's Digest,* June 2007.

111 "'Just let me go ahead and get on with the work'": *Bare Bones,* p. 70.

111 "or what's going to happen with it": Ibid., p. 74.

112 "I didn't know *how* long": *Complete Encyclopedia of Stephen King,* p. 18.

113 "it takes for them to work out their problem": *Writer's Digest,* September 1991.

113 "But you never know when it's going to happen": *Paris Review,* Fall 2006.

113 "it's short and it's mean": *Times of London,* October 21, 2006.

113 "It was tougher to react sympathetically to the woman": *Feast of Fear,* p. 234.

114 "But what's there is honest enough": Ibid.

115 "And I like it that way": *Bare Bones,* p. 199.

115 "because it pushes the old buttons": Ibid., p. 200.

115 "The bl-o-o-d-y parts!": *Feast of Fear,* p. 223.

115 "only because their father's famous": Ibid.

115 "It'll be interesting to see what happens": Ibid.

116 "as part of the company's highest-level strategy": *Publishers Weekly,* February 26, 2007.

117 "what is this tower and why does this guy need to get there?": "An Interview with Stephen King," by Janet Beaulieu, November 17, 1988.

117 "toss out our nightmares for the consumption of others": *Castle Rock,* March 1987.

117 "who would watch *Attack of the Crab Monsters* four times": *Feast of Fear,* p. 127.

118 "about ten pounds hanging off it": *Stephen King Country,* p. 58.

118 "it was so funny": Ibid., p. 59.

118 "you know when you're doing a bad job": *Feast of Fear,* p. 138.

118 "how Wile E. Coyote looks when he falls off a cliff?": *Stephen King at the Movies,* p. 29.

119 "so he went to work": *Bare Bones,* p. 81.

119 "For a little kid, it was a blast": *New York Times,* March 18, 2007.

119 "That's right, just a movie, officers": *Stephen King at the Movies,* p. 80.

120 "not the way they did": Ibid.

121 "and really screw our eyes out": *Bare Bones,* p. 45.

121 "I don't really need to fool around": Ibid.

121 "I wouldn't *dare* cheat on her!": Ibid., p. 46.

121 "Infidelity is a shooting offense": *Publishers Weekly,* February 10, 1997.

121 "it just slammed shut and cut your penis off": *Bare Bones,* p. 189.

121 "before I got up on the goddamn scales": *Kingdom of Fear,* p. 142.

122 "make me do all these terrible things to save my life": Ibid.

122 "somebody started to lose weight and couldn't stop": Ibid.

122 "and I use everything": *Bare Bones,* p. 90.

123 "because they loved it too": *Times of London* podcast, January 28, 2007.

123 "And you don't miss what's not there": *Nightline,* November 15, 2007.

123 "maybe that's just a lot of horseshit, I don't know": *The Province, Dienstag,* April 22, 1997.

123 "because their fathers are gone": *Dream Makers,* p. 278.

124 "with a real tendency toward violence": *Salon,* September 24, 1998.

124 "I'm pretty sure my father's dead": *Bare Bones,* p. 35.

124 "after you've done your important work": *Dream Makers,* 2: 281.

125 "all the things that are not the story": *On Writing,* p. 57.

125 "and at that point they'll be right": *Dream Makers,* 2: 282.

125 "Nobody ever talked about Plymouth cars anymore": *Twilight Zone,* February 1984.

126 "any mainstream Hollywood actor I could think of": *Fangoria,* July 1984.

127 "it makes us forget it is supernatural": *Chicago Sun-Times,* October 26, 1983.

128 "she'll accuse me of stealing one of her ideas": *Monsterland Magazine,* May 1985.

128 "imagine what it would be like to be such a person": *Castle Rock,* August 1987.

128 "don't write anything like he does": Ibid.

128 "merely another flawed human being": Ibid.

128 "if it was okay to have breakfast": Ibid.

129 "balls-to-the-wall rock music can provide": *Castle Rock,* October 1987.

129 "like I'm on my student driver's permit": *Feast of Fear,* p. 195.

129 "That book came out of a real hole in my psyche": *Times of London* podcast, January 28, 2007.

130 "and I don't really believe that": *USA Today,* May 10, 1985.

CHAPTER EIGHT: MAXIMUM OVERDRIVE

132 "I'm the Firestarter, I'm Charlie McGee": *Creepshows,* p. 38.

132 "and a resounding failure as a film": Ibid., p. 39.

132 "attacking these movies": Ibid.

132 "much less than the sum of those parts": Ibid.

132 "the most astonishing thing in the movie is how boring it is": *Chicago Sun-Times,* January 1, 1984.

133 "our own repertory company of dragons, vampires, assorted Things": *Murderess Ink,* 1979.

133 "there was nothing there to watch": *Feast of Fear,* p. 94.

133 "It'll pass": Ibid., p. 101.

133 "and the ultimate comedy at the same time": *Boston Globe,* April 15, 1990.

134 "I got the job for a while": Ibid.

134 "in the window of a live sex show on Forty-second Street": *Fantasy Review,* January 1984.

134 "whore duty for some marketing guy": Ibid.

135 "And in a small town, you only have one": *Talk of the Nation,* February 9, 1999.

135 "I should just write under a different name": *New York Times,* March 18, 2007.

136 "It's not the fucking *Mona Lisa*": *New York Times,* August 13, 2000.

136 "maybe that's why they live science fiction": *Dream Makers,* 2: 275.

137 "It became a mission for me to respect Steve's privacy": *Kingdom of Fear,* p. 129.

137 " 'You *can't* copy him,' they said": *A Good Read,* Maine Public Television, August 2004.

137 "The poor guy was one ugly son of a bitch": *Kingdom of Fear*, p. 124.

138 "This is what Stephen King would write like if Stephen King could really write":
     Ibid., p. 132.

138 "I was about eighty percent convinced Bachman was Stephen King": Ibid., p.
     124.

138 "Let's talk": Ibid., p. 125.

138 "they all have downbeat endings": Ibid., p. 132.

138 "and his fear was that he would lead his audiences astray": Ibid.

138 "died of cancer of the pseudonym": *Castle Rock*, June 1987.

139 "in this case, Richard Bachman": *Creepshows*, p. 54.

139 "I deserved to be because it was lazy": *Writer's Digest*, September 1991.

139 "you think is a dead giveaway, it's a trick": Stanley Wiater interview, 1984 World
     Fantasy Convention.

139 "unsure myself who had written what": *Encyclopedia of Stephen King*, p. 58.

140 "carried in their back pockets to work": *Fangoria*, p. 10.

140 "if the actor happens to be a Mack truck": *Feast of Fear*, p. 186.

141 "would be easier than working with actors": *Castle Rock*, September 1986.

141 "always gave me more than I expected": *Feast of Fear*, p. 186.

141 "and sort of allow you to mess up": *Talk of the Nation*, February 9, 1999.

141 "or the other thing if it's bad news": *Stephen King at the Movies*, p. 72.

142 "I just can't see going through that kind of thing again": *Feast of Fear*, p. 262.

142 "as if the Porn Fairy had visited in the middle of the night": *Castle Rock*, July 1986.

142 "I really didn't know what I was doing": *Hollywood's Stephen King*, p. 20.

142 "he did seem to be strung out": *Entertainment Weekly*, September 27, 2002.

143 "we're renting them": *Feast of Fear*, p. 279.

143 "Then it might seem real": *Newsweek*, June 10, 1985.

143 "and take another walk in the afternoon": *Faces of Fear*, p. 256.

143 "that I always have in mind": Ibid.

144 "they changed the batteries in the smoke detector?": Ibid., p. 239.

144 "I'm afraid of what it's doing to my life": Ibid.

144 "but it puts you on a pedestal": *Castle Rock*, August 1986.

144 "I'm just another woman driving around with a dog in her car": *Castle Rock*, January 1986.

145 "If keeping him in the car until the bell rings makes him feel better, then okay": *Bare Bones*, p. 56.

145 "they *know* what you're going to do": *Bare Bones*, p. 13.

145 "they'll get sucked in": Ibid., p. 95.

145 "I put all the monsters in that book": Ibid., p. 176.

146 "I wanted to write about a real troll under a real bridge": *Secret Windows*, p. 322.

146 "dropped it into the book, and didn't change a thing": *Writers Dreaming*, pp. 137–38.

147 "it's still in the books today": *Salon*, September 24, 1998.

147 "I started to get a lot of that stuff back": *Writers Dreaming*, p. 141.

147 "I don't seem to have so much to say about kids anymore": *Feast of Fear*, p. 199.

149 "we don't get locked in dark closets": *Castle Rock,* August 1986.

149 "that's the honest truth": Ibid.

149 "It definitely motivated me to write more": *SDCC,* July 27, 2007.

150 "His eyes are everywhere, trying to take in everything at once": *The Lost Work of Stephen King,* p. 249.

CHAPTER NINE: THE LONG WALK

151 "She has very little interest in my vampires, ghoulies, and slushy crawling things": *Castle Rock,* February 1987.

151 "if she won't come to me, I'll go to her": *Fangoria,* p. 34.

152 "have the author do more than just answer it": *Castle Rock,* March 1987.

152 "The book is the boss": Ibid.

152 "any more than I could stop breathing": *Fangoria,* p. 36.

152 "He plans to continue writing but publish less": *Castle Rock,* September 1987.

153 "or my life or my bedroom or anything else. *Fangoria,* p. 80.

153 "what I have achieved was really meant for them": *Fresh Air,* November 21, 2003.

153 "I hope he's still discovering the unknown in me": *Castle Rock,* August 1987.

153 "how much you do and do not know about another person": Ibid.

153 "she actually generated a lot more sympathy in my heart than I expected": *Weekly Reader Writing* magazine, October 2006.

153 "and didn't have a clue": Ibid.

154 "I write like fat ladies diet": *New Yorker,* September 7, 1998.

154 "it can lead to self-indulgence": Ibid.

154 "you better be pretty careful": *Writer's Digest*, September 1991.

154 "I never did that with a book": *Stephen King Companion*, p. 292.

155 "Everything I wrote for the next year fell apart like tissue paper": *Fangoria*, p. 47.

155 "constantly wanting to push things past the edge": *Faces of Fear*, p. 256.

155 "Don't you know I'm the king of the fucking universe?": *Guardian*, September 14, 2000.

156 "There was something in that tar that she, that I, needed": Ibid.

157 "If it would change your consciousness, I was all for it": *Fresh Air*, October 10, 2000.

157 "Then he decided to save himself": *Good Housekeeping*, September 2001.

158 "Needless to say I was not successful in this": *Guardian*, September 14, 2000.

158 "that stuff eats you from the inside out": Ibid.

160 "It's like it wasn't my voice": *Entertainment Weekly*, September 27, 2002.

160 "I think it would take away a lot of the good stuff": *Paris Review*, Fall 2006.

160 "right away I knew it was a problem": *Guardian*, September 14, 2000.

160 "who have three or four martinis when they get in from work": Ibid.

161 "He covered well": *USA Today*, February 12, 2007.

161 "I wrapped the whole book around that spine": *Waldenbooks Magazine*, November/December 1989.

162 "other than it's not normal": *Castle Rock*, August 1987.

163 "But now I feel like myself again, only with wrinkles": BBC, *An Audience with Stephen King*, November 12, 2006.

163 "it would have been a thirty-two-hour miniseries": *Talk of the Nation*, February 9, 1999.

164 "gone into a total panic": *Fangoria*, p. 48.

164 "I think the door has been finally opened for him": *Entertainment Weekly*, September 27, 2002.

164 "had coaxed the best nonfiction writing of my life out of me": *Nightmares and Dreamscapes*, p. 811.

166 "since I was sixteen without drinking or drugging": *Paris Review*, Fall 2006.

166 "you ended up paying with your soul": *A Good Read*, Maine Public Television, August 2004.

166 "maybe it just wasn't a very good book": *Paris Review*, Fall 2006.

167 "I think you have to grow up here": *A Good Read*, Maine Public Television, August 2004.

CHAPTER TEN: IT GROWS ON YOU

168 "There was something very Snidely Whiplash about the whole thing": *Fresh Air*, October 10, 2000.

168 "I told her I was doing an experiment": Ibid.

168 "because she has been chained in a certain kind of life": *Times of London* podcast, January 28, 2007.

169 "you feel so grateful to have it return": Amazon.com, September 1998.

169 "and find ways to revitalize it": *Age*, November 25, 2006.

169 "you'll miss the surprises, and some of them are wonderful": *Good Housekeeping*, September 2001.

169 "I was taught that charity begins at home": *Boston Globe*, November 22, 1991.

174 "I haven't done to stay alive creatively": *USA Today*, December 1992.

174 "if they're all saying something's a piece of shit, they're right": *Writer's Digest*, September 1991.

174 "they have to do *Carrie 2* or *Children of the Corn VI*": *Creepshows*, p. 177.

175 "And I didn't even know it got made": *USA Today*, June 20, 2007.

175 "while they wonder what the fuck to do with them": *Hollywood's Stephen King*, p. 8.

176 "there's just not enough life or enough time": *Talk of the Nation*, February 9, 1999.

176 "With *The Green Mile*, I made twenty-five million": *Hollywood's Stephen King*, p. 7.

176 "if they bring a watermelon and a barrel for him to sit on": *Guardian*, September 14, 2000.

176 "who was going to be the lead dog": *A Good Read*, Maine Public Television, August 2004.

177 "He's also taught me the legitimacy of ordinary things in fiction": *New Hampshire Sunday News*, June 27, 1993.

179 "The tour felt like it never happened": *Mid-Life Confidential*, p. 188.

180 "I'd rather not write at all": *Writer's Digest*, September 1991.

180 "I hardly slept at all": *America Online Chat*, 1996.

180 "the stories are found articles and the story basically will tell itself": *A Good Read*, Maine Public Television, August 2004.

180 "if you're really careful and lucky, you can get most of it": *Writers Dreaming,* p. 137.

180 "brushing them off and looking at the carvings on them": *Writer's Digest,* September 1991.

180 "then I remember that I can't, because of something in the story": Ibid.

181 "I'm Stephen King, it doesn't happen to me": Ibid.

181 "more work than any two or three novels I've ever done in my life": *Fangoria,* p. 93.

181 "apparently, he didn't want to change a word": Ibid., p. 99.

182 "I've played a lot of hick morons in my career": Ibid., p. 98.

182 "No, you didn't": Amazon.com, March 2003.

183 "being put at the head of a float on National Whore's Day": *Fangoria,* p. 109.

183 "is like learning to talk after you've had a stroke": Ibid., p. 110.

CHAPTER ELEVEN: THE GOLDEN YEARS

184 "when did Stephen King stop being scary?": *Entertainment Weekly,* June 16, 1995.

184 "There are a lot of people who are dedicated to keeping the clubhouse white": *Entertainment Weekly,* September 27, 2002.

184 "It made me feel like an impostor, like someone made a mistake": *New York Times,* August 13, 2000.

185 "mom and dad went in to throw the pizza dough every day": *Times of London,* March 10, 2007.

185 "I don't think they were all that surprised": *Bangor Daily News,* July 11, 2005.

185 "yet they were treated as part of the community": Ibid.

186 "they'd prefer to have their privacy": *Bangor Daily News,* August 23, 1994.

186 "Peltry is where I have to get some urgent work done": *Publishers Weekly,* February 10, 1997.

186 "there's such an emphasis on stripped-down stories, because people's lives aren't": Ibid.

186 "are usually pretty minor tweaks": Ibid.

187 "knowing I would be hung if it didn't": *Stephen King from A to Z,* p. 32.

187 "I want to stay dangerous, and that means taking risks": *America Online Chat,* 1996.

188 "performing *King Lear* one night and *Bus Stop* the next": Ibid.

188 "that cop killed them all": Powells.com, October 2006.

189 "these guys have had no problems with vampires, demons, golems, and werewolves in the past": *World of Fandom,* September 1996.

189 "So I choose to believe": *Fresh Air,* October 10, 2000.

189 "I never said anything about signing them": Hillhousepublishers.com, "Collecting Stephen King."

190 "What if she also found a number of canceled checks?": Ibid.

191 "killing off a major character right at the start!": *London Observer,* August 9, 1998.

191 "like a buried body, they start to smell bad": *Omaha World Herald,* June 29, 1998.

191 "which I haven't used very much in my longer fiction": Ibid.

192 "the writing works is very similar": Amazon.com, March 2003.

192 "it's always a little further along": Interview by Stanley Wiater, September 1998.

192 "or to live confined in an emotional spiritual cage": Sermon, "Holding Thee More Nearly," September 23, 2007.

192 "After that, people encouraged me to go to seminary": *Fort Lauderdale Sun-Sentinel,* September 15, 2007.

193 "no gay girl kid was going to be able to do that": Sermon, "The Magic of Thomas Potter," September 30, 2007.

193 "is what I see out of the corners": *60 Minutes,* February 16, 1997.

194 "in the movie he was hit once but she wasn't": *World of Fandom,* September 1996.

195 "the way one puts down any savage animal that cannot stop biting": Keynote address, annual meeting, Vermont Library Conference, May 26, 1999.

195 " 'That's it for me, that book's off the market' ": BBC, December 19, 1999.

195 "Because we always have": *Bangor Daily News,* January 19, 2008.

195 "and see what they're getting hit with up North": *A Good Read,* Maine Public Television, August 2004.

195 "If it stops, it's over, forget it": *Province,* April 22, 1997.

195 "at least you don't have to linger in a burn ward": *Dennis Miller Live,* April 3, 1998.

196 "except in the film at the beginning": Ibid.

196 "something you wrote twenty-eight years ago was your best book": *Paris Review,* Fall 2006.

196 "different events, personalities, and things that you can flip together": *Writers Dreaming,* p. 136.

197 " 'I've got the idea, now let me out of here' ": BBC, *An Audience with Stephen King,* November 12, 2006.

198 "Let sleeping dogs lie, I say": *Guardian,* September 14, 2000.

CHAPTER TWELVE: MISERY

199 "I really enjoyed the process": *Talk of the Nation*, February 9, 1999.

200 "generally that works pretty well": Ibid.

200 "if you whine enough, you do": Ibid.

200 "I've done most of the promotion that they've asked me to do": Ibid.

200 "should have been changed to *Story That Lasts a Century*": *San Francisco Chronicle*, February 12, 1999.

200 "A lot of people will not let me rest until I finish with Roland": Ibid.

201 "it would be *The Girl Who Loved Tom Gordon*": *Weekly Reader Writing* magazine, October 2006.

202 "If he hit those rocks, he would have died": *Bangor Daily News*, June 21, 1999.

202 "I thought, 'Oh, boy, I'm in trouble here'": *Nightline*, November 15, 2007.

202 "I loved all your movies": *Fresh Air*, October 10, 2000.

202 "he was still talking and coherent": *Dateline*, November 1, 1999.

203 "then it started up again, all different": *Good Housekeeping*, September 2001.

203 "after they had intubated me and pumped up my lung": *Fresh Air*, October 10, 2000.

203 "Not today": *Dateline*, November 1, 1999.

204 "with the exception of my head, which was only concussed": Ibid.

204 "it was that I had to take them again": *Fresh Air*, October 10, 2000.

204 "I'm going to take it": Ibid.

204 "it put chills in my heart": Ibid.

205 "It's almost funny": *On Writing*, p. 256.

205 "I'd tell her I couldn't and to let me stop, and she wouldn't": *Dateline*, November 1, 1999.

206 "I didn't know if I knew how to do this anymore": Ibid.

207 "so you just kind of let go": Ibid.

207 "my brain began inventing pain just to get these painkillers": *Age*, November 25, 2006.

207 "that was a very frightening place to be": *Fresh Air*, October 10, 2000.

208 "you're awake nights, you twitch, and then it's gone": BBC, *An Audience with Stephen King*, November 12, 2006.

CHAPTER THIRTEEN: SOMETIMES THEY COME BACK

209 "They all wanted to see my leg": *New York Times*, August 13, 2000.

210 "because we can reduce each other to helpless laughter": Tenebres.com, 2000.

210 "It's just a question of trying to find the time": *Lilja's Library*, January 16, 2007.

210 "an idea of what this market is like now": *Publishers Weekly*, March 14, 2000.

210 "but also in terms of length": Ibid.

210 "it was a way of keeping things fresh": *Paris Review*, Fall 2006.

213 "It's more like 'I'm taking my leg to New York": *Guardian*, September 14, 2000.

213 "The death of a forty-three-year-old man can only be termed untimely": CNN .com, September 25, 2000.

213 "Facts don't bother a novelist": *Boston Globe*, November 22, 1991.

213 "You'd rather do it than write about it": *Guardian,* September 14, 2000.

213 "Is this all you really have to say about the art and craft of writing?": *A Good Read,* Maine Public Television, August 2004.

213 "trying to teach women how to behave": *Entertainment Weekly,* September 27, 2002.

214 "they take it more seriously": *A Good Read,* Maine Public Television, August 2004.

214 "because if I stop, I'll never start again": *Guardian,* September 18, 2004.

214 "Tabby keeps the monsters away": *60 Minutes,* February 16, 1997.

214 "Tabby's not afraid of him, or anything": *Good Housekeeping,* September 2001.

215 "and keeps us from knowing things": *Boston Globe,* June 4, 2006.

215 "contemplate some god-awful things in my fiction": *Talk of the Nation,* February 9, 1999.

215 "I can always rip it out later": *Feast of Fear,* p. 99.

215 "what the consequences were when the man leaves": *Age,* November 25, 2006.

215 "and then I would shoot him": *Publishers Weekly,* February 10, 1997.

215 "the thought has crossed my mind": *Augusta Chronicle,* October 20, 1998.

215 "he just bullies his way into what he wants like a freight train": *Writer's Digest,* June 2007.

216 "I ended my involvement immediately": *Onyx Reviews,* May 2006.

216 "and that's the end of it": Ibid.

216 "what it means to be a man among other men": *CBS Morning Show,* March 20, 2001.

216 "they would rather kill all of us than tell us the truth": *Hollywood's Stephen King*, p. 7.

217 "I found myself pulling back a bit": *Guardian*, September 14, 2000.

218 "Nothing did really": *Lilja's Library*, January 16, 2007.

218 "You see little flashes of their style": *Paris Review*, Fall 2006.

219 "there might have been an element of that involved": *All Things Considered*, March 16, 2005.

219 "So to hell with it": *Portland Press Herald*, June 4, 2006.

219 "who's been following the Red Sox forever": Ibid.

220 "I've become sort of a Red Sox mascot": *All Things Considered*, March 16, 2005.

220 "there was no reason not to publish them as soon as possible": Amazon.com, March 2003.

220 "these books are going to come in fairly rapid succession": Ibid.

221 "has to come out some other way": *Talk of the Nation*, NPR, February 9, 1999.

221 "I'd kick his body into the street and dance on it!": *Castle Rock*, December 1987.

221 "I don't need the money": *Entertainment Weekly*, September 27, 2002.

222 "might be his last novel for the year": Ibid.

222 "I would publish it": *Time*, March 24, 2002.

222 "the idea that this guy was going to retire is a laugh": *Time*, March 24, 2002.

222 "like my mind and body is trying to scare me back to work": *Age*, November 25, 2006.

222 "so I tried to simplify it a little bit": Amazon.com, March 2003.

222 "all they're doing is remaking them at this point": *Boston Globe*, June 4, 2006.

223 "And he's a kindred spirit": *A Good Read,* Maine Public Television, August 2004.

224 "the shocking process of dumbing down our cultural life": *Boston Globe,* September 24, 2003.

224 "to a girl who's not going to be Miss America": *Nightline,* November 15, 2007.

224 "there's still a fair amount of resentment toward that": Ibid.

224 "I was going to accept it and make my speech": *Age,* November 25, 2006.

224 "and got rotten and infected the rest": Ibid.

225 "The writing was the best part of the day": Ibid.

225 "She knew I couldn't argue": BBC, *An Audience with Stephen King,* November 12, 2006.

225 "when my mother died of cancer": *Age,* November 25, 2006.

CHAPTER FOURTEEN: THE END OF THE WHOLE MESS

226 "the pressure of being a famous guy's kid": *New York Times,* March 18, 2007.

226 "horror stories with few adverbs": Ibid.

226 "and it's the same comments": Ibid.

227 "the fulfillment of a very intense childhood fantasy": *SDCC,* July 27, 2007.

227 "out of me that I'm very proud of": *Onyx Review,* June 2005.

227 "a nepotistic exercise and for you to suck": *Telegraph,* May 21, 2006.

227 "not make any bread off his name": *Bangor Daily News,* July 11, 2005.

227 "how he'd get his point across": Ibid.

227 "which makes me work more": "Interview with Susan Henderson," MySpace .com, May 4, 2006.

228 "surrounded by all of these urns of ancient olive oil": Ibid.

228 "flavor-of-the-month New York relationships": *New York Times,* August 13, 2000.

228 "thank God he's good": *Entertainment Weekly,* June 24, 2005.

228 "Everything else is commentary": *Fort Lauderdale Sun-Sentinel,* September 15, 2007.

228 "I had to stop making jokes about it": BBC, *An Audience with Stephen King,* November 12, 2006.

228 "and she just laughs": *New York Times,* August 13, 2000.

229 "those of us who are also people, created and beloved of God": *Fort Lauderdale Sun-Sentinel,* September 15, 2007.

229 "I tell stories through sermons": *Miami Herald,* August 12, 2007.

229 "my basic standard of parenthood was nobody's in jail": *Good Housekeeping,* September 2001.

230 "which really was an instant book": *Times of London* podcast, January 28, 2007.

230 "Don't give me a pixie!": *New York Daily News,* June 18, 2007.

230 "not to sound good inside that environment": BBC, *An Audience with Stephen King,* November 12, 2006.

213 "but sooner or later it ends": *Times of London* podcast, January 28, 2007.

231 "That turned out to be Dooley in *Lisey's Story*": Ibid.

231 "it's too good not to publish": BBC, *An Audience with Stephen King,* November 12, 2006.

232 "because I love this book": *Paris Review,* Fall 2006.

232 "That takes a generosity that isn't common": *Writer's Digest,* June 2007.

232 "that no sane person expects to reach": *Boston Globe,* June 4, 2006.

233 "that much time with people not looking at you": *Portland Press Herald,* June 4, 2006.

233 "Paging Dr. Alzheimer": *Times of London* podcast, January 28, 2007.

233 "that's all that I wanted out of it": *New York Post,* March 8, 2007.

233 "almost impossible to visualize on-screen": *Lilja's Library,* February 6, 2007.

234 "like not getting published. *Sun-Herald* (Australia), July 23, 2007.

234 "a case of my pen name doing its job": *Telegraph,* October 20, 2007.

234 "it just didn't work out that way": *New York Times,* March 18, 2007.

234 "But he did it": *USA Today,* February 12, 2007.

234 "that shows there's hope for you": *Bangor Daily News,* January 19, 2008.

234 "as a stand-in for himself": *USA Today,* February 12, 2007.

234 "there'll be some comparison": *Telegraph,* October 20, 2007.

235 "I'd kill the whales to do this": *New York Times,* June 4, 2007.

235 "more of a hobby than work": *A Good Read,* Maine Public Television, August 2004.

235 "I'm just a hood ornament on this band": *New York Times,* June 4, 2007.

236 "good makeup won't hide bad writing": BBC, *An Audience with Stephen King,* November 12, 2006.

237 " 'Because we could!' ": *Bangor Daily News,* January 19, 2008.

238 "a skill I once had had slipped away": *Leonard Lopate Show,* WNYC, October 18, 2007.

238 "than I did on this one": Ibid.

238 "to see the magazine reach a wider reading public": Ibid.

239 " 'Oh, my God, this is wonderful!' ": *Nightline*, November 15, 2007.

239 "What if giant bugs started to fly into the glass?": Ibid.

239 "the world that had been created in that story": Ibid.

239 "the last thing I need in my books is another author": *Bangor Daily News,* January 19, 2008.

239 "I got this image of two dead girls": Ibid.

240 "David Baldacci and the born-again books?": *Paris Review,* Fall 2006.

240 "would make anybody a healthy human being": *Weekly Reader Writing* magazine, October 2006.

240 "that's not easy to achieve all the time": *Lilja's Library,* January 16, 2007.

240 "It's grow or die": *Leonard Lopate Show,* WNYC, October 18, 2007.

240 "more than just the box-step waltz": *A Good Read,* Maine Public Television, August 2004.

241 "try different things and formats": *Time,* November 23, 2007.

241 "and we're big mouths too": *Rolling Stone,* January 31, 2008.

241 "But I'm not crazy enough to do it again": *The Mist* press conference, November 13, 2007.

241 "the most horrible, awful things that I can think about": *Highway Patrolman,* July 1987.

242 "that'll kick your ass every time": *The Mist* press conference, November 13, 2007.

242 "it's the teaspoon against the sea": *Portland Press Herald,* June 4, 2006.

242 "on every gallon of gas you buy": UMO commencement address, May 7, 2005.

242 "every time I sit down at a typewriter": *Time,* October 6, 1986.

242 "He writes like old people fuck": *Guardian,* September 14, 2000.

243 "That's the bottom line": *Hollywood's Stephen King,* p. 5.

243 "it's time to stop": *Castle Rock,* April 1989.

Beahm, George. *Stephen King: America's Best-Loved Boogeyman*. Kansas City, MO: Andrews McMeel Publishing, 1998.

———, ed. *The Stephen King Companion*. Kansas City, MO: Andrews McMeel, 1989.

———. *Stephen King Country*. Philadelphia: Running Press, 1999.

———. *Stephen King from A to Z: An Encyclopedia of His Life and Works*. Kansas City, MO: Andrews McMeel Publishing, 1998.

———. *The Stephen King Story: A Literary Profile*. Kansas City, MO: Andrews Mc-Meel Publishing, 1992.

Collings, Michael R. *The Annotated Guide to Stephen King: A Primary and Secondary Bibliography of the Works of America's Premier Horror Writer*. Mercer Island, WA: Starmont House, 1986.

———. *The Films of Stephen King*. Mercer Island, WA: Starmont House, 1986.

———. *The Many Facets of Stephen King*. Mercer Island, WA: Starmont House, 1985.

———. *Stephen King as Richard Bachman*. Mercer Island, WA: Starmont House, 1985.

———. *The Stephen King Phenomenon*. Mercer Island, WA: Starmont House, 1987.

Collings, Michael R., with David Engebretson. *The Shorter Works of Stephen King*. Mercer Island, WA: Starmont House, 1985.

Epel, Naomi. *Writers Dreaming: 26 Writers Talk About Their Dreams and the Creative Process*. New York: Vintage, 1994.

Hoppenstand, Gary, and Ray B. Browne. *The Gothic World of Stephen King: Landscape of Nightmares*. Bowling Green, OH: Bowling Green State University Popular Press, 1987.

Horsting, Jessie. *Stephen King at the Movies*. New York: Starlog Press, 1986.

Jones, Stephen. *Creep Shows: The Illustrated Stephen King Movie Guide*. New York: Watson-Guptill Publications, 2001.

King, Stephen. *Danse Macabre*. New York: Everest House, 1981.

———. *On Writing: A Memoir of the Craft*. New York: Scribner, 2000.

———. *Secret Windows: Essays and Fiction on the Craft of Writing*. New York: Book-of-the-Month Club, 2000.

Magistrale, Tony. *Hollywood's Stephen King*. New York: Palgrave Macmillan, 2003.

———. *Landscape of Fear: Stephen King's American Gothic*. Bowling Green, OH: Bowling Green State University Popular Press, 1988.

———. *The Moral Voyages of Stephen King*. Mercer Island, WA: Starmont House, 1989.

Marsh, Dave, ed. *Mid-Life Confidential: The Rock Bottom Remainders Tour America with Three Chords and an Attitude*. New York: Viking Penguin, 1994.

Platt, Charles. *Dream Makers*, vol. 2. New York: Berkley Books, 1983.

Spignesi, Stephen J. *The Complete Stephen King Encyclopedia: The Definitive Guide to the Works of America's Master of Horror*. Chicago: Contemporary Books, 1991.

———. *The Essential Stephen King: A Ranking of the Greatest Novels, Short Stories, Movies, and Other Creations of the World's Most Popular Writer*. Franklin Lakes, NJ: New Page Books, 2003.

———. *The Lost Work of Stephen King: A Guide to Unpublished Manuscripts, Story Fragments, Alternative Versions, and Oddities*. New York: Birch Lane Press, 1998.

———. *The Second Stephen King Quiz Book*. New York: Signet, 1992.

———. *The Stephen King Quiz Book*. New York: Signet, 1990.

Terrell, Carroll F. *Stephen King: Man and Artist*. Orono, ME: Northern Lights, 1990.

Timpone, Anthony, ed. *Fangoria: Masters of the Dark: Stephen King, Clive Barker*. New York: HarperPrism, 1997.

Underwood, Tim, and Chuck Miller, eds. *Bare Bones: A Conversation on Terror with Stephen King*. New York: McGraw-Hill, 1989.

———, eds. *Feast of Fear: Conversations with Stephen King*. New York: Carroll & Graf, 1992.

Wiater, Stanley, Christopher Golden, and Hank Wagner. *The Complete Stephen King Universe: A Guide to the Worlds of Stephen King*. New York: St. Martin's Griffin, 2006.

Winn, Dilys. *Murderess Ink: The Better Half of the Mystery*. New York: Workman, 1979.

Winter, Douglas E. *Faces of Fear: Encounters with the Creators of Modern Horror*. New York: Berkley Books, 1985.

———. *Stephen King*. Mercer Island, WA: Starmont House, 1982.

———. *Stephen King: The Art of Darkness*. New York: New American Library, 1984.

Wood, Rocky. *The Complete Guide to the Works of Stephen King*. 3rd ed. Melbourne, Australia: Kanrock Publishing, 2004. www.horrorking.com/order/index.html.

———. *The Stephen King Collector's Guide*. Melbourne, Australia: Kanrock Publishing, 2008. www.horrorking.com/collector.

———. *Stephen King: Uncollected, Unpublished*. Forest Hill, MD: Cemetery Dance Publications, 2005. Revised version, Melbourne, Australia: Kanrock Publishing, 2006. www.horrorking.com/skuu.

Wood, Rocky, and Justin Brooks. *Stephen King: The Non-Fiction*. Forest Hill, MD: Cemetery Dance Publications, 2008. www.cemeterydance.com.

Note: SK stands for Stephen King. Women are listed under their maiden names. Fictional characters are listed by first name, e.g., "Annie Wilkes." Literary works cited are by King unless otherwise stated.